ADMINISTRATIVE LAW
FOR PUBLIC MANAGERS

Essentials of Public Policy and Administration Series

Series Editor: Jay Shafritz
University of Pittsburgh

Westview Press proudly announces a new series of textbooks for public policy and administration courses. Written for students at both the advanced undergraduate level and graduate level, these texts follow a standard design and format which allows them to be incorporated easily into multiple courses. Each text covers a core aspect of public policy and administration that is commonly discussed in the classroom. They are written by authorities in their fields and will serve as both core and supplemental texts.

New titles in the series include:

Administrative Law for Public Managers
David H. Rosenbloom
Organizational Development in the Public Sector
David G. Carnevale
Managing Diversity in Public Sector Workforces
Norma M. Riccucci
Comparative Public Administration and Policy
Jamil E. Jreisat
The Regional Governing of Metropolitan America
David Miller

ADMINISTRATIVE LAW
FOR PUBLIC MANAGERS

David H. Rosenbloom
American University

Westview
PRESS

A Member of the Perseus Books Group

Essentials in Public Policy and Administration

Copyright © 2003 by Westview Press, A Member of the Perseus Books Group

Westview Press books are available at special discounts for bulk purchases in the United States by corporations, institutions, and other organizations. For more information, please contact the Special Markets Department at the Perseus Books Group, 11 Cambridge Center, Cambridge MA 02142, or call (617) 252–5298 or (800) 255-1514 or by email j.mccrary@perseusbooks.com.

Published in 2003 in the United States of America by Westview Press, 5500 Central Avenue, Boulder, Colorado 80301-2877

Find us on the World Wide Web at www.westviewpress.com

A Cataloging-in-Publication data record for this book is available from the Library of Congress.
ISBN 0–8133–4072–1 (HC) ISBN 0–8133–9805–3 (Pbk.)

The paper used in this publication meets the requirements of the American National Standard for Permanence of Paper for Printed Library Materials Z39.48-1984.

CONTENTS

Detailed Table of Contents

PREFACE

The first textbook on public administration in the United States, Leonard D. White's *Introduction to the Study of Administration*, asserted that "the study of administration should start from the base of management rather than the foundation of law, and is therefore more absorbed in the affairs of the American Management Association than in the decisions of the courts" (White 1926:56). The gist of White's statement may still be true, but there is no denying that law is far more important now than in his day or that the practice of public administration has become heavily infused with law. The single body of law that public administration students need to understand most is administrative law, broadly construed as the constitutional and statutory provisions, court decisions, and official directives that generically define individuals and organizations' rights vis-à-vis administrative agencies; regulate administrative procedures; and provide for executive, judicial, and legislative review of administrative actions. Administrative law imbues day-to-day public administration with due process, public participation, interest representation, freedom of information, open meetings, and additional democratic-constitutional values. It structures administrative rulemaking, adjudication, enforcement choices, and other decisionmaking. A solid grounding in administrative law is a prerequisite for understanding a substantial number of contemporary public administrative processes in the United States; like other aspects of administrative practice, it is better to learn it in the classroom than on the job.

Administrative law has such a major impact on public administration that it cannot be left to the lawyers alone. One does not need to be a lawyer to learn or teach it from the perspectives of public management. The purpose of this book is to make administrative law more accessible to public administration students. This book focuses on the essentials that public managers should know about administrative law—why we have administrative law; the broad constitutional constraints on public administration; administrative law's frameworks for rulemaking, adjudication, enforcement, and transparency; and the parameters of internal executive and external judicial and legislative review. The book views administrative law from the perspective of administrative practice rather than lawyering. One will not find chapters on "getting into court" and "staying in court" here (Fox 2000). Instead, the emphasis is on how various administrative law provisions promote their underlying goal of improving the fit between public administration and U.S. democratic constitutionalism.

The discussion is organized around federal administrative law, which in general is more elaborate than state-level equivalents. Where appropriate, state approaches are noted as alternatives to federal practices. After reading this book, one should have a firm grip on federal administrative law and no difficulty learning the administrative law of any particular state. Unlike most administrative law texts, the book neither contains legal cases nor devotes much attention to the development of case law. Federal court decisions are readily available on websites (e.g., www.findlaw .com) and can be flexibly selected by instructors to augment the text. Books dealing comprehensively with case law tend toward overkill in general public administrative education, sometimes running to a thousand pages or more. This book also differs from others by including a chapter titled "The Constitutional Context of American Public Administration," which explains the constitutional constructs and doctrines under which today's public administration and administrative law operate.

The book is intended for classroom use in two ways. First, as a supplement, it will efficiently cover the main dimensions of administrative law in general introductory public administration classes and in courses on bureaucratic politics or the political context of public management. Second, it can serve as a core text in public administration courses dealing with administrative law or the legal basis of public administration. As a core text, it could be coupled with selected legal cases of the instructor's choice. It is unlikely that the book will be used in law school classes, though law students may find it refreshingly concise and helpful in explaining the political and administrative contexts and larger purposes of administrative law.

The challenge in writing this book has been to explain the essentials of administrative law clearly and accurately, in nontechnical terms and with sufficient depth to provide readers with a sophisticated, lasting under-standing of the subject matter. The fact that I am not a lawyer has proba-bly been an advantage. However, the manuscript benefited greatly from the comments and suggestions of three lawyers, all of whom have acade-mic or applied expertise in both public administration and administrative law: Lucille Streeter; Maria Buzdugan; and my wife, Deborah Rosen-bloom. I am very grateful for their assistance and encouragement. I am also thankful to Suzanne J. Piotrowski, with whom I coauthored other works, for her substantial help with the research, critiques of the initial chapter drafts, and copious editorial attention. Professor Jeffrey Lubbers of American University's Washington College of Law generously pro-vided assistance with some of the finer points along the way. Thanks also go to Professor Christine Reed of the University of Nebraska–Omaha for her very helpful and encouraging review of the manuscript for Westview Press. The book is much better for all their efforts, and I am fully responsi-ble for whatever shortcomings may remain.

David H. Rosenbloom

1

What Is Administrative Law?

Introduction: What Is Administrative Law?

In the late 1990s, the Federal Aviation Administration (FAA) was considering whether to adopt a rule requiring that all children under age two be strapped into specially designed safety seats when flying on regularly scheduled U.S. commercial airlines. FAA Administrator Jane Garvey favored the seats because "the heart and soul of the FAA's mission is aviation safety—for the young and old alike" (Garvey 1999). In her view, the ideal was a child seat that parents could use interchangeably in both cars and planes. Garvey noted that although such a seat was not yet available, it was technically feasible. Who could argue with such a measure to protect babies' and toddlers' lives?

Quite a few people, it turned out. Opponents of the safety-seat requirement were not callous or cold-blooded about saving children. They argued that requiring safety seats would actually lead to *more* deaths—not because the seats were unsafe or would be misused (as car seats often are) but because they would raise the price of taking infants on flights. Parents would no longer be permitted to fly with under-two-year-olds snuggled on their laps. Instead, they would have to pay for an additional plane seat for each child. They might also have to buy the safety seats, depending on whether or not the airlines decided to supply them. The higher cost would lead some families to drive rather than fly to their destinations—and because driving is statistically more dangerous than flying, the risk of infants (and their parents) being killed in accidents would rise. In fact, some data suggested that young children were sixteen times more likely to be killed in automobile accidents than plane crashes (*USA Today* 1999).

Administrative policymaking often involves tough choices like the one that confronted the FAA. Administrators make a great number of decisions that directly affect the health, safety, and welfare of the population or sections of it. They have to address complex issues regarding transportation, environmental protection, economic practices, labor relations, and much, much more. What they decide is of fundamental consequence to the nation's quality of life, and it attracts a great deal of political and media attention. Equally important to our constitutional democracy, though generally less visible and interesting to the public, is *how* administrators should make and enforce their decisions.

The "how" rather than the "what" is the essence of administrative law. What steps should an administrator such as Garvey be required to take before making a decision on child safety seats? What values should she weigh, and how heavily? How much evidence should she need to support her conclusion? How open to public scrutiny and participation should the FAA's decisionmaking be? For instance, should Garvey be required to consult with the airline industry, the manufacturers of safety seats, public health officials, and/or children's advocacy groups? How relevant is it that between 1978 and 1994 the deaths of only five infants could possibly be attributed to the lack of safety seats on airplanes? Given this small number, should the entire matter be left up to parents, rather than subject to government regulation? If the FAA requires safety seats, should it have to show that their benefits clearly outweigh their costs, and, if so, how will the costs and benefits be measured? In addition to safety and cost, should Garvey consider whether a safety-seat regulation would be family-friendly? What would its impact be on families' ability to get together with grandparents or have reunions with other relatives who live beyond a four- or five-hour drive?

Additional administrative law questions focus on accountability and review of agency decisionmaking. How should Garvey be held accountable for whatever decision she makes? Should the decision be subject to review by Congress and/or a unit within the executive branch, such as the Office of Management and Budget (OMB)? Presuming that a safety-seat requirement were challenged in court, should the FAA have to show statistically that it would prevent "X" number of injuries and deaths, or only that it is a reasonable means of protecting very young children? Should the documents relied on in adopting such a requirement be available to the public? If an airline were caught violating such a rule, what steps should the FAA be required to take before fining or otherwise penalizing it? Concerns like these are the crux of administrative law.

Administrative law can be defined as the body of constitutional provisions, statutes, court decisions, executive orders, and other official directives that: first (a) regulate the procedures agencies use in making rules and related policy decisions, (b) control the exercise of their authority to enforce laws and regulations, and (c) govern the extent to which administration is open to public scrutiny (i.e., transparent); and second, provide for review of agency decisions respecting these matters. For the most part, administrative law is generic in that one size fits all. Although there are apt to be exceptions, it more or less applies across the board to administrative agencies within a government, as opposed to being tailored to match each agency's mission individually. The phrase "administrative law," as used in the United States, does not refer to the substantive content of rules and regulations created by agencies. In other words, the procedures used by the FAA in adopting a rule for child safety seats is a matter of administrative law, but the rule's specific requirements for the design and strength of such seats is not. Moreover, administrative law, with the exception of some forms of adjudication, is not concerned with agency decisions regarding internal personnel, organizational, budgetary, outsourcing, and similar administrative matters. All levels of government in the United States rely on some forms of administrative law to regulate their administrative activities. In the absence of U.S. Supreme Court constitutional decisions applying to all jurisdictions, the requirements of federal, state, and local administrative law need not be uniform. In fact, there is substantial variation.

Why We Have Administrative Law
Statutes: Delegation and Discretion

Delegation

Administrative law statutes regulate administrative procedures and the review of agency actions. In the United States such statutes were adopted largely to control agencies' use of delegated legislative authority and their exercise of discretion. Although administration is usually associated with the executive branch of government, administrative activities nowadays also involve *legislative functions*. Rulemaking is the preeminent example. Agency rules, such as one for child safety seats, are the equivalent of legislation and are essentially a substitute for it. Thus administrative rulemaking is sometimes called "supplementary lawmaking." A safety-seat requirement could be imposed by statute as well as by an administrative

rule. But at the federal level, where agencies have no independent constitutional authority, such a rule can be issued only pursuant to a congressional delegation (i.e., grant) of legislative authority to an agency.

At first thought, it may seem odd that legislatures would give up their
own lawmaking authority to public administrators. After all, bureaucrats
are hardly popular among the American public. They are often derided
for usurping power and issuing undesirable rules written in impenetrable gobbledygook. However, there are several reasons why legislatures
find it necessary or desirable to delegate legislative authority to administrative agencies. First, as the scope and complexity of public policy increase, legislatures have difficulty keeping abreast of the need to adopt
and amend legislation. Legislative processes are typically cumbersome,
especially in bicameral legislatures such as Congress and those of forty-
nine of the fifty states (Nebraska being the sole exception). A bill typically
has to work its way independently through each house. It has to win majority support in both before being submitted to the president or governor for approval or veto. Legislative procedure is intended to provide
ample checks and balances, but where the workload is heavy, it can overwhelm a legislature's capacity to deal with all the demands it faces. By
delegating legislative authority to administrative agencies, legislatures
can unload some of the lawmaking burden on administrators.

Second, legislatures cannot be expected to have the level of detailed
technical expertise often required in contemporary public policy making.
Environmental, health, and safety regulation can involve setting standards based on elaborate scientific analysis. Trade-offs, such as the impact of child safety seats on families' decisions to fly or drive, are also
complex. Available science and statistical evidence may be imperfect. For
example, it may take years of technical analysis to determine how many
parts per million of a substance can be considered safe in drinking water
or in the ambient atmosphere at a factory. In time, new information may
require reevaluation of that determination. Expert administrators are in a
better position than legislators and their staffs to deal with such matters.
Moreover, the range of regulatory standards and related policy concerns
is too broad to be addressed by legislatures. It takes the attention of numerous, and frequently large, agencies.

Third, legislators may find it politically advantageous to delegate legislative authority to administrative agencies in order to avoid taking firm
stands on controversial issues. It is easier to maintain constituents' favor
by supporting broad objectives that are widely shared, such as protecting
the environment, than to set regulatory standards that will raise prices or

cause unemployment in one's home district. Legislators may even score points with the voters by denouncing decisions made by the very agencies and administrators that their legislation has empowered (Fiorina 1977:48–49).

As necessary and convenient as delegations of legislative authority are, they raise a number of political questions. Constitutionality is one. The separation of powers at the federal level and in the states is intended to establish checks and balances as a means of protecting the people against the aggregation of power in one branch of government. Parliamentary systems fuse legislative and executive powers, but the Framers of the U.S. Constitution thought such a combination could produce tyranny. Following their lead, Americans have preferred to keep these powers separate, though less so at the local government level. Consequently, when legislative authority is delegated to administrative agencies, even though voluntarily on the part of legislatures, it can be seen as a threat to the constitutional order. As the U.S. Supreme Court once summarized the problem, "The Congress is not permitted to abdicate or to transfer to others the essential legislative functions with which it is . . . vested" and there must be "limitations of the authority to delegate, if our constitutional system is to be maintained" (*Schechter Poultry Corp. v. United States* 1935:529–530). Yet modern government requires at least some delegation. Large-scale administration would be impossible without it.

At the federal level, the formal constitutional solution to the tension between the separation of powers and the vesting of legislative authority in administrative agencies requires delegations to be accompanied by "an intelligible principle to which [an agency] . . . is directed to conform." (*J. W. Hampton, Jr., & Co. v. United States* 1928:409). In theory, this "intelligible principle" doctrine ensures that Congress will clearly establish the broad objectives of public policy, relying on the agencies, when necessary, only to fill in the details. In practice, however, finding an intelligible principle in some delegations may be impossible. For instance, the federal Occupational Safety and Health Act of 1970 provides that the secretary of labor, "in promulgating standards dealing with toxic materials or harmful physical agents . . . shall set the standard which most adequately assures, *to the extent feasible*, on the basis of the best available evidence, that no employee will suffer material impairment of health or functional capacity even if such employee has regular exposure to the hazard dealt with by such standard for the period of his working life" (*Industrial Union Department, AFL-CIO v. American Petroleum Institute* 1980:671 [emphasis added]). With obvious frustration, Justice William Rehnquist parsed this language in an unsuccessful quest for an intelligible principle: "I believe that the legislative history demonstrates that the feasibility requirement . . . is a legislative mirage, appearing to some Members [of Congress] but not to others, and assuming any form desired by the beholder" (*Industrial Union Department, AFL-CIO v. American Petroleum Institute* 1980:681).

Rehnquist called the feasibility requirement "precatory," meaning that it essentially entreated the secretary of labor to take a balanced approach (*Industrial Union Department, AFL-CIO v. American Petroleum Institute* 1980:682). Such "legislative mirages" are not unusual. Statutes are loaded with key "standards" such as " 'adequate,' 'advisable,' 'appropriate,' 'beneficial,' 'convenient,' 'detrimental,' 'expedient,' 'equitable,' 'fair,' 'fit,' 'necessary,' 'practicable,' 'proper,' 'reasonable,' 'reputable,' 'safe,' 'sufficient,' 'wholesome,' or their opposites" (Warren 1996:370). The Federal Communications Commission (FCC) is charged with regulating communications by wire and radio in "the public interest"—a term with no fixed meaning that can accommodate any reasonable action (Office of the Federal Register 1999:524). The greatest certainty regarding the meaning of the phrase "stationary source" in the Clean Air Act Amendments of 1977 is that such sources of pollutants are not mobile. The U.S. Environmental Protection Agency (EPA) interpreted these same words very differently in different programs and at different times (*Chevron U.S.A., Inc. v. Natural Resources Defense Council, Inc.* 1984; see Chapter 6).

Discretion

Delegations of legislative authority call on administrators to use discretion in formulating standards and policies. The weaker the intelligible principle in the statutory delegation, the greater the potential range of administrative discretion. However, administrative discretion also goes well beyond the rulemaking function. Agencies may exercise a great deal of it in implementing or enforcing laws, rules, and other regulations. They often lack the resources to do everything legally required of them. Universal enforcement may be impossible or impracticable. It is an uncomfortable fact that selective application of the law is often inevitable. Equally important, the legal acceptability of many matters is determined by "street-level" administrators, such as safety and health inspectors, or weighed on a case-by-case basis through adjudication within administrative agencies.

The use of discretion by thoroughly trained, professional, competent administrators can be highly beneficial—society has come to depend on it. We have master of public administration/policy programs to provide public managers and policy analysts with the tools and ethical bases to exercise discretion soundly. We rely on merit systems and career civil services to reduce the likelihood that discretion will be abused. From a public administrative perspective, discretion is essential to the implementation of laws and the successful achievement of a government's policy objectives.

There is also another view. The motto "Where Law Ends Tyranny Begins" is prominently engraved on the U.S. Department of Justice headquarters building in Washington, D.C. From the vantage point of U.S. democratic constitutionalism, then, discretion is often at "war" (Warren 1996:365) with the bedrock principle of the rule of law. The Supreme Court has even called unconstrained discretion in enforcement an "evil" (*Delaware v. Prouse* 1979).

Administrative law is a major means of checking the exercise of administrative discretion to ensure that it is used rationally and fairly. It does this primarily in two ways: first, by structuring administrative decisionmaking processes; and second, by providing for procedural and substantive review of administrators' decisions.

Administrative Decisionmaking

The federal Administrative Procedure Act of 1946 (APA) is representative of U.S. administrative law statutes in trying to promote rationality and lawfulness in agency decisionmaking without imposing overly encumbering procedural requirements. It specifically seeks to prevent decisions that are

> (A) arbitrary, capricious, an abuse of discretion, or otherwise not in accordance with law; (B) contrary to constitutional right, power, privilege, or immunity; (C) in excess of statutory jurisdiction, authority, or limitations, or short of statutory right; (D) without observance of procedure required by law; (E) unsupported by substantial evidence . . . ; (F) unwarranted by the facts. (section 706)*

These objectives are often augmented by other statutes and executive orders that require agencies to use the best science available, engage in

---

*Citations to codified statutes in the text are to their section number in the *United States Code* (U.S.C.). Rather than repeat the title number of the *Code* in which the statute is found in each citation, this information is provided in the References section at the end of the book. The full citation to this section of the APA is 5 U.S.C. 706.

cost-benefit analysis, prepare environmental and other impact statements, or promote substantive values such as vibrant federalism or environmental justice. (These matters are addressed in Chapter 3, on rulemaking.)

In administrative law, agency decisions may be either "formal" or "informal." Although the distinction is imperfect, decisions resulting from activities whose procedures are substantially regulated by administrative law, such as rulemaking and adjudication, are considered formal. Informal decisions are more likely to involve questions such as which firm to investigate or inspect, how carefully, when, and what enforcement actions, if any, should be taken. Except where constitutional law is involved (e.g., the Fourth Amendment's protection against unreasonable searches and seizures), informal decisions are overwhelmingly regulated by individual agency protocol rather than administrative law.

Administrative decisions can also be categorized as retrospective, prospective, or present-tense. Administrative law uses a variety of processes to structure formal decisions of each type and to constrain the administrators making them. Retrospective decisions require assessing the past behavior of an individual, firm, group, governmental unit, or other entity. They involve questions such as whether a corporation engaged in illegal false advertising or an unfair labor practice. Retrospective decisions are often made in an adjudicatory framework. The agency and the regulated party make their cases before a hearing examiner, an administrative law judge, or a commission or board of some kind. The process can be undertaken in written form only, and it can involve presenting oral statements as well. It can range from an almost cursory review of the facts and issues by the decisionmaker to a full-fledged hearing that resembles courtroom procedure. It may also include a right to appeal adverse decisions to a higher unit within the agency. In all cases, however, the objective is to establish the facts, including motives where relevant, and to apply the law to them in an unbiased fashion. Consequently, administrative law may specify a great deal about the procedures to be used, the kind of information that can be considered, and the credentials and neutrality of the decisionmaker. (Adjudication is discussed in Chapter 4.)

Prospective decisions apply to events in the future. Rulemaking, such as the FAA's consideration of child safety seats, is the clearest example. Administrative law requirements are generally based on the assumption that prospective decisionmaking on complex matters will be more rational when it is open to public scrutiny and participation. Ideally, open rulemaking and related decisionmaking will bring a greater range of perspectives and information to the administrators' attention. Administrative law can require that the decisionmakers respond to public input and explain their evaluation of it. Rules may also be subjected to a rationality standard upon judicial review, such as being supported by substantial evidence (reasonableness).

Present-tense decisions often involve questions of eligibility or immediate compliance with a regulatory requirement. Many licensing decisions are present-tense and strongly regulated by administrative law statutes. However, much present-tense decisionmaking is informal, and some is more likely to be regulated by constitutional law decisions than by administrative procedure acts. For example, eligibility for social welfare benefits, such as Social Security Disability Insurance, is not ordinarily regulated by administrative law. Rather, it is established by a separate statute or administrative regulation specifically for the program involved. The denial or termination of these benefits, by contrast, may raise equal protection, due process, or other constitutional concerns. Many law enforcement decisions by police and health, safety, and housing inspectors are also present-tense. Their discretion whether to issue citations is generally not regulated by administrative law, and it is constrained by constitutional law only within broad parameters (Lipsky 1980; Bardach and Kagan 1982).

It is often difficult to establish or maintain the balance that administrative law seeks to secure between constraining discretion and allowing administrators enough flexibility to carry out their legislative mandates cost-effectively. Administrators may complain that the procedural requirements for rulemaking and adjudication are counterproductive and too complex, whereas regulated entities may want even more elaborate procedures to protect their interests. The compromises reached in administrative law statutes upon their enactment can also become outdated or upset by future legislation. Finding and keeping a satisfactory balance between the underregulation and overregulation of administrative decisionmaking is part of the challenge and vibrancy of administrative law.

Procedural and Substantive
Review of Administrative Decisions

Administrative law provisions regarding the procedural and substantive review of agency decisions also seek a balance of competing concerns. On the one hand, the political system relies on administrators to bring a high level of specialized expertise to the formulation and implementation of public policies. Subjecting their decisions to review by generalists who know less about the specifics of these policy areas and enforcement can result in delay, expense, and poor decisions. On the other hand, administrators' judgments can be distorted by self-interest; untoward internal or external influences; a failure to recognize competing priorities; over- or underconfidence; and many other factors that negatively affect individual and group decisionmaking. It is easy to find excellent as well as shockingly bad examples of administrative decisionmaking. Administrators have sent astronauts to the moon and back; they have also allowed children to play in highly toxic radioactive fallout (Ball 1986). The trick is to protect against the bad decisions while not upsetting the good ones or wasting time, effort, and money reviewing them.

Administrative law focuses on four venues for review of agency decisions. First, review may be available within the agency itself. For instance, decisions by administrative law judges (ALJs) in the federal government can be overturned by agency heads, boards, or commissions on procedural and substantive grounds. This allows political appointees, who are often generalists, to substitute their judgment for that of more specialized ALJs in the career civil service. They can correct decisions for failure to see public policies from a big-picture perspective, as well as for simple errors of judgment. Of course, political appointees' decisions themselves may be subject to review by the courts, and so appointees normally consult with agency attorneys and experts before making them.

Second, administrative law may provide for review by specific units within the executive branch. Currently, the OMB plays this role with regard to aspects of rulemaking and information gathering by many federal agencies. Its Office of Information and Regulatory Affairs (OIRA) reviews agency proposals to engage in major rulemaking, that is, rules that will have an annual economic impact of $100 million or more. Agencies are also required to obtain OIRA's clearance to use forms and other instruments for collecting information from individuals and organizations outside the federal government (see Chapter 3). The primary purposes of executive review of this kind are to coordinate agency activity and to ensure that it is in keeping with the goals of a president, governor, or other elected executive.

Third, administrative law statutes can establish the scope of judicial review of agency decisions, although the courts have independent authority under the federal and state constitutions to hear cases alleging violations of constitutional rights and powers. Judicial review has become so common at the federal level that for some agencies (e.g., the EPA), it can be considered part of the administrative process (Coglianese 1997: 1296–1309). (Judicial review is discussed in Chapter 6.)

Finally, there are procedures in Congress and some state legislatures for reviewing agency rulemaking decisions. Their logic is clear enough. The agencies' use of delegated legislative power ought to be reviewed by the legislature, which empowered them, in order to ensure conformance with legislative intent. (Legislative review is further discussed in Chapter 6.)

The Development of U.S. Administrative Law

The United States began to develop a substantial administrative component in the 1870s and 1880s. In time, administrative agencies engaged in so much policy formulation and implementation that the phrase "administrative state" was adopted to convey their centrality to modern government. Industrialization, urbanization, and population growth led governments to become increasingly involved in the economy and society and to rely more heavily on administrative agencies to do much of their work. As noted earlier, the Congress and state legislatures were unable to keep up with the continual need for new legislation, often involving complex health, scientific, or technological issues. The courts, which once engaged in a good deal of regulation of economic practices under common law doctrines, were overwhelmed by the changes industrialization caused in production, employment, transportation, and marketing. Vesting rulemaking and adjudicatory functions in administrative agencies was the nation's solution to the ever-expanding scope and complexity of government. More government activity also meant more enforcement by the executive branch.

A key feature of the administrative state is that agencies engage in legislative, judicial, and executive functions. In other words, the constitutional separation of powers, which largely places these functions in different branches, *collapses* into administrative agencies. Administrators make rules, adjudicate alleged violations of laws and rules, and execute and implement public policy. After the massive federal administrative growth during the New Deal (1933–1938) and U.S. involvement in World War II (1941–1945), it was fair to say, along with Supreme Court Justice Robert Jackson, that the agencies "have become a veritable fourth branch of the

Government, which has deranged our three-branch legal theories as much as the concept of a fourth dimension unsettles our three-dimensional thinking" (*Federal Trade Commission v. Ruberoid* 1952:487). By 1946, Congress viewed the power and independence of administrative agencies as a threat to its own role in government and to the overall constitutional scheme (Rosenbloom 2000). In response, it enacted the APA, which still frames federal administrative law.

There are several basic premises underlying the APA and state administrative law: When agencies engage in legislative functions, they should be informed by legislative values; when they adjudicate, they should follow judicial procedure; and enforcement should be fair, relatively nonintrusive, and subject to review. Importantly, Congress was willing to sacrifice some administrative cost-effectiveness to promote these values. As the APA's chief sponsor in the Senate approvingly noted, the Senate Judiciary Committee had "taken the position that the bill must reasonably protect private parties even at the risk of some incidental or possible inconvenience to, or change in, present administrative operations" (U.S. Congress 1946:2150).

In terms of rulemaking, as another APA supporter explained, "Day by day Congress takes account of the interests and desires of the people in framing legislation; and there is no reason why administrative agencies should not do so when they exercise legislative functions which the Congress has delegated to them" (U.S. Congress 1946:5756). Prior to the APA, administrative rulings might be made "in the form of letters, and nothing in the way of even an informal hearing [was] required. If the citizen [had] a hearing it [was] at the grace of the administrator or bureau chief" (U.S. Congress 1940:13668). From this perspective, the act could be seen as "a bill of rights for the hundreds of thousands of Americans whose affairs are controlled or regulated in one way or another by agencies of the Federal Government" (U.S. Congress 1946:2190). Its provisions for administrative adjudication model judicial procedure and constitutional procedural due process.

The APA did not provide for legislative or executive review, but it adopted a strong presumption of judicial review of enforcement and other actions: "A person suffering legal wrong because of agency action, or adversely affected or aggrieved by agency action within the meaning of a relevant statute, is entitled to judicial review thereof" (section 702). The act also contained a number of transparency provisions, including the general expectation that agencies would publish information about their organization, rules, adjudicatory decisions, and methods of operation, as well as make their public records available to "persons properly and directly concerned" (section 3). (Transparency is the subject of Chapter 5.)

The APA continues to serve as a platform for requiring federal administrative processes to embrace the basic democratic-constitutional values of openness for accountability; representativeness and public participation in policy formulation; reviewability for adherence to the rule of law; procedural due process for the fair treatment of individuals; and rationality when regulating private parties and other entities. Over the years the APA has been amended and augmented by several additional statutes. The following list provides a snapshot of the development of and scope of federal administrative law:

1. The Freedom of Information Act (1966; significantly amended in 1974, 1986, and 1996). The act vastly expanded the provisions for transparency contained in the APA.
2. The Federal Advisory Committee Act (1972; FACA) promotes representativeness and transparency in the agencies' use of advisory committees in policymaking.
3. The Privacy Act (1974) protects against unwarranted administrative invasions of personal privacy and the release of information on private individuals without their consent.
4. The Government in the Sunshine Act (1976) requires multi-headed federal boards and commissions to hold open meetings.
5. The Regulatory Flexibility Act (1980) requires agencies to consider the impact of potential rules on small businesses.
6. The Paperwork Reduction Acts (1980, 1995) seek to reduce the intrusiveness and burdensome quality of agency efforts to collect information from individuals and organizations outside the federal government.
7. The Administrative Dispute Resolution Act (1990) provides for alternative dispute resolution of matters that might otherwise be adjudicated within federal agencies.
8. The Negotiated Rulemaking Act (1990) outlines the general process through which agencies may attempt to negotiate rules with parties whose interests will be directly affected by them.
9. The Government Performance and Results Act (1993) requires agencies to engage in strategic planning and annual performance measurement and reporting.

10. The Small Business Regulatory Enforcement Fairness Act (1996) requires agencies to solicit information from small entities when writing rules and contains a title, known as the Congressional Review Act, that provides for congressional review of agency rules.

11. A variety of executive orders providing for executive review of agency rulemaking and information-gathering, as well as seeking to promote substantive values. These tend to change with different presidential administrations.

12. A substantial body of judicial decisions dealing with constitutional constraints on agencies and the appropriate scope of judicial review of agencies' interpretation of statutes, rulemaking, adjudication, and other actions.

The subjects listed above are the focus of the remainder of this book. There are parallel administrative law provisions in the states, though with a good deal of variation. North Dakota and California adopted administrative procedure acts in the 1940s, prior to the federal APA. Many more states followed suit between the mid-1950s and 1980. At least half of the state acts are based on the 1961 Model State Administrative Procedure Act. Some include provisions incorporated into the Model State Administrative Procedure Act of 1981, which placed more emphasis on protecting individual rights against administrative abuse. The state APAs typically apply to most or all state agencies but not to local governments. The discussion here centers on federal administrative law but highlights significant alternatives or differences found in the states where equivalent values and approaches may be stronger, weaker, or even nonexistent (Bonfield 1986, chapter 1; Bonfield and Asimow 1989; Asimow, Bonfield, and Levin 1998).

Conclusion

Public administration courses and programs generally emphasize management and the political context in which administrators operate. They sometimes view administrative law as a dry, technical matter for lawyers and judges. It may even be seen as interfering with cost-effective professional public management. In legal education, administrative law is taught from the perspectives of protecting private parties from administrative abuse and of suing agencies for some type of relief. Both of these approaches tend to consider administrative law from the outside-in, that is, as something imposed on agencies that is external to their central missions, professional expertise, and administrative values. This book treats administrative law from the inside-out. It explains how administrative law's underlying values, as well as typical requirements, are an integral part of contemporary public administration. It also emphasizes how administrative law helps make public administration comport more fully with the core values and processes of U.S. democratic constitutionalism. Administrative law helps prevent the modern administrative state from "becoming a government by the government and not by the people" (U.S. Congress 1940:4648). Administrative law makes bureaucracy safe for democracy.

2

The Constitutional Context of U.S. Public Administration

In 1887, Woodrow Wilson, who is often considered the founder of the academic field of public administration in the United States, could write that "public administration . . . at most points stand[s] apart . . . from the debatable ground of constitutional study" (Wilson 1887:18). Perhaps then, but no longer. Today public administrative practice is infused with constitutional concerns—and as the following cases illustrate, sometimes in surprising ways.

- In 1952, President Harry Truman (1945–1953) issued an executive order authorizing his secretary of commerce to seize the nation's steel mills in order to resolve a labor dispute that threatened to harm the U.S. military effort in the Korean War.
- President Richard Nixon (1969–1974) sent a budget message to Congress in 1973 that included no funds for the Office of Economic Opportunity (OEO). OEO's acting director, Howard Phillips, started closing down the agency. He wanted to prevent wasteful spending on activities he thought would come to a screeching halt at the end of the fiscal year.
- In 1987, Theodore Olson, a former assistant attorney general in the EPA, was subpoenaed by a grand jury at the behest of an independent counsel who believed he had given false and misleading testimony to Congress. Olson, who later became solicitor general in the George W. Bush administration (2001–), challenged the subpoena on the grounds that independent counsel's position violated the constitutional separation of powers.

The independent counsel was appointed to the Department of Justice by a special federal court, and she could be dismissed by the attorney general only for very limited, performance-related causes.

- Seeking to make federal procurement more efficient and economical, President Bill Clinton (1993–2001) issued an executive order in 1995 authorizing the secretary of labor to bar purchases from firms that hired workers permanently to replace employees who were legally on strike. The National Labor Relations Act of 1935 protects an employer's right to utilize permanent replacements, but Clinton claimed the Procurement Act of 1949 and his position as chief executive empowered him to override federal labor law when establishing policies for federal contracting.

- In 1995, Patricia Garrett, who had breast cancer, was forced to give up her position as director of Nursing, OB/Gyn/Neonatal Services, at the University of Alabama Hospital because her boss felt that her illness and the medical treatment she was receiving for it made her an undesirable employee. Garrett sued the hospital in federal court, claiming a violation of her rights under the Americans with Disabilities Act of 1990 (ADA).

- In 1993, Mayor Reid Paxon of Northlake, Illinois, removed John Gratzianna's company from the town police's tow truck rotation list. Paxon's action deprived Gratzianna of the business generated by the town's enforcement of parking and other traffic regulations. Gratzianna had a preexisting commercial relationship with Northlake, but no contract. The mayor was showing his displeasure with Gratzianna's refusal to contribute to his reelection bid and for supporting an opposition candidate instead.

Each of these cases raised a substantial constitutional issue. Presidents Truman and Clinton lacked constitutional and legal authority for their executive orders. The head of the OEO was bound to follow the law, not the chief executive's budget message. Olson overstated the extent to which the separation of powers compartmentalizes the branches of government or places federal administration under the president. Although Garrett could sue a private employer who did the same thing, the Eleventh Amendment bars such suits against states. The mayor violated Gratzianna's constitutionally protected freedom of speech.

These outcomes were not self-evident. Some made new law; others clarified or integrated existing principles. Together, they provide a sampling of how constitutional law frames many aspects of public administration in this country. The cases involving Truman, Nixon, Olson, and Clinton speak to the limits of executive authority. Garrett was done in by the doctrine of state sovereign immunity, which is an important component of contemporary U.S. federalism. Paxon's action illustrates that administrative decisionmaking is constrained—sometimes in surprising ways—by individuals' constitutional rights. Constitutional law is ever-changing, and even practices as old as the American republic itself, such as partisanship in hiring, firing, and contracting, can one day be ruled unconstitutional (*Rutan v. Republican Party of Illinois* 1990; *O'Hare Truck Service, Inc. v. City of Northlake* 1996).

This chapter explains four key aspects of public administration's constitutional framework: (1) the separation of powers, which places administrative agencies under executive, legislative, and judicial authority; (2) federalism, which affects the relationships between state and federal administrators; (3) individuals' rights in the context of different administrative encounters; and (4) public administrators' liabilities for violating individuals' constitutional rights. Together, these constitutional features define and confine U.S. public administration. They make it clear that although politicians, reformers, and media pundits often call for running government like a business, constitutional law makes the public's business very different from others.

The Separation of Powers

The U.S. Constitution's separation of powers has a tremendous impact on federal and state administration. It divides authority over public agencies and administrators. Legislatures and courts, as well as executives, are constitutionally mandated to play substantial roles in public administration. Each branch brings a somewhat different value-set to administration. Almost everybody wants the efficient, economical, and effective government associated with good public management. But at what cost to other concerns? Legislatures write administrative law to promote representativeness, public participation, transparency, and fairness in public administration. These values are also widely shared by Americans. The same is true of the courts' efforts to protect constitutional integrity and individual rights. Maximizing all these values simultaneously is often impossible. One person's open, participatory public administration is another's delay and hurdle to achieving programmatic results. A judge's procedural due process is an executive's red tape. And so on and so on. Yet the separation of powers is not merely about executive, legislative, and judicial controls over public administration; it goes directly to the matter of what public administration should be.

The U.S. Constitution's scheme for the separation of powers is extreme in its impact on federal administration. Its main provisions were written at a time when no one possibly could have foreseen the development of the modern administrative state. The number of civilian federal employees at its historical highpoint—4 million in 1945—was just about equal to the *entire U.S. population* when the Constitution took effect in 1789. Although the Framers' provisions for public administration were rudimentary at best, they remain largely in place today. By contrast, the states have found it easier to amend their constitutions or even adopt new ones in order to keep pace with political change, including administrative growth. They have been in a better position to clarify powers over public administration, especially those of the governor. By and large, local governments avoid the separation of powers altogether or rely on a much weaker version than the federal government. The following discussion focuses on Congress, the president, and the federal judiciary because the division of authority among them provides the clearest example of the impact of separation of powers on public administration.

Congress

It is fair to say that the Constitution makes Congress the source or author of federal administration (Willoughby 1927; 1934). Legislation is required to establish, empower, structure, staff, and fund federal agencies. Article I, section 9, clause 7 is unequivocal in providing that "No Money shall be drawn from the Treasury, but in Consequence of Appropriations made by Law." Article II, section 2, clause 2 requires that all federal positions not specifically established by the Constitution "shall be established by Law." These provisions were written to check presidential power. In the absence of an appropriations statute the president cannot constitutionally draw a dime from the Treasury; without delegated legislative authority, the president cannot create and legally empower a single administrative office.

Relying on its constitutional powers, Congress has substantially enhanced its role in federal administration. Since 1946, it has reorganized and staffed itself for continuous oversight of the agencies. It also created the Congressional Research Service (CRS) and the Congressional Budget Office to obtain better information regarding federal administration and public policy. Additionally, the General Accounting Office (GAO), another legislative agency, gained greater capacity to investigate and evaluate federal administrative operations. Congress has also relied on inspectors general, who have been dubbed "congressional moles," and chief financial officers in the agencies to keep it informed about administrative activities (Moore and Gates 1986:10). The Congressional Review Act (1996) enables Congress to permanently block agency rules (see Chapter 6).

The President

Some political scientists maintain that Congress, as a result of its constitutional authority and oversight activity, has gained dominance over federal agencies (see Wood and Waterman 1994: chapter 3). That may sound strange to the many Americans who look to the president to control and manage the executive branch. However, it is in keeping with what several presidents and high ranking federal executives have had to say. When Vice President Dick Cheney was chief of White House staff in the Gerald Ford administration (1974–1977), he commented that

> there's a tendency before you get to the White House or when you're just observing it from outside to say, "Gee, that's a powerful position that person has." The fact of the matter is that while you're here trying to do things, you are far more aware of the constraints than you are of the power. You spend most of your time trying to overcome obstacles getting what the President wants done. (Edwards and Wayne 1985:351)

President Jimmy Carter (1977–1981) may not have been the most effective president, but presidential power over federal administration may have hit its nadir when he complained, "I can't even get a damn mouse out of my office" due to a bureaucratic jurisdictional dispute between the Department of the Interior (White House grounds) and the General Services Administration (White House building) (Barger 1984:145).

Carter's successors have done better, but both President Ronald Reagan (1981–1989) and President Bill Clinton met considerable frustration in trying to promote fundamental administrative change. Reagan vowed to make the federal government smaller. When he left office it was larger in terms of the number of cabinet departments, civilian employees, budget deficit, and spending as a percent of the nation's gross domestic product (GDP). With Vice President Al Gore leading Clinton's Reinventing Government initiative, a wide variety of reforms were implemented, including downsizing, outsourcing, deregulating and decentralizing the personnel system, streamlining procurement, and setting customer service standards (Gore 1993; Gore 1995). Yet surveys of federal employees indicated that the reform effort had only a modest overall impact. Although 72 percent of the civil service knew about the reinvention effort, just 35 percent thought their own agencies made it a priority (Barr 2000:A27). It seems noteworthy that Gore barely mentioned the reinvention effort during his unsuccessful 2000 presidential campaign.

The president's problem is that the Constitution's provisions regarding the scope of executive authority over federal administration are very general. Article II, section 1 vests "executive Power" in the president without specifying its content. President Theodore Roosevelt (1901–1909) declared that this gave him the "duty to do anything that the needs of the Nation demanded unless such action was forbidden by the Constitution or by the laws" (Olson and Woll 1999:15). In terms of federal administration, one wonders just what this might be without legal authority to spend money or hire staff. Article II, section 3 is even more obtuse in authorizing the president to "take Care that the Laws be faithfully executed." Notice the "be." The Framers did not charge the president with faithfully executing the laws but apparently overseeing and coordinating their execution— and not necessarily on an exclusive basis. In so doing the president "may require the Opinion, in writing, of the principal Officer of each of the executive Departments, upon any Subject relating to the Duties of their respective Offices" (Article II, section 2, clause 1). The president also has "the Power to fill up all Vacancies that may happen during the Recess of the Senate, by granting Commissions which shall expire at the End of their next Session" (Article II, section 2, clause 3). This alternatively suggests that the president is either in charge of federal administration or merely a caretaker when Congress is not in session.

When federal administrators are caught between competing congressional and presidential commands, they are constitutionally required to take refuge in the law. A Supreme Court decision issued in 1838 remains good constitutional principle today: "It would be an alarming doctrine, that [C]ongress cannot impose upon any executive officer any duty they may think proper, which is not repugnant to any rights secured and protected by the [C]onstitution; and in such cases, the duty and responsibility grow out of and are subject to the control of the law, and not to the direction of the President" (*Kendall v. United States* 1838:610).

Howard Phillip's mistake, as acting director of the OEO, was precisely listening to the president rather than the law. He believed it was his "duty to terminate that agency's functions to effect the least 'waste' of funds" (*Local 2677, American Federation of Government Employees* [AFGE] *v. Phillips* 1973:73). To the contrary, ruled the district court: "No budget message of the President can . . . force the Congress to act to preserve legislative programs from extinction prior to the time Congress has declared they shall terminate, either by its action or inaction. . . . An administrator's responsibility to carry out the Congressional objectives of a program does not give him the power to discontinue that program, especially in the face of a Congressional mandate that it shall go on" (*Local 2677, AFGE v. Phillips* 1973:75; 77–78). (In the end, some of the OEO's functions were transferred to other agencies and it was disbanded.)

Clinton's executive order barring federal contracting with firms that permanently replace lawful strikers ran into a similar problem. Clinton claimed the order's purpose was "to ensure the economical and efficient administration of Federal Government contracts" (Executive Order 12,954 [1995]: section 1) and that it was congruent with the purposes of the Procurement Act of 1949. Again a federal court saw things differently:

> It does not seem possible to deny that the President's Executive Order seeks to set a broad policy governing the behavior of thousands of American companies and affecting millions of American workers. The President has, of course, acted to set a procurement policy rather than a labor policy. But the former is quite explicitly based—and would have to be based—on his views of the latter. . . .
>
> No state or federal official or government entity can alter the delicate balance of bargaining and economic power that the NLRA [National Labor Relations Act of 1935] establishes, whatever his or its purpose may be.
>
> *If the government were correct [in its arguments supporting Clinton], it follows . . . that another President could not only revoke the Executive Order, but could issue a new order that actually* required *government contractors to permanently replace strikers, premised on a finding that this would minimize unions' bargaining power and thereby reduce procurement costs.* (*Chamber of Commerce of the United States, et al. v. Reich* 1996:1337–1338 [emphasis added])

In short, the executive power does not give the president authority to use administrative processes, such as procurement, to contravene or circumvent federal statutes—even in the name of efficiency, economy, or effectiveness. If it did, as the court suggests, national policy could be unstable and the rule of law might dissolve. Moreover, the president's de facto lawmaking power would be vast: In the mid-1990s, federal contracts accounted for 6.5 percent of the nation's GDP and 22 percent of its employment (*Chamber of Commerce, et al. v. Reich* 1996:1338).

Morrison v. Olson (1988)—the independent counsel case—limits presidential power over federal administration from another angle. It essentially holds that the executive branch does not belong to the president but rather is subordinate to Congress and the federal courts as well. In a sense, the agencies are under the "joint custody" of all three branches, though *Morrison v. Olson* does not use that term specifically (Rourke 1993). The Ethics in Government Act of 1978 provided for the appointment of independent counsels by a federal court, called the Special Division. Independent counsels were vested with the "full power and independent authority to exercise all investigative and prosecutorial functions and powers of the Department of Justice, the Attorney General, and any other officer or employee of the Department of Justice" (*Morrison v. Olson* 1988:662). They could be dismissed only by impeachment and conviction or by the *"personal action"* of the attorney general "for good cause, physical disability, mental incapacity, or any other condition that substantially impairs the performance of such independent counsel's duties" (*Morrison v. Olson* 1988:663 [emphasis added]). No wonder Theodore Olson thought that Alexia Morrison, the independent counsel, was vexing him unconstitutionally. She was engaged in a core executive function—execution/enforcement of the law—and able to draw on the resources of the Department of Justice. Yet she was appointed by a court, provided by Congress with substantial legal protection from dismissal by her nominal superior, the attorney general, and could not be fired directly by the nation's chief executive, the president, at all.

The Supreme Court found this arrangement perfectly acceptable. The Constitution's Appointment Clause specifically provides that "Congress may by Law vest the Appointment of . . . inferior Officers, as they think proper, in the President alone, in the Courts of Law, or in the Heads of Departments" (Article II, section 2, clause 2). Its wording left three main questions open.

- Was Morrison an "inferior officer" (as opposed to a principal officer such as a department head who must be appointed by the president with the advice and consent of the Senate, except when the latter is in recess)? Yes.

- Was there "some 'incongruity' between the functions normally performed by the courts and the performance of their duty to appoint" independent counsels? No.
- Did the independent counsel provisions "interfere impermissibly" with the president's "constitutional obligation to ensure the faithful execution of the laws"? No. (*Morrison v. Olson* 1988:676, 693)

In a lone dissent, Justice Antonin Scalia protested, "There are now no lines. If the removal of a prosecutor, the virtual embodiment of the power to 'take care that the laws be faithfully executed,' can be restricted, what officer's removal cannot? This is an open invitation for Congress to experiment" (*Morrison v. Olson* 1988:726). Precisely; that is the nature of joint custody. In the context of some administrative processes, such as dismissals and rulemaking, whole units—the independent regulatory commissions—may be beyond the direct reach of presidential executive powers (Moreno 1994). In *Humphrey's Executor v. United States* (1935:628), the Supreme Court held that members of the Federal Trade Commission, which has quasilegislative and quasijudicial functions, occupy "no place in the executive department" and exercise "no part of the executive power vested by the Constitution in the President." By implication, the independent regulatory commissions are sometimes considered a "headless fourth branch" of the government.

Constitutional joint custody of administration hardly renders the president powerless. President Truman's effort to take over the steel mills was beyond his constitutional authority—even as commander in chief during a major war. However, his action yielded an important formula for assessing presidential powers that continues to inform analysis of the scope of executive authority today. As explained by Justice Robert Jackson in a concurring opinion:

1. When the President acts pursuant to an express or implied authorization of Congress, his authority is at its maximum, for it includes all that he possesses in his own right plus all that Congress can delegate. . . .

2. When the President acts in the absence of either a congressional grant or denial of authority, he can only rely upon his own independent powers, but there is a zone of twilight in which he and Congress may have concurrent authority, or in which its distribution is uncertain. . . .

3. When the President takes measures incompatible with the expressed or implied will of Congress, his power is at its lowest ebb, for then he can rely only upon his own constitutional powers minus any constitutional powers of Congress over the matter. (*Youngstown Sheet & Tube Co. v. Sawyer* 1952:636–637)

The president's large role in federal administration is primarily a product of the circumstances in Jackson's first category. Congress delegates a great deal of initiative and authority over administration to the president. It looks to presidents for faithful execution of the laws it enacts, day-to-day cost-effective management, and coordination of the agencies' activities. Through legislation, Congress has given the president leadership roles in federal budgeting, personnel administration, and, to a lesser extent, agency organizational design. Within this framework, presidential power is exercised with a tool kit of sorts, consisting of the Executive Office of the President (EOP), political appointees, and executive orders.

The EOP was created in 1939 in response to massive administrative expansion under President Franklin D. Roosevelt (1933–1945) and the New Deal, which resulted in some 100 agencies reporting directly to the president. Its primary purpose was to give the presidency the organizational capability to direct, coordinate, and monitor federal administrative activity. Today, its main units of importance to the agencies are as follows:

1. The White House Office, which promotes the president's policy agenda within the agencies, coordinates their activities, generates solutions to administrative and policy problems, and resolves conflicts among the president's appointees. It also includes the president's top advisers, the press secretary, legal advisers, and others who assist the president on a day-to-day basis. The White House Office has generally had more than 400 employees under recent presidents.

2. The Office of Management and Budget is perhaps the president's major source of control over contemporary federal administration. In 1970, the OMB replaced and expanded on the activities of the Bureau of the Budget, a unit first created in the Treasury Department in 1921 and later moved to the EOP in 1939. OMB plays a major role in: formulating the federal budget for submission by the president to Congress; supervising agencies' spending, rulemaking, policy, and regulatory initiatives;

and coordinating administrative activity. Its Office of Information and Regulatory Affairs is especially important in overseeing and coordinating agencies' rulemaking and their use of forms and similar instruments for collecting information. It is characteristic of the separation of powers that although OMB is a quintessential presidential agency the director, deputy director, and the head of OIRA require Senate confirmation. In recent years OMB has housed more than 500 employees.

3. The National Security Council, established in 1947, advises the president on the coordination and integration of domestic, foreign, and military policy as it relates to national security. Its leadership is composed mainly of federal officials with other responsibilities, including the president, vice president, secretaries of the departments of state and defense, the Director of Central Intelligence, and the chair of the Joint Chiefs of Staff.

4. The Office of Policy Development, and similarly named units, have had a checkered history since 1970, when first established. Their basic purpose is to help formulate, coordinate, and implement the president's domestic policy agenda. By and large, domestic policy units have been overshadowed by OMB.

Other EOP units include the Office of the Vice President, the Council of Economic Advisers, the Council on Environmental Quality, and offices for drug control, science and technology policy, and foreign trade. Presidents have considerable flexibility in using these units to promote their policies, although several of the top EOP appointees outside the White House Office require confirmation by the Senate. In 2001, the Office of Homeland Security (OHS) was established by President George W. Bush (who took office that year) to coordinate the nation's defense against terrorism. However, because OHS was carved out of existing presidential authority and budget, rather than based on new legislation, its role was largely advisory. The federal budget for homeland security was spread across 2,000 separate agency and department accounts (Miller 2002a). The inherent problems in this arrangement were a direct outgrowth of the constitutional limits on presidential power. In mid-2002, Bush called on Congress to enact a statute establishing the cabinet-level Department of Homeland Security to replace the OHS.

Political appointees to the departments and agencies also help the president direct and coordinate federal administration. Presidents rely on them to implement policy initiatives and to manage and monitor the career civil service on a day-to-day basis. There are several types of political appointees of varying importance. Top-level appointees, such as department and agency heads or commissioners, require Senate confirmation, whereas most others do not. In recent years, the overall number of political appointees has generally been upward of 2,500, which some consider so large as to impede efficiency and effectiveness (Light 1995). In practice, all but a few department and agency heads have limited access to the president. They basically receive presidential direction through the White House Office and OMB. In terms of administration, the relatively short tenure of political appointees—about two years or less in several recent presidential administrations—can be destabilizing or even disruptive to program implementation by the career civil service (Heclo 1977; Aberbach and Rockman 2000).

Executive orders are often a highly effective means of directing and controlling administrative activity. Presidents have issued more than 13,000 of them since 1862, when the term "executive order" was first used. They are a staple of presidential efforts to exercise authority over administrative agencies and processes. Among other matters, executive orders have been used to reorganize agencies; to require agencies to pay attention to particular values such as vibrant federalism and customer service; to regulate agencies' rulemaking processes; and to deal with federal personnel matters. They are often issued pursuant to congressional delegations of legislative authority, though they may be based on the president's assertion of Article II authority alone. To be valid, their implementation cannot contravene the Constitution or statutory law. They can be challenged in federal court, as were Truman's order dealing with the steel mills and Clinton's regarding permanent scabs. Unless they are in an area of exclusive presidential authority under the Constitution, Congress can negate them by statute (which is subject to presidential veto and override by a two-thirds vote in both the House of Representatives and the Senate). To regulate the behavior of ordinary private citizens or businesses, an executive order must be based on a statute or a special connection to the government, such as being a contractor with it. For example, Executive Order 8802 (1941) declared that "there shall be no discrimination in the employment of workers in defense industries or Government because of race, creed, color, or national origin," although prohibiting such discrimination in most private-sector employment had to wait several years for congressional legislation, namely, the Civil Rights Act of 1964. Overall, and perhaps by legislative default, executive orders have become a very powerful tool for regulating administrative processes and activity (Olson and Woll 1999).

Taken as a whole, then, Article II, delegations of legislative authority, and the tool kit put the president at the center of federal administration. Nevertheless, it is a mistake to assume that the executive branch is solely the president's. On most administrative matters, presidential power is shared with Congress—and sometimes with the courts as well.

The Judiciary

The judiciary is central to public administration and administrative law in the United States. At the federal level, and perhaps in many states, litigation is a normal rather than extraordinary feature of the administrative process. Individuals and regulated entities often sue the agencies that regulate them. Agencies use litigation to enforce statutes and administrative rules. Perhaps to the taxpayers' disbelief, sometimes federal agencies even sue each other (e.g., *Department of Defense v. Federal Labor Relations Authority*, discussed in Chapter 5). Litigation is so institutionalized that there is a specialized U.S. Court of Appeals for the Federal Circuit that hears appeals dealing with patents, federal contracts, international trade, claims against the United States, federal personnel matters, and veterans' affairs. Through hundreds, if not thousands, of suits, federal and state judges define the constitutionality and legality of administrative procedures, decisions, and enforcement activities. Court decisions are part of the overall fabric of U.S. administrative law. Consequently, their substantive holdings and requirements are fully integrated into this book's discussion of rulemaking, adjudication, and transparency. However, because it is easy to get lost in the details of myriad judicial rulings and doctrines, the discussion here explains the overall framework and coherence of the judiciary's impact on contemporary public administration.

Since the 1950s, the federal judiciary has responded to the post–New Deal and post–World War II role of public administration in the society, economy, and governmental structure primarily in four ways. First, it declared (or "created") a vast array of new constitutional rights for individuals in their encounters with public administrators. Prior to the 1950s, agencies' clients or customers, public employees, and those confined to prisons and public mental health facilities had very few constitutional protections against abusive administrative action. The same was true of individuals involved in street-level interaction with enforcement officers, such as police and health and safety inspectors. There has been, however, a dramatic turnabout (discussed below in the section "Individual Constitutional Rights in Administrative Encounters").

Second, the courts made it easier for individuals to gain *standing* (see Chapter 6) to sue administrators for violations of their newfound rights. Under Article III of the Constitution, the judicial power extends only to "cases and controversies." Consequently, the federal district courts, circuit courts of appeal, the Supreme Court, and other Article III courts do not give advisory opinions. To bring a case against an administrative agency—that is, to have standing to sue the agency—the plaintiff must show that he/she has been, or will be, injured by the agency in some concrete and particular way that can be redressed appropriately through a lawsuit. The courts can tighten or loosen the standards for standing when assessing the nature of the injury; its cause; the extent to which it is borne by particular individuals or an identifiable class of persons; and whether the remedy sought is appropriate. Merely being a taxpayer whose taxes increase due to an agency's action is insufficient to create standing to sue federal agencies. Such an injury is shared with millions of other individuals and, therefore, is not particularized. One may also lack standing because the injury is too limited to create a sufficient stake in the outcome of a suit; the injury was not caused by the party being sued; or the requested relief will not remedy the injury. However, at one point in the mid-1970s, the threshold for suing an agency in federal court was reduced "to the simple proposition that one who is hurt by governmental action has standing to challenge it" (Davis 1975:72). That opened the door to more suits and, consequently, more judicial involvement in administration. Today, the door remains open wider than throughout most of U.S. history (but somewhat narrower than in the 1970s).

Third, the federal judiciary developed a new type of lawsuit that facilitates its direct intervention in public administration as a means of protecting the constitutional rights of discrete categories of people, such as prisoners or applicants for employment in a government agency. These suits, called remedial lawsuits, are aimed at creating thoroughgoing reforms in administrative institutions and processes. Public school desegregation suits are a familiar example, in which judges become deeply involved in the operation of school systems in order to remedy previous violations of some students' constitutional right to equal protection of the laws. Courts sometimes retain jurisdiction for years and may make decisions about neighborhood school boundaries, teachers' salaries, curriculum, the location of new schools and the closing of older ones, and even the architecture of school buildings. Prisons, jails, public mental hospitals, and public personnel systems have also been subject to such judicial oversight (Rosenbloom and O'Leary 1997:283–289).

Fourth, as is discussed later in this chapter, the federal courts greatly increased the personal liability that most public administrators face for violating individuals' constitutional rights. The administrators' best defense against suits alleging an injury to one's constitutional rights is not to violate these rights in the first place. Because constitutional law "is what the courts say it is," as Justice Lewis Powell once remarked, potential liability provides a strong incentive for administrators to follow judicial decisions affecting the rights of their clients, customers, subordinates, contractors, or inmates, along with any others upon whom they may act in their official capacities (*Owen v. City of Independence* 1980:669). Public administrators also need to integrate into their daily practices the constitutional values that underlie those decisions.

These four developments amount to a judicial response to the modern administrative state. Judges have declared new constitutional rights to protect individuals against administrative abuses; made it easier for them to sue agencies and administrators; developed a type of lawsuit that enables judges to intervene directly in administrative operations; and made administrators who ignore the constitutional rights of others far more vulnerable to liability. Much of their reasoning has been premised on the concern that "today's mounting bureaucracy, both at the state and federal levels, promises to be suffocating and repressive unless it is put into the harness of procedural due process" (*Spady v. Mount Vernon* 1974:985). It is also based on a desire to ensure that "where an official could be expected to know that certain conduct would violate statutory or constitutional rights, he should be made to hesitate" (*Harlow v. Fitzgerald* 1982:819). Taken as a whole, the judiciary has "constitutionalized" public administration throughout the United States by establishing constitutional law as a basis for constraining administrative activity and defining its processes, values, and ethical requirements (Rosenbloom, Carroll, and Carroll 2000; Rosenbloom and O'Leary 1997; Rohr 1989).

Federalism

Federalism—the division of authority between the federal government and the states—is another constitutional arrangement of great importance to U.S. public administration. The constitutional law of federalism is defined by the Commerce Clause and Spending Clause in Article I, along with the Tenth and Eleventh Amendments. The Tenth Amendment most succinctly underscores the basic theory of federalism in this country. The federal government is one of limited, enumerated powers, whereas the states have largely open-ended residuary sovereignty over a very broad range of policy areas: "The powers not delegated to the United States by the Constitution, nor prohibited by it to the States, are reserved to the States respectively, or to the people." The key issue in assessing federalism is determining which powers are denied to the states and which are vested in the federal government.

Because the states' powers are open-ended, it is easier to say what they cannot do (as opposed to what they can do) under the Constitution. Prohibitions on state activity in Article I, section 10 include: entering treaties, alliances, and confederations; coining money; passing ex post facto laws, bills of attainder, and laws impairing the obligation of contracts; and granting titles of nobility. The section permits the states to do the following, but only with congressional consent: levy duties on imports and exports (except what is "absolutely necessary" for executing its inspection laws); keep troops or warships during peacetime; enter into compacts with other states or foreign powers; and engage in war, except if imminently threatened by invasion or actually invaded.

In addition to these limitations, the states are directly constrained by several constitutional amendments. In terms of contemporary administration, the Fourteenth Amendment is most important. It reads, in part: "Nor shall any State deprive any person of life, liberty, or property, without due process of law; nor deny to any person within its jurisdiction the equal protection of the laws" (section 1). The word "liberty" has been interpreted by the federal courts to "incorporate" much of the Bill of Rights (i.e., the first ten amendments) and to apply their restrictions, which originally pertained to the federal government, to the states. For example, the First Amendment's provisions that "Congress shall make no law respecting an establishment of religion, or prohibiting the free exercise thereof; or abridging the freedom of speech, or of the press" applies to the states through the Fourteenth Amendment. As a consequence, the U.S. Constitution and federal courts now play a much greater role than the Framers anticipated in 1787 in protecting individuals' fundamental rights from infringement by the states. Several other amendments also directly limit the states. The Thirteenth (1865) bans slavery; the Fifteenth (1870), Nineteenth (1920), Twenty-fourth (1964), and Twenty-sixth (1971), respectively, prohibit abridgment of the right to vote on account of race, sex, failure to pay a poll tax, or age (for those eighteen and older). The Twenty-first (1933), by contrast, empowers the states to regulate the delivery and use of intoxicating liquors.

The Commerce Clause

Federalism is more complicated when the states are denied powers because they are constitutionally vested in the federal government. The Commerce Clause, in particular, has been central to defining the scope of federal and state powers. It authorizes Congress "to regulate Commerce with foreign Nations, and among the several States, and with the Indian Tribes" (Article I, section 8, clause 3). However, it does not define "commerce" or "among." The Supreme Court's interpretation of these words changes over time and thereby alters the balance between federal and state power.

At the low point of federal power, "commerce," defined as buying and selling, did not include production, manufacturing, and mining. Regulation of these activities, including working conditions within them, was a matter for the states. Commerce could be regulated by the federal government if it was interstate or had a direct effect on interstate trade. In the 1930s, the New Deal effort to overcome the Great Depression was frustrated by such a narrow Commerce Clause interpretation, which put a great deal of economic activity beyond the reach of federal regulation. For example, in 1936 the Supreme Court strongly rebuffed Congress's attempt to regulate labor practices, wages, and other working conditions in coal mining:

> The distinction between a direct and an indirect effect turns, not upon the magnitude of either the cause or the effect, but entirely upon the manner in which the effect has been brought about. If the production by one man of a single ton of coal intended for interstate sale and shipment . . . affects interstate commerce indirectly, the effect does not become direct by multiplying the tonnage, or increasing the number of men employed, or adding to the expense or complexities of the business, or by all combined. (*Carter v. Carter Coal Co.* 1936:308)

Under this approach, if production was local, there was no difference between one ton and a million tons, and a "production crisis in every part of the country simultaneously could never add up to a national problem with which Congress could deal" (Pritchett 1977:193). Regulation would have to come from the states, which for economic reasons might want to be more lax, or at least not significantly more stringent than their neighbors.

The Supreme Court's constricted reading of the Commerce Clause in the 1930s triggered a great deal of criticism. President Roosevelt sought to pack the Court (i.e., expand its size in order to appoint up to six new justices, who presumably would be more amenable to New Deal measures). The court-packing plan proved unnecessary. In 1937, the Court began to accept a broader role for the federal government in regulating the economy. By 1942, the Commerce Clause could be used to regulate a farmer's production of wheat on his farm in one state, even though almost all of it was consumed there and only a trivial amount ever entered any market. In the Court's new and expansive interpretation of the Commerce Clause, "even if [the] activity be local, and though it may not be regarded as commerce, it may still, whatever its nature, be reached by Congress if it exerts a substantial economic effect on interstate commerce, and this irrespective of whether such effect is what might at some earlier time have been defined as 'direct' or 'indirect'" (*Wickard v. Filburn* 1942:125). The Court's underlying theory was that if a large number of farmers grew and consumed wheat on their farms in excess of federal crop quotas, it would have a substantial effect on the national market for wheat.

Today, the federal government can regulate: (1) the channels of interstate commerce, such as motels and other places of public accommodation; (2) persons, things, and the instrumentalities of interstate commerce, including vehicles and thefts from interstate shipments; and (3) activities having a substantial relation to interstate commerce, either individually or in the aggregate, as in the case of farmers who exceed crop quotas. Based on these principles, the Commerce Clause gives Congress power to enact such landmark legislation as the Civil Rights Act of 1964, which prohibits discrimination based on sex and the factors mentioned earlier in most employment, by labor unions, and in public accommodations and transportation. The clause also supports federal law against discrimination based on age or disability.

The breadth of the post–New Deal Commerce Clause raised two main questions. First, are there any limits to what Congress can regulate? After all, if sufficiently repeated or aggregated, almost any behavior Congress might want to control could have a substantial effect on interstate commerce. And second, when does congressional legislation entirely preempt the states from regulating in the same policy area?

Until the 1990s, there appeared to be no clear limits to the federal government's Commerce Clause powers. However, in *United States v. Lopez*

(1995) and *United States v. Morrison* (2000), the Supreme Court emphasized that the act regulated must be *economic* in character. In *Lopez* the
Court held that the Commerce Clause could not sustain a federal statute
banning the possession of a gun in any school zone in the United States.
The Court's majority contended that if the statute were valid, "we are
hard-pressed to posit any activity by an individual that Congress is without power to regulate" and, therefore, federal powers would endlessly
overlap those of the states (*United States v. Lopez* 1995:564). Similarly, in
Morrison the Court found a section of the 1994 Violence Against Women
Act unconstitutional because Congress may not regulate "noneconomic,
violent criminal conduct based solely on that conduct's aggregate effect
on interstate commerce" (*United States v. Morrison* 2000:617).

Preemption doctrine is more complex. The fact that Congress regulates
something, such as the environment, does not automatically mean that
the states lose all power to address the same policy area. For instance, a
state might want its groundwater to be even freer of toxins than is required under EPA standards. However, when federal legislation comprehensively occupies a policy field, the states are preempted—that is, excluded—from asserting jurisdiction over it. In general, states are more
likely to be preempted by federal legislation when: (1) the policy area requires uniform national regulation; (2) the policy area has not historically
been dominated by the states (e.g., nuclear energy); (3) dual regulation
will promote conflict; and (4) a federal agency has been created to regulate the policy area. Business interests often favor national regulation that
preempts the states from setting a variety of separate standards, but both
the federal and state governments are active in regulating health, safety,
labor, the environment, transportation, and other matters.

Federal preemption can also be based on the Commerce Clause alone.
A judicial construct called the "negative" or "dormant" Commerce
Clause prohibits state and local governments from passing regulations
that discriminate against interstate commerce or impose burdens on interstate commerce that are "clearly excessive in relation to the putative
local benefits" (*C & A Carbone, Inc. v. Town of Clarkstown* 1994:390). The
usual motive for discrimination is to retain as much economic activity as
possible within a state. For instance, a state might try (probably unsuc-
cessfully) to require that all timber or shrimp harvested within its bor-
ders be processed there as well. The excessive burden test requires a subjective balancing by the courts. In one example, Arizona sought to
enhance its reputation for fine agricultural produce by requiring cantaloupes grown there to be packed in boxes clearly showing their origin.

In order to ensure effective enforcement, the packaging would have to be done in Arizona as well. The Supreme Court found the regulation excessively burdensome to a grower who, lacking a packing facility in Arizona, shipped his cantaloupes to a nearby one in California and would have had to make a $200,000 capital investment to comply with it (*Pike v. Bruce Church, Inc.* 1970).

The Tenth Amendment

The Tenth Amendment ratifies the concept of dual sovereignty, whereby the federal government is sovereign in some areas and the states in others. The residuary state powers it protects necessarily vary with judicial interpretation of the Commerce Clause. As Justice Sandra Day O'Connor explained: "If a power is delegated to Congress in the Constitution, the Tenth Amendment expressly disclaims any reservation of that power to the States; if a power is an attribute of state sovereignty reserved by the Tenth Amendment, it is necessarily a power the Constitution has not conferred on Congress" (*New York v. United States* 1992:156). The broader state sovereignty under the Tenth Amendment, the narrower the Commerce Clause, and vice versa.

State sovereignty under Tenth Amendment interpretation waned in the wake of the New Deal. In 1985, the Supreme Court came close to holding that the amendment was no longer judicially enforceable. Rather, the states should look to their representation in Congress—the Senate, in particular—for protection against federal encroachment: "The Framers chose to rely on a federal system in which special restraints on federal power over the States inhered principally in the workings of the National Government itself, rather than in discrete limitations on the objects of federal authority" (*Garcia v. San Antonio Metropolitan Transit Authority* 1985:552).

Tenth Amendment jurisprudence was resuscitated by the Supreme Court in the 1990s. Today, the amendment's main ramification for public administration is to prohibit the federal government from compelling "the States to enact or administer a federal regulatory program" (*New York v. United States* 1992:188). This means Congress cannot conscript or press state officers to implement federal laws (other than those statutes regulating the states themselves). For example, Congress cannot compel state law enforcement officers to perform the background checks required by federal gun control legislation. Rather, the federal government must either gain the states' cooperation or administer such a law through its own employees or agents. Even though the benefits of requiring state employees to administer federal laws might far outweigh the costs, the Supreme Court rejected a "balancing analysis" where "the very *principle* of state sovereignty" is offended (*Printz v. United States* 1997:932). This interpretation of the Tenth Amendment highlights the importance of the Spending Clause as a vehicle for exercising federal power.

The Spending Clause

The Spending Clause (Article I, section 8, clause 1) authorizes Congress to "lay and collect Taxes, Duties, Imposts and Excises, to pay the Debts and provide for the common Defence and general Welfare of the United States." The clause has been interpreted expansively to permit Congress to use conditional grants to the states to achieve indirectly purposes it could not pursue directly under the Commerce Clause or its other enumerated powers. For example, even if Congress cannot constitutionally set a national drinking age (something that is uncertain), it can induce the states to set the age at twenty-one by withholding federal highway funds from those declining to do so (*South Dakota v. Dole* 1987). The key restrictions are: (1) The spending must be in pursuit of a general public purpose; (2) the conditions must be unambiguous so that the states clearly understand their obligations; (3) the conditions must be related to a "federal interest in particular national projects or programs"; and (4) the conditions cannot be prohibited by other constitutional provisions, such as the Fourteenth Amendment's guarantee of equal protection of the laws (*South Dakota v. Dole* 1987:207). It is also important that congressional use of the Spending Clause buys, rather than effectively extorts or coerces, state compliance. However, within these limits Congress has very broad power to influence state policy and administrative operations through conditional grants.

The Eleventh Amendment

The Eleventh Amendment (1795) protects the states' sovereign immunity by preventing suits against them in federal court. It provides that "the Judicial power of the United States shall not be construed to extend to any suit in law or equity, commenced or prosecuted against one of the United States by Citizens of another State, or by Citizens or Subjects of any Foreign State." Supreme Court decisions have expanded this immunity to cover suits by the states' own citizens as well. However, there are several exceptions to the states' immunity from suits in federal court: (1) Suits may be brought in federal court against named state officials for their violations of rights protected by the U.S. Constitution; (2) a state court decision involving a constitutional issue or question of federal law can be appealed to the U.S. Supreme Court; (3) the states may voluntarily waive their immunity; and (4) Congress can override state sovereign immunity via the enforcement clauses of the Thirteenth, Fourteenth, and Fifteenth Amendments.

This framework contains some additional qualifications. State officers and administrators cannot be sued in their official capacities in federal court for constitutional violations if the relief requested would require the *state* to pay money damages for *past* conduct. (As explained later in this chapter, state officers and administrators can be sued in their *personal capacities* for such damages in federal court.) Suits are not barred if the remedy sought could require *prospective* state spending, as in remedial law decisions requiring prison reform.

Another complication involves congressional legislation under the enforcement clauses mentioned above. These specifically give Congress the power to enforce the amendments "by appropriate legislation." One means of enforcement is to authorize private individuals to sue a state in federal court for money damages for its violations of their rights under any of the three amendments. However, in nurse Garrett's case, the Supreme Court emphasized that for enforcement clause legislation to be "appropriate" there must be "congruence and proportionality between the injury to be prevented or remedied and the means adopted to that end" (*Board of Trustees of the University of Alabama v. Garrett* 2001:958). In applying this standard, the Court concluded that the Americans with Disabilities Act was constitutionally defective in authorizing state employees like Garrett to sue their states in federal court. In developing the ADA, Congress failed to show a pattern of discrimination in state employment that would violate the Equal Protection Clause. Consequently, the ADA's override of the Eleventh Amendment was not congruent and proportional to the harm it was trying to stem.

By preventing private individuals from vindicating their rights in federal court under statutes like the ADA, the Eleventh Amendment complicates public administration in the United States. Enforcement of such federal laws may require a federal agency to sue a recalcitrant state or attempt to gain compliance through conditional grants. Either approach requires a greater federal administrative presence. Both are more costly and probably less efficacious than authorizing injured parties to sue the states directly. Furthermore, Eleventh Amendment immunity creates an incongruity of its own. It applies only to the states and affords no protection to local governments. Consequently, the means available for safeguarding individuals' federally protected rights depends on which level of government has violated them. If a state wanted to reduce the overall vulnerability of its public sector to suits for money damages, it could put a higher proportion of local-level administrators on its payroll (*McMillian v. Monroe County* 1997).

Individuals' Constitutional Rights in Administrative Encounters

Constitutional law currently affords individuals broad rights in the context of their interactions with public administrators. At all levels of government, public administrators' encounters with clients and customers, coworkers, contractors, patients confined to public mental health facilities, prisoners, and individuals involved in street-level administrative regulation are significantly bounded by constitutional law (Rosenbloom and O'Leary 1997; Rosenbloom, Carroll, and Carroll 2000).

Relationships with Clients and Customers

Public administrative relationships with clients and customers are governed by the constitutional doctrines of equal protection, "new property," and unconstitutional conditions. Each of these was developed or substantially strengthened during the 1950s to the 1970s and continues to apply today.

Equal Protection. Contemporary equal protection doctrine has a three-tiered structure. The threshold issue is whether a government is classifying people by some characteristic such as race, sex, wealth, residency, or age. The classification may be implicit in a policy or its implementation rather than explicitly stated in legislation or formal regulations. However, if there is no classification, there is no equal protection issue. A "classification of one" is possible under equal protection, but unfair treatment of particular individuals is typically litigated under procedural due process protection against arbitrary or capricious administrative decisionmaking (*Village of Willowbrook v. Olechon* 2000).

Classifications based on race or ethnicity are considered *suspect*. In view of the nation's history, it is likely that they will be used to disadvantage minorities. They are subject to *strict scrutiny* (the courts' most exacting level of judicial review) and are constitutional only when *narrowly tailored* to promote a *compelling governmental interest*. A heavy burden of persuasion rests on the government, and the courts will not be deferential to its claims. These requirements apply whether the purpose of the classification is benign, as in the case of affirmative action, or invidious, as in the case of racial segregation.

Narrow tailoring is intended to ensure that a classification does not do significantly more damage to equal protection rights than is necessary to serve a compelling governmental interest. It is somewhat more flexible than a similar test (the *least restrictive alternative* analysis, which is sometimes applied to abridgements of First Amendment rights and requires government to use the least invasive means of achieving its compelling interests). Neither test (i.e., narrow tailoring and the least restrictive alternative) places much emphasis on the financial cost to government of finding ways to promote its interests that are less harmful to constitutional rights. Narrow tailoring generally requires that the use of a classification: (1) is more efficacious than other possible policy approaches; (2) has a fixed stopping point, either in terms of time or the achievement of a specific policy goal; (3) is sufficiently flexible so that irrational outcomes can be avoided; and (4) in the case of affirmative action, is proportionate to the beneficiaries' representation in the relevant population and does not excessively harm the interests of nonbeneficiaries.

Classifications based on factors that are not immutable, such as wealth and residency, are constitutional when they are rationally related to the achievement of a legitimate governmental purpose. The burden of persuasion is typically on the challenger, and the courts grant considerable deference to the government's claims. This analysis turns on *mere rationality* or *rational basis*. It also applies to classifications based on age. An exception occurs if a nonsuspect classification directly interferes with the exercise of a protected constitutional right. For example, a residency requirement for welfare eligibility might abridge the constitutional right of indigents to travel and relocate across state lines. In such a case, the classification is subject to strict judicial scrutiny and must serve a compelling governmental interest in a way that is narrowly tailored or, possibly, the least restrictive of the protected constitutional rights involved.

Classifications based on gender are *quasisuspect* and face an intermediate test. They must be *substantially related to the achievement of important governmental objectives.* The courts may ask the government to provide an *exceedingly persuasive* justification for such classifications, many of which are legacies of earlier practices and beliefs about gender differences that society no longer supports. For instance, women were once excluded from juries in order to shield them from hearing about the grisly acts of depraved criminals.

Contemporary equal protection interpretation constrains administrative behavior with respect to clients and customers in a range of circumstances. Most obviously, it prohibits racial and ethnic discrimination in public education, housing, welfare, health, recreation, occupational licensing, and other programs, except where the government can meet the compelling governmental interest and narrow tailoring tests under strict judicial scrutiny. Invidious discrimination is likely to be justified, if ever, under only the most extraordinary circumstances. Benign or remedial racial and ethnic classifications, as in affirmative action and minority business set-asides, face the same test, but it is plausible that some may serve a compelling governmental interest in a narrowly tailored fashion. Even though classifications based on gender do not require a compelling governmental interest and narrow tailoring, it is highly unlikely that invidious discrimination against females or males will be constitutional in client and customer relationships. Theoretically, the weaker standard for gender classifications makes it easier to justify affirmative action programs for women and girls than for minorities. However, in practice there may be no real difference. Allowing affirmative action on the basis of gender, which would substantially benefit white women, but not on the basis of race would run counter to the historical purpose of the Fourteenth Amendment. By contrast, the weaker standard might permit single-sex public schools or classes even though racially segregated ones would be unconstitutional. Classifications based on other factors, such as age, will most likely be constitutional unless they are clearly irrational or interfere with the exercise of another protected constitutional right.

New Property and Procedural Due Process.   New property theory treats an individual's governmental benefits as his or her own property, rather than as a privilege or gratuity (Reich 1964). As such, the benefits are covered by the Due Process Clauses of the Fifth and Fourteenth Amendments, which protect against the deprivation of "life, liberty, or property, without due process of law." Consequently, welfare benefits, public housing, public education, a variety of occupational and other licenses, and similar benefits cannot be withheld or terminated (during the period for which they were offered) without a fair procedure.

Procedural due process requires a balancing of three factors: (1) the individual's interest in the benefit and/or the severity of the deprivation at issue; (2) the risk that the procedure in place, if any, will result in erroneous decisions *and* the probable value of additional procedures in reducing errors; and (3) the government's administrative and financial interests in avoiding additional or alternative procedures. The underlying assumption in this formula is that, in general, the more elaborate the procedures, the lower the risk of error. Once a statute or administrative regulation establishes a continuing new property interest, it can be withheld or terminated only in accordance with constitutional due process. In other words, statutory procedures for terminating a benefit, such as public housing, will be inadequate if they do not afford sufficient procedural due process.

The application of procedural due process is subjective. One must weigh both the individual's and the government's interests. Typically, two issues arise. First, is the client entitled to procedural due process *prior* to the termination of a benefit during the term for which it was offered? Recipients of means-tested welfare benefits, which may be vital to their survival or ability to use posttermination procedures, generally enjoy a procedural due process right to some pretermination protection against erroneous administrative decisions. An exception exists when there is no factual dispute about their continuing eligibility.

Second, how elaborate must the due process be? Procedures can range from highly informal notice and opportunity to respond, to a formal response in writing only, to the rudiments of a nonjury judicial trial with a right to counsel, presentation of evidence and witnesses, confrontation and cross-examination of adverse witnesses, a written transcript, a decision by an impartial decisionmaker, and a right to appeal (*Goldberg v. Kelly* 1970; *Goss v. Lopez* 1975; *Mathews v. Eldridge* 1976; *Board of Curators of the University of Missouri v. Horowitz* 1978). Impartiality prevents biased officials or those who investigated or prosecuted the case from making adjudicatory decisions (see Chapter 4). Sometimes pre- and posttermination requirements are linked. For example, because elaborate posttermination procedures are available to social security disability recipients, only limited procedure is required before these non–means tested benefits are cut off.

The impact of new property doctrine on administration depends on the specific context. Pre- or posttermination hearings are common in decisions to terminate welfare, disability benefits, and occupational licenses. Suspensions and expulsions from public schools are also controlled by procedural due process. It is important to remember that when benefits terminate because they were offered for a fixed term or the recipients have aged, moved, married, or otherwise changed their eligibility status, procedural due process may require nothing more than notice, if that (procedural due process is discussed at greater length in Chapter 4).

Unconstitutional Conditions.   The conditions attached to governmental benefits sometimes interfere with clients' and customers' constitutional rights. For instance, a state might mandate that applicants for unemployment compensation be available for work on Saturday despite their Sabbatarian religious beliefs, or that public school students recite prayers or pledge allegiance to the flag. The unconstitutional conditions doctrine seeks to limit a government's ability to use client and customer relationships as leverage for regulating behavior that it could not reach directly without violating individuals' constitutional rights. Thus, under the unconstitutional conditions doctrine, U.S. governments, which lack the power to establish religion directly, cannot do so indirectly through the manipulation of benefits.

The problem public administrators and lawmakers face is knowing which conditions imposed on clients or customers will be adjudged unconstitutional. Essentially, the courts apply a two-part test, but as in the case of procedural due process, a good deal of subjectivity is involved. Specific requirements vary with the nature of the benefit and type of condition. Conditions that gratuitously infringe on protected rights by failing to serve a significant governmental purpose or by prohibiting more than necessary in order to achieve a legitimate or compelling public interest are very likely to be unconstitutional. Conditions involving freedom of speech, association, religion, or protection from unreasonable searches must generally promote at least an important, if not compelling, governmental interest. Conditions attached to building permits that constitute a Fifth Amendment taking of private property must be roughly proportional to the impact that the proposed development will have on legitimate governmental interests, such as traffic congestion (*Dolan v. City of Tigard* 1994).

Together, contemporary equal protection, new property theory, and the unconstitutional conditions doctrine bring constitutional law directly into the relationships between public administrators and their clients and customers. This complicates public administration by expanding the set of values that administrators and programs must protect and, some-times, by requiring elaborate procedure. It also broadens the role of courts and judges in public administration.

Public Personnel Management

Public employees first began to gain significant constitutional rights in the context of their employment during the 1950s–1970s as equal protection was applied to public employment; civil service jobs were considered part of the new property; and the unconditional conditions doctrine was invoked to protect public employees' First Amendment rights. However, the constitutional doctrine that regulates public personnel management differs from that affecting relationships with clients and customers.

Constitutional rights within the framework of public employment are assessed through a *public service model*. Its core premise is that the administrative values of efficiency and effectiveness are more important to governments when they act as employers than when they seek to regulate the behavior of ordinary citizens. Government, like any employer, needs greater authority over its employees than it can exercise over its clients, customers, or the general public. But there are also limits to that authority.

The public service model balances three considerations: (1) the interest of the employee in exercising his or her constitutional rights, that is, in being free of governmental controls; (2) the government's interest in achieving some important purpose as an employer; and (3) the public's interest in the way government and public administration operate. The crux of the public service model is that the public's interest may coincide with either that of the employee or the government. For example, in the realm of free speech, the public has a very clear interest in strong constitutional protection of whistle-blowing by public employees. The public is better able to assess governmental performance when public employees can freely expose illegality, gross waste, fraud, abuse, and specific and immediate dangers to public health and safety. By contrast, the public has only a minimal interest, if any, in public employees' partisan campaign speeches, routine office gossiping, and grousing about political bosses and administrative higher-ups. Under the public service model, whistle-blower speech is constitutionally protected, whereas partisan speech and speech that is of minimal or no public concern are not. (Whistle-blowing is discussed in Chapter 5.)

The same kind of balancing applies to public employees' free exercise of religion and association as well as to their Fourth Amendment privacy rights and equal protection guarantees. In constitutionally evaluating constraints on personnel management in these contexts, one always considers the individual's interest in exercising or retaining protected rights, the government's interests that could justify abridgments, and the public's interest. It is important that public personnelists, managers, and employees bear in mind that the governmental interest, though often stated as serving the taxpayers, is not necessarily synonymous with the public interest. Even in the context of public employment, a governmental interest in cost-effective administration may not justify infringements on constitutionally protected rights. If there is no clear public interest one way or the other, then the balance is simply between the interests of the employee and the government. The employee will sometimes win because judges may place a higher value on protecting the robustness of constitutional rights than on obtaining administrative results or maximizing values such as efficiency and economy (*Stanley v. Illinois* 1972).

First Amendment Rights.   Public employees enjoy broad First Amendment rights to speak openly on matters of public policy, politics, administration, and other matters. Under the public service model, the major limitations on their freedom of speech are: (1) In order to enjoy constitutional protection, expressive activity must be on a matter of public concern; and (2) speech as part of a partisan political campaign may be banned. Disruptive remarks on matters only of private concern are not protected because they serve no public interest. Restrictions on the partisan political activity of public employees are constitutionally justified by the public interest in administrative impartiality and efficiency, as well as by the protection they afford government workers against being coerced by political appointees and supervisors to support political parties and partisan candidates.

In general, public employees' speech on matters of public concern is most vulnerable to being the basis for a successful adverse action when it impairs discipline or harmony in the workplace, jeopardizes close working relationships, interferes with normal operations, or detracts from the employee's ability to do his/her job. In balancing the interests of government, employee, and public attention must be paid to the nature of the employee's position in the organization (*Rankin v. McPherson* 1987). Identical remarks by those at the top and bottom of an organizational hierarchy may be treated differently. When disciplining employees for their off-the-job remarks or other protected activities, the government should be able to show a nexus between its significant interests as an employer and the conduct involved (*United States v. National Treasury Employees Union* 1995).

The public service model also broadly protects employees' freedom of association and religious freedom. Restrictions on these freedoms have to be justified by the balance among the interests of employee, public employer, and public. Constitutional law extends extensive protection to employees' freedom of association on the premise that membership alone is not a proxy for behavior. Consequently, employees may join labor unions (though there is no constitutional right to collective bargaining), employee associations, antisocial groups such as the Ku Klux Klan, and even subversive organizations. Exceptions are permissible for categories of employees whose membership in particular organizations would significantly harm the employer's or the public's interests. For instance, supervisors and managers can be banned from joining labor unions representing rank-and-file employees because such membership might conflict with their hierarchical responsibilities. Employees also have the right not to join organizations, and consequently union-shop labor agreements are unconstitutional in the public sector (*Chicago Teachers Union v. Hudson* 1986). Since the late 1970s, public employees' freedom of association has been interpreted to make job actions based on political partisanship unconstitutional unless the government can show that relying on party affiliation is the means of ensuring effective job performance that is least restrictive of constitutional rights or narrowly tailored to avoid excessive intrusion on those rights (*Rutan v. Republican Party of Illinois* 1990).

The parameters of public employees' religious freedom are less clear. A government employer cannot coerce employees to engage in prayer or other religious activity. Neither can it gratuitously restrict their religious expression or behavior. Because discrimination based on religion is prohibited by federal equal employment opportunity law, civilian public employees at all levels of government ordinarily are permitted to wear religious jewelry or headgear, even if other workers find it objectionable. Restrictions on religious activity might be justified when overt religious proselytizing or vocal praying at work is disruptive or otherwise interferes with the employer's legitimate interests in workplace harmony and cost-effectiveness.

Fourth Amendment Privacy. Public employees retain protections against unreasonable searches and seizures even while at work in public buildings. The threshold question is whether the employee has a reasonable expectation of privacy under the circumstances, that is, an expectation of privacy that society is prepared to support (according to judges). Absent such an expectation, public employers are free to search an employee's workspace, desk, files, computer, and so forth. Where there is a reasonable expectation of privacy, the governmental search must be reasonable in its inception and scope. Employees have a reasonable expectation of privacy in their bodily fluids, but suspicionless drug testing is constitutionally permissible when it reasonably promotes national security, law enforcement, or public safety.

Procedural Due Process.   Civil service systems typically provide public employees with new property rights in their jobs. Consequently, procedural due process protects them against arbitrary, capricious, or abusive dismissal or demotion. Pretermination notice and opportunity to respond are generally required, as are more elaborate posttermination procedures (*Cleveland Board of Education v. Loudermill* 1985). Depending on the circumstances, a public employee may not have a right to procedural due process prior to suspension without pay for wrongdoing. However, the employee should be offered a hearing of some kind within a reasonable time after the suspension takes effect (*Gilbert v. Homar* 1997).

For the most part, the constitutional requirements for public employees' procedural due process are now written into civil service laws and regulations. However, once a new property right in public employment is created by the government, its termination or diminution is controlled by constitutional rather than statutory law. Where public employees do not have civil service or tenured status, adverse actions may be at will only insofar as they do not violate First Amendment, Fourth Amendment, equal protection, or other constitutional rights.

Equal Protection.   The three-tiered equal protection analysis previously discussed applies to public employees as well as to clients and customers. Racial and ethnic classifications, whether benign or invidious, are subject to strict scrutiny. To date, the Supreme Court has not held that promoting workforce diversity is a compelling governmental interest. It has permitted benign racial classifications only as a remedy for past, proven, egregious violations of equal protection. These and other racial/ethnic classifications must be narrowly tailored. For instance, the public service model does not generally permit personnel assignments based on race or ethnicity, but such criteria might be acceptable when necessary for the achievement of a specific and important governmental purpose, as in undercover police work (see *Baker v. City of St. Petersburg* 1968).

Residency and age requirements are subject to rational basis analysis. They will be constitutional if they are rationally related to the achievement of a legitimate governmental interest. Gender-based classifications face a higher standard—they must be substantially related to the achievement of important governmental purposes.

Substantive Due Process Rights.   The Fifth and Fourteenth Amendments protect individuals against governmental deprivations of "life, liberty, or property, without due process of law." The body of constitutional interpretation defining "liberty" in this context is *substantive due process*. It enables the courts to identify and protect fundamental rights that are not specifically mentioned elsewhere in the Constitution. Consequently, substantive due process is open-ended, and specific decisions under it are often controversial. In the context of public personnel management, the Supreme Court invalidated overly restrictive maternity leave policies on the grounds that the "Court has long recognized that freedom of personal choice in matters of marriage and family life is one of the liberties protected by the Due Process Clause of the Fourteenth Amendment. . . . There is a right 'to be free from unwarranted governmental intrusion into matters so fundamentally affecting a person as the decision whether to bear or beget a child" (*Cleveland Board of Education v. La Fleur* 1974:639–640). In another case, the Court found no substantive due process barrier to short-hair grooming regulations for police (*Kelley v. Johnson* 1976). There is little judicial guidance on how to analyze substantive due process claims within the public service model. As a threshold matter, the government should be able to demonstrate a reasonable connection between its interests and the prohibited behavior.

Relationships with Contractors

Contractors also have constitutional protections against governmental infringements on their rights. Some of these are well-settled. Governments cannot engage in invidious racial, ethnic, or gender discrimination when contracting out. Contracts that establish new property interests cannot be terminated without procedural due process. Since the late

1980s, the Supreme Court strengthened the Constitution's application to contractor relationships in three ways.

First, the Court unequivocally held that benign racial and ethnic classifications in governmental contracting are subject to strict scrutiny (*Adarand Constructors v. Pena* 1995). They must serve a compelling governmental interest in a narrowly tailored fashion. This severely restricted the use of minority business set-asides and other preferences. Even though the constitutional test for gender classifications is weaker, preferences for women-owned businesses will also be difficult to sustain.

Second, the Court made it clear that contractors and those engaged in preexisting commercial relationships with governments, such as Gratzianna's with the city of Northlake, retain First Amendment rights. Using unconstitutional conditions analysis, the Court held that the Constitution protects contractors' public criticism of a government and their political campaigning against its officials. Essentially, the same constitutional test that applies to public employees' speech is used to determine the free speech rights of contractors and others engaged in ongoing business relationships with government. A government can terminate its commercial relationship with such parties in response to their speech only if it can show that, on balance, such action is justified by the speech's detrimental impact on its ability to deliver public services.

Third, the Court clarified the application of *state action doctrine* to contractors. With the exception of the Thirteenth Amendment, the Constitution ordinarily does not govern relationships among purely private parties. However, under some circumstances, contractors may be considered *state actors* (i.e., governmental actors, regardless of whether at the state, local, or federal level) and are thereby bound by constitutional requirements. The basic premise is that the Constitution applies to private parties if "there is such a 'close nexus between the State and the challenged action' that seemingly private behavior 'may be fairly treated as that of the State itself'" (*Brentwood Academy v. Tennessee Secondary School Athletic Association* 2001:930). Unfortunately for those who like their constitutional law to come with bright lines, determining what constitutes state action is often "a matter of normative judgment" (*Brentwood Academy v. Tennessee Secondary School Athletic Association* 2001:930).

In general, a contractor may become a state actor when it: (1) engages in a public function, such as incarceration; (2) exercises government's coercive power (e.g., to seize property); (3) acts as a government's agent for some unconstitutional purpose, such as promoting racial discrimination;

(4) is nominally private but largely or wholly controlled by a government agency; or (5) is entwined with government or acts as a joint participant with it (*Brentwood Academy v. Tennessee Secondary School Athletic Association* 2001).

Private parties will not be state actors merely because they are heavily regulated or funded by government. Neither will governmental subsidization of their clients or customers transform them into state actors. If the widespread outsourcing and development of public-private partnerships of the 1990s continues, then state action doctrine will probably be further applied, perhaps in ways that dampen private parties' interest in contracting or partnering with government. For instance, in *West v. Atkins* (1988), a private physician on part-time contract with a state prison became a state actor with Eighth Amendment obligations to the prisoners.

Public Mental Health Patients

Since the early 1970s, patients confined to public mental health facilities have had a constitutional right to treatment. Earlier, they were often warehoused indefinitely or otherwise inadequately treated. In *Wyatt v. Stickney* (1971), a federal district court held that confining such patients without treatment constitutes a violation of their right to liberty under the Fourteenth Amendment. Although the decision applied directly only to the Alabama mental health system, its logic was soon adopted nationwide.

The constitutional right to treatment was eventually defined in broad terms. It includes reasonable care, safety, and freedom from confinement, as well as individualized treatment (or training for the mentally disabled). Implementation requires a humane physical and psychological environment as well as adequate staffing. In practice this may require far-reaching architectural and medical reforms. The *Wyatt* litigation eventually required Alabama either to release patients or to provide the following: (1) protection of patients' right to wear their own clothes, freedom of religious worship, and opportunity to have physical exercise; (2) physical building conditions in which there were no more than six patients per room, at least one toilet for each eight patients and one shower or tub for every fifteen of them, not less than fifty square feet per person in the dayroom, at least ten square feet per person in the dining room, and a temperature range between sixty-eight and eighty-three degrees Fahrenheit; and (3) various per-patient staffing ratios for professionals, clerical workers, and other staff.

Initially, judicial involvement in public mental health care was sometimes characterized as misguided interference in professional psychiatry. However, eventually the American Psychiatric Association supported the constitutional right to treatment. Along with other factors, including better psychoactive drugs, crowding was reduced through deinstitutionalization and shorter stays, and the overall conditions in public mental health facilities improved substantially. On the downside, deinstitutionalization contributed to homelessness (Rosenbloom and O'Leary 1997: chapter 7).

Prisoners' Constitutional Rights

Since the 1970s, the treatment of prisoners has been thoroughly constitutionalized. The Eighth Amendment prohibition of cruel and unusual punishment was reinterpreted to apply to the conditions of confinement rather than to the sentence alone. This required prison reforms in more than forty states to reduce overcrowding; provide adequate medical care and safety; and guarantee inmates at least a minimal level of nutrition, hygiene, and civilized life's other necessities. The scope of what is prohibited by the Eighth Amendment changes as society progresses and standards of decency evolve. For instance, in the 1990s prisoners gained the right to challenge exposure to secondhand tobacco smoke when it poses a risk of serious harm due to their personal respiratory or other health problems (Rosenbloom and O'Leary 1997: chapter 7).

In addition to Eighth Amendment protections, prisoners have a right to procedural due process when proposed discipline creates extraordinary hardships within the framework of normal prison life. Similarly, within the confines of what incarceration requires in practice, they have the right to free exercise of religion and to marry. The general test is whether restrictions on the prisoners' constitutional rights serve legitimate penological interests, including their impact on other inmates and guards. Prison administration has become so thoroughly infused with constitutional concerns that some prison systems engage in constitutional audits to assure their compliance with the latest judicial decisions.

Street-Level Regulatory Encounters

Street-level public employees engage in face-to-face regulatory interaction with the public. They are police, social workers, public school teachers, public health workers, health and safety inspectors, and others who

(1) tend to work in the absence of close proximate supervision; (2) have a great deal of discretion in dealing with members of the public; (3) are largely self-reporting; and (4) are often in a position to have a substantial positive or negative impact on the individuals with whom they deal. It is also common for street-level employees to work with heavy caseloads and inadequate resources. Their work environment may be charged with physical and/or psychological threats (Lipsky 1980).

The Fourth Amendment and the Equal Protection Clause are most relevant to individuals' rights in street-level encounters. However, these protections are porous and subject to circumvention.

Fourth Amendment Constraints. Fourth Amendment law is notoriously uneven because it is fact-specific in its application. It applies only when an individual has a reasonable expectation of privacy. The courts treat this expectation as a continuum. On one end, individuals who are in their own homes with the windows and doors closed and curtains drawn have a great expectation of privacy. On the other hand, the same individuals would have a minimal expectation of privacy in their baggage when seeking to board a scheduled commercial airplane at a U.S. airport. In between, there are many gradations. The slope from a conventional home, to a permanently parked mobile home, to one moving on an interstate highway, to a minivan camper, to a public bus can prove slippery. Moreover, some individuals have reduced Fourth Amendment protections due to their special relationship with an administrative function and its personnel. For example, public school administrators have greater leeway to search students because the schools have special custodial and tutelary responsibilities (*Vernonia School District 47J v. Acton* 1995; *Board of Education of Independent School District No. 92 of Pottawatomie County v. Earls* 2002).

A distinction is usually drawn between law enforcement searches and administrative inspections. Whenever practicable, the Fourth Amendment requires law enforcement officers to seek a warrant from a judge, magistrate, or other judicial official. The warrant is issued upon *probable cause*, which essentially means there is specific evidence that a violation of law may exist. When time or other considerations make obtaining a warrant impractical, law enforcement agents can proceed upon probable cause alone. Administrative inspections of nonpervasively regulated businesses may also require warrants. However, it is not necessary to show probable cause, as these warrants may be issued when reasonably necessary for the enforcement of the statute involved. Administrative searches involving special relationships or needs, such as public school discipline, are generally governed by a reasonableness standard. Pervasively or closely regulated entities have a reduced expectation of privacy and, therefore, may be inspected without a warrant under a rational regulatory scheme (see the "Enforcement" section in Chapter 4). Precisely what constitutes such an entity is sometimes a judgment call.

The constraints on street-level administration generated by this framework often appear inconsistent and, sometimes, close to nonexistent. On the one hand, for instance, an individual can be arrested for *any* traffic infraction, however minor, and consequently subjected to a legitimate personal and vehicle search. The Supreme Court has eschewed inquiry into whether such stops or arrests following them are merely pretexts used by the police to search individuals and their vehicles. Even arrest for a nonjailable offense, such as not wearing a seatbelt, is permitted (*Atwater v. City of Lago Vista* 2001; *Whren v. United States* 1996). On the other hand, a federal Occupational Safety and Health Administration (OSHA) inspector may need a warrant in order to inspect a workplace—depending in part on how open the facility is to the public or how pervasively the government regulates it (*Marshall v. Barlow's Inc.* 1987). The constitutionality of a public hospital's drawing of bodily fluids from patients may depend on its purpose. For law enforcement, the hospital needs the patients' consent or a warrant, though apparently the same fluids can be taken for diagnostic purposes without implicating the Fourth Amendment (*Ferguson v. City of Charleston* 2001).

Equal Protection Constraints. The main problem for individuals who challenge street-level administrators' behavior on equal protection grounds is that the burden of persuasion rests on the challenger to demonstrate that the government employees have explicitly or implicitly created a classification. Explicit invidious racial, ethnic, or gender classifications are highly unusual in contemporary street-level administration. Public personnel and governments know better than openly to categorize people by such social characteristics in order to discriminate against them. Implicit classifications, based on these characteristics, may be inferred from patterns of administrative behavior. However, establishing their existence to a court's satisfaction is difficult. This is why the Equal Protection Clause has been relatively ineffective in combating racial and ethnic profiling by law enforcement agents when there is no written or verbal evidence. Unless profiling is the only plausible explanation for the administrative behavior at issue, it may be impossible to show that an implicit classification exists. Of course, equal protection is a more effective constraint against street-level behavior that follows directly from racist, ethnically derogatory, or sexist statements (Larrabee 1997).

Public Administrators' Liability for Constitutional Torts

There is often a notable gap between formal constitutional requirements and actual administrative practice. Constitutional law may be unclear or poorly communicated to administrators. As already noted, sometimes it is highly subjective or requires an elaborate balancing of multiple factors. Specific constraints may seem counterintuitive to administrators or impractical due to scarce resources or lack of time. They may also run counter to deep-seated administrative and organizational values. Furthermore, individuals whose constitutional rights are violated may lack the incentive or resources to sue the government or its employees for redress.

In a series of decisions crystallizing in the 1980s, the Supreme Court sought to protect individuals' constitutional rights in their encounters with public administrators by invigorating *the law of constitutional torts* (i.e., injuries to constitutional rights). The Court made it far easier for individuals to sue most public administrators personally in federal court for money damages for violations of their constitutional rights. In terms of legal doctrine, the Court changed the presumption that public employees and officials are absolutely immune from civil suits for money damages (meaning they could not be sued for their constitutional torts) to one that affords them only a *qualified immunity* from such suits. The Court reasoned that making it easier to bring constitutional tort suits serves to deter breaches of constitutional law as well as to compensate victims. The current standard for qualified immunity requires public administrators, at all levels of government, to have reasonable knowledge of constitutional law and to factor it into decisionmaking.

Since 1982, most public administrators in the United States have been potentially *personally* liable for money damages for conduct violating "clearly established [federal] statutory or constitutional rights of which a reasonable person would have known" (*Harlow v. Fitzgerald* 1982:818). This standard expands the requirements of administrators' job competence to include constitutional law. In the Supreme Court's words, "A reasonably competent public official should know the law governing his conduct" (*Harlow v. Fitzgerald* 1982:819). Suits may be for punitive as well as compensatory damages (*Smith v. Wade* 1983). The major exception is that public administrators cannot be sued for constitutional torts committed while engaging in adjudicatory or legislative functions. There are also some technical differences in how local, state, and federal employees may be sued. However, the vast majority of public administrators are subject to suit, and constitutional torts produce considerable litigation. Local governments and their agencies are also liable to such suits for compensatory damages when their policies directly cause violations of individuals' constitutional rights (*Pembaur v. City of Cincinnati* 1986). Under limited circumstances, cities and counties can also be sued for failure to train their employees to protect individuals' constitutional rights (*City of Canton v. Harris* 1989). They cannot be sued for punitive damages in constitutional tort cases.

It should be emphasized that the "clearly established" constitutional law a reasonable administrator should know is not synonymous with the latest judicial precedent on some matter. In *Hope v. Pelzer* (2002:2), the Supreme Court emphasized that "officials can be on notice that their conduct violates established law even in novel factual situations." Conduct may be obviously unconstitutional even though it has never been the subject of litigation. The broad purpose of qualified immunity is to encourage public administrators to follow the case law and be responsive to the judiciary's constitutional reasoning and values. Qualified immunity is designed to give federal judges a greater role in defining appropriate public administrative behavior. The courts labor hard to give substance to constitutional rights. They do not want their decisions to be hollow. Knowing that they face personal suits for constitutional torts gives public administrators a strong incentive to think twice before taking an action that might tread on someone's constitutionally protected rights.

Relatively speaking, qualified immunity protects the public interest in allowing public administrators to act without fear of frivolous or other unwarranted lawsuits. Private individuals engaged in state action have no immunity at all; they are vulnerable to suit regardless of whether the constitutional law was clearly established or likely to be known by a reasonable person (*Richardson v. McKnight* 1997).

Conclusion

The U.S. Constitution is central to the organization and practice of public administration in this country. The separation of powers defines the scope of legislative, executive, and judicial authority for public administration.

Each branch brings different—and often competing—core values to public administrative practice. Constitutional federalism allocates sovereignty and power between the federal government and the states. It also adds to the complexity of public administration. During the second half of the twentieth century the federal courts, often led by the Supreme Court, vastly expanded individuals' constitutional rights in their encounters with public administration. Constitutional law became relevant, if not central, to administrative decisions and operations regarding clients and customers; public personnel systems; outsourcing; the treatment of patients in public mental health facilities; incarceration; and the exercise of regulatory authority in street-level encounters. The courts also greatly strengthened the opportunity for aggrieved individuals to vindicate their newfound rights through constitutional tort suits.

Constitutional law is dynamic rather than static. It affords the federal judiciary continual opportunities to exercise influence over public administrative decisionmaking and values at all levels of government. Perhaps most important, the federal judiciary expects public administrators to follow the development of constitutional law; to understand how it bears upon their official functions; and to treat it as a central element of job competence. It is no longer true—if it ever was—that U.S. public administration "at most points stands apart even from the debatable ground of constitutional study" (Wilson 1887:18). Rather, contemporary public administration is informed by and infused with constitutional concerns.

Additional Reading

Barron, Jerome, and C. Thomas Dienes. *Constitutional Law in a Nutshell*, 4th ed. St. Paul: West Group, 1999.

Rosenbloom, David H., and Rosemary O'Leary. *Public Administration and Law*, 2nd ed. New York: Marcel Dekker, 1997.

3

Administrative Rulemaking

Introduction: Smoking Whitefish

A lot of people like smoked whitefish. Some 2.75 million pounds of it were produced annually in the United States during the 1960s and 1970s. Between 1960 and 1963, a problem arose—eight cases of botulism, the only U.S. cases involving whitefish since 1899. All eight involved a vacuum-packing process, which the industry soon abandoned. From 1964 through 1970, no botulism whatsoever was reported in the 17.25 million pounds of U.S.-produced whitefish. Nevertheless, in 1970 the Food and Drug Administration (FDA) issued time-temperature-salinity rules requiring heating fish that have been brined to 3.5 percent salinity at 180 degrees Fahrenheit for at least thirty minutes, or, alternatively, at only 150 degrees for the same period when their salinity was at 5 percent.

The Nova Scotia Food Products Corporation, however, maintained that the time-temperature-salinity standards would kill more than just the very remote possibility that toxic Clostridium botulinum Type E spores would form in its smoked whitefish; the new standards would kill its business. According to Nova Scotia and the industry interest group, the Association of Smoked Fish Processors, Inc., the FDA's requirements "could not be met if a marketable whitefish was to be produced" because they would "completely destroy the product." The company sued to block FDA enforcement action against its smoked whitefish.

The legal issues were specific to whitefish but common to much rulemaking. With remarkable clarity, the reviewing court averred that

> The key issues were (1) whether, in the light of the rather scant history of botulism in whitefish, that species should have been considered separately rather than included in a general regulation which failed to distinguish

species from species; (2) whether the application of the proposed [time-temperature-salinity] requirements to smoked whitefish made the whitefish commercially unsaleable; and (3) whether the agency recognized that prospect, but nevertheless decided that the public health needs should prevail even if that meant commercial death for the whitefish industry. The procedural issues were whether, in light of these key questions, the agency procedure was inadequate because (i) it failed to disclose to interested parties the scientific data and methodology upon which it relied; and (ii) because it failed utterly to address itself to the pertinent question of commercial feasibility.

In the court's view, the FDA failed on two counts. First, "when the basis for a proposed rule is a scientific decision, the scientific material which is believed to support the rule should be exposed to the view of interested parties for their comment. One cannot ask for comment on a scientific paper without allowing the participants to read the paper." Second, the rule was not accompanied by a "concise general statement" explaining the rationale behind it, as is required by the Administrative Procedure Act. Nowhere did the FDA address the issue of commercial feasibility. As the court noted, "It is not in keeping with the rational process to leave vital questions, raised by comments which are of cogent materiality, completely unanswered. The agencies certainly have a good deal of discretion in expressing the basis of a rule, but the agencies do not have quite the prerogative of obscurantism reserved to legislatures." The whitefish industry (though not the whitefish) won a reprieve (*United States v. Nova Scotia Food Products Corp.* 1977:250, 252).

Rulemaking: Definitions and General Concerns

To a very large extent, public policy in the United States is established through administrative rulemaking. Federal rules govern the purity of the food we eat, the water we drink, and the air we breathe. They regulate the safety of our workplaces, homes, vehicles, and many of the products we use and consume. They determine much about the health care available to us and the practices used in banking, industry, business, agriculture, and many other areas of economic life. During the 1990s, federal agencies routinely promulgated more than 4,000 rules per year, which significantly exceeded the volume of congressional lawmaking (Kerwin 1999:18, 21). Many rules are highly specific to particular technologies and processes used in broadcasting, generating energy, farming, extracting natural resources, fishing, manufacturing, refining, and so forth. Cumulatively, along with rules having more general effects on the overall economy and environment, they do much to determine the quality of American life.

There is no single definition of administrative rules. The federal APA (section 551[4]) defines them as "the whole or part of an agency statement of general or particular applicability and future effect designed to implement, interpret, or prescribe law or policy or describing the organization, procedure, or practice requirements of an agency." Its definition also includes the "approval or prescription for the future of rates, wages, corporate or financial structures or reorganizations thereof, prices, facilities, appliances, services, or allowances" as well as the accounting and other practices relating to them. Several general characteristics of rules are buried in this language.

1. Rules are usually prospective. Their requirements will become effective and enforced at some future date, giving those directly governed by them time to comply. U.S. administrative and constitutional law especially disfavors rulemaking as a means of determining the legality of past behavior. Adjudication rather than rulemaking is typically used to determine the legal status of past or continuing activity. Adjudication is often called "order-making" to distinguish it from rulemaking. Sometimes, however, when there is good cause, rules may go into effect immediately.

2. There are three general types of rules. *Legislative rules* (or *substantive rules*) are like statutes and have the force of law. The FDA's time-temperature-salinity rule was a legislative rule. Such rules regulate conduct, impose performance standards on products and processes, and establish eligibility for licenses and benefits. For instance, the U.S. Occupational Safety and Health Administration enacts a wide range of legislative rules to regulate hazards and toxic substances in the workplace; the National Highway Traffic Safety Administration similarly issues rules governing motor vehicle safety; Federal Aviation Administration rules regulate the safety of air travel; Securities and Exchange Commission rules regulate financial reporting by companies whose stock is sold publicly; the FDA issues rules regarding food purity; and Federal Trade Commission rules regulate advertising and other economic practices.

Procedural rules govern an agency's internal organization and operations, such as how it will process requests from the public for information or benefits of various kinds, deal with its own employees' labor grievances or equal employment opportunity complaints, or prioritize its enforcement actions.

Interpretative rules (as the APA calls them) are essentially policy statements establishing an agency's understanding of the terms of its statutory mandate. Better known as *interpretive rules*, in theory they should not establish new legal obligations but rather explain the basis for existing ones. Sometimes, however, the distinction is blurry. For instance, the 1964 Civil Rights Act specifically allows employers to use hiring and promotion examinations that are "professionally developed"—a term subsequently defined by the Equal Employment Opportunity Commission (EEOC) as requiring the exams to be actually job-related, something that is often very difficult for employers to prove (*Griggs v. Duke Power Co.* 1971:433–434).

3. Rules can be of general or particular application. They can regulate a very wide range of industry and activity (clean air) or a single process (use of a pesticide). As the application of a rule narrows to only a few firms or persons, constitutional due process may require the rulemaking agency to provide notice and a hearing of some sort to those directly affected (*Bi-Metallic Investment Co. v. State Board of Equalization of Colorado* 1915).

As suggested by the FDA's experience with smoked whitefish, a key political and legal question is how administrative rules should be made. How should a time-temperature-salinity standard be formulated and applied? What voice in the development of such a rule should a food-processing company have? What voice, if any, should consumers and/or public health professionals have? What scientific or other information should underlie the rule? How much of that information should be disclosed? To what level of rationality should an agency be held?

If whitefish doesn't appeal to you, then try peanut butter. Any product labeled as "peanut butter" must have peanuts in it. But how should an agency go about determining how much of it can be derived from non-peanut products? Should it take nine years and a 7,736-page transcript to determine whether the appropriate level is 87.5 percent or 90 percent? Should the allowable nonpeanut products include up to thirty insect fragments per 100 grams, fewer, or more (Warren 1996:253; Rosenbloom and Kravchuk 2002:454)?

There is a wide range of options for regulating administrative rulemaking. Agencies can be left completely to their own devices and allowed to make rules however they see fit. Alternatively, their processes and decision criteria can be so heavily regulated that they have very limited discretion in formulating and enacting rules. In between, there are many possibilities. In administrative law, these are often viewed as existing on a continuum from *informal* (less regulated) to *formal* (more regulated) processes. Each end of the continuum and every step along the way will maximize some values at the expense of others. The following are of major concern, as are the potential trade-offs among them:

1. *Flexibility.* When agencies make rules like those for smoked whitefish and peanut butter, they are exercising delegated legislative authority. Flexibility enables administrators to bring their expertise and discretion to the resolution of public policy problems, such as food purity. Decisions sometimes rest on different views of the public interest, contested science, or competing assumptions about behavior. Some degree of uncertainty is generally present. (When is peanut butter no longer peanut butter?) Flexibility allows agencies to use their best judgment in determining what kinds of information should be used, from where, and from whom, and which criteria should be met, in formulating rules. Flexibility would place the burden of persuasion on those opposed to an agency's rule. For example, the FDA has more flexibility if the burden is on food companies to demonstrate that a regulation is commercially infeasible than if it has to show that a rule, as applied to each product, is feasible.

2. *Policy criteria.* In contrast to unfettered flexibility, rulemakers can be required to consider specific policy criteria, such as costs and benefits, the interests of small entities, and the impact of rules on the environment, economic competitiveness, and specific groups such as farmers or minorities.

3. *Faithfulness to legislative intent.* Rules can be more or less in keeping with the legislative intent behind them. Gross deviations from statutory intent or criteria are problematic in terms of the rule of law and democracy. Unelected administrators, who often have civil service protection, should not take the place of legislators.

However, legislative intent and statutory standards may be vague, or it may be necessary to reinterpret them in light of new knowledge, conditions, and technologies. Judicial and legislative review of agency rules can be applied, in varying degrees, to hold rulemakers accountable to legislative intent (see Chapter 6).

4. *Rationality*. Rulemaking can be subject to a variety of standards of rationality. An agency can be required to explain the rationale for a rule, the information or science used, the likely costs and benefits, and the level of probability that the rule will achieve its intended purpose. Rulemaking may include mandatory consideration of various alternative means of achieving the desired objective, such as safe smoked whitefish. Legislatures can use the same criteria when passing laws, but typically majority support is a surrogate for legislative rationality. Requiring high levels of rationality may undercut flexibility.

5. *Participation*. Rulemaking can be limited to one or a few agency personnel or opened up to the universe of interested or affected parties. Broad participation may yield better information and greater acceptance of the legitimacy of administrative rulemaking. Agencies can be required to include enforcement agents in their rulemaking. Participation also has costs; for example, it can reduce flexibility by encumbering and delaying rulemaking. Although it is easy to poke fun at the FDA for taking nine years to issue its peanut-butter standard, not all of the snail's pace was of its own making.

6. *Efficiency*. Rulemaking can be an efficient alternative to legislative processes, which are usually cumbersome and laden with opportunities to block action. Rulemaking can be more timely and precise. Agencies can be required to produce rules within a fixed time frame. However, as policy criteria and opportunities for participation multiply, efficiency may suffer. Higher standards of rationality may also impede efficiency. Nova Scotia urged the FDA to adopt specific processing requirements for each species of fish, which would have been more rational but also have required much more science and time. The fish could have consumed a huge amount of the agency's resources.

7. *Enforceability and the ability to conform*. Administrative law can encourage agencies to produce rules that are clear, coherent, and enforceable. The ability of regulated parties to conform, and at

what cost, are always relevant to rulemaking, though rulemakers may give them limited attention. Nova Scotia flatly refused to comply with the FDA's regulations. Agencies can be required to assess the impact of proposed rules on the different categories of entities that will be affected by them, such as small businesses and local governments, arid versus wet regions, and those who process a particular species of fish.

A good general checklist of rulemaking criteria is contained in Executive Order 12,866 issued by President Bill Clinton in 1993. It provides that federal agencies' regulatory action should be guided by twelve principles: (1) identify the problems addressed; (2) assess the contributions, if any, of existing regulations to those problems; (3) identify alternatives to regulations; (4) consider risks; (5) assess cost-effectiveness; (6) weigh costs and benefits; (7) base decisions on the best obtainable information; (8) assess alternatives among regulatory possibilities; (9) seek the views of state, local, and tribal governments; (10) avoid inconsistency; (11) impose the least burden on society; and (12) write regulations in simple, understandable language.

Clinton's order operated against the backdrop of APA requirements for legislative rulemaking. These rest on an idealized model of the legislative process itself. Prior to enactment of the APA in 1946, there was no single, standardized federal rulemaking process. Many agencies had great flexibility. Within the framework of broad delegations of legislative authority, they established the specific policy criteria and trade-offs, chose the participants, and set the level of rationality. Agency procedures varied so widely that an attorney might have to be specially certified to practice before any particular one, such as the Interstate Commerce Commission. A committee of the American Bar Association summarized federal rulemaking in 1934:

Practically every agency to which legislative power has been delegated (or sub delegated [by the president]) has exercised it, and has published its enactments, sometimes in the form of official printed pamphlets, bound or looseleaf, sometimes in mimeograph form, sometimes in privately owned publications, and sometimes in press releases. Sometimes they exist only in sort of an unwritten law. Rules and regulations, upon compliance with which important privileges and freedom from heavy penalties may depend, are amended and interpreted as formally or informally as they were originally adopted. (American Bar Association 1934:228)

In one congressman's view, the federal bureaucracy was "becoming greater as a lawmaking institution than the Congress of the United States itself" (U.S. Congress 1940:4672). The bigger problem, as another said, was that the agencies "not only pay too little attention to the viewpoint of the public, but pay less attention to the clearly expressed intention of Congress" (U.S. Congress 1939:46).

Congress's solution was to require the agencies, "when acting in a quasi-legislative capacity," to "follow the legislative practice of Congress, which from the beginning has held open public hearings on proposed legislation of general public interest" (U.S. Congress 1940:4591). In this model, administrative rulemaking is a search for the broad public interest. It draws on the insights, information, knowledge, and perspectives of the community at large, especially those who have the greatest stake or concern in the substance of a rule. Just as congressional committees hold hearings on proposed legislation or policy issues, administrators should approach rulemaking with open minds, listen to the public, and be responsive to it. In short, administrative rulemaking is a legislative process, and, therefore, it should be informed by legislative values.

A major difficulty with the idealized model is precisely that—it is idealized. Politics in the United States tends to flow to the point of policy decision (Lowi 1969). When administrative rules make important policy choices, political influence—rather than a neutral search for the public interest—will be exerted (Stewart 1975). Political parties and groups will seek to protect and promote their interests. They will attempt to ensure that rulemakers pay attention to particular values, such as vibrant federalism, preventing environmental degradation, and protecting small businesses. Groups with enough political clout may convince Congress, the president, or an agency such as the Office of Management and Budget to impose impact statements or other procedures that will slow or block the adoption of rules that offend their interests or values. They may also try to achieve their favored substantive policy outcomes or generate delay by influencing an agency's choice among available administrative procedures for rulemaking. Additionally, they may litigate and, over time, essentially compel agencies to use expansive procedures in order to establish comprehensive and defensible rulemaking records that reviewing courts will find convincing. After *Nova Scotia*, presumably the FDA was less likely to withhold the scientific basis for its rules or fail to issue a more comprehensive "concise general statement" of their purpose. Eventually, organized groups seeking to promote their own interests will tend to make rulemaking more elaborate.

It is highly unlikely that in enacting the APA in 1946 Congress could have foreseen what federal rulemaking would look like fifty-plus years later. The APA is based on an idealized model. It established three rulemaking processes and, for better or worse, left ample flexibility to build upon them. To varying degrees, the same general approaches are available at the state level.

Rulemaking Processes

The APA's rulemaking processes range from unregulated to highly formalized, trial-like procedures.

Limited or No Procedural Requirements

Rules relating to military and foreign affairs, agency management, personnel, public property, loans, grants, benefits, and contracts are exempt from APA requirements. Rulemaking on these matters may nevertheless be regulated by other statutes and/or internal agency procedures. The only APA requirement for procedural and interpretive rules is publication in the *Federal Register*. The constitutionality or legality of specific exempt, procedural, and interpretive rules can be challenged in federal court, but how they are made is up to the agencies. Of course, an agency may want to consult with outside interests, or even hold hearings on such rules, but it is not required to do so.

Agencies can also make legislative rules in unrestricted fashion (other than required publication in the *Federal Register*) when they have "good cause," meaning more elaborate procedure is "impracticable, unnecessary, or contrary to the public interests" (section 553[a][3][b]). This is a large loophole. The U.S. General Accounting Office found that in 1997 the good-cause provision was used in about half of all potentially covered rulemakings. Most instances involved administrative or technical matters of limited applicability. However, eleven substantial rules were published with no prior public notice or participation. In some cases, the agencies use one of two variants for obtaining public input *after* a rule is made. In *direct final rulemaking*, a rule is published in the *Federal Register* and goes into effect at a specified future date, unless adverse comments are filed. *Interim final rules* are immediately effective but subject to post-publication comments and potential withdrawal or revision (U.S. General Accounting Office 1998:2–3, 6–8).

Informal Rulemaking

Informal rulemaking requirements are modest but subject to considerable amplification. Also known as *notice and comment rulemaking*, informal rulemaking imposes five requirements on the agencies. First, they
must either specifically notify affected persons or publish a notice of the
proposed rulemaking (NPRM) in the *Federal Register*. The notice must
contain "(1) a statement of the time, place, and nature of public rule making proceedings; (2) reference to the legal authority under which the rule
is proposed; and (3) either the terms or substance of the proposed rule or
a description of the subjects and issues involved" (section 553[b]). Second, "the agency shall give interested persons an opportunity to participate in the rule making through submission of written data, views, or arguments with or without opportunity for oral presentation" (section
553[c]). Third, "after consideration of the relevant matter presented, the
agency shall incorporate in the rules adopted a concise general statement
of their basis and purpose" (section 553[c]). Fourth, after publication of a
final rule in the *Federal Register* at least thirty days must elapse before it
can take effect, unless there is good cause, explained with the published
rule, for it to apply sooner. Fifth, the agencies have to "give an interested
person the right to petition for the issuance, amendment, or repeal of a
rule" (section 553[e]). If the agency significantly revises a proposed rule
after receiving initial comments, it may publish a new version in the *Federal Register* to obtain additional feedback. On their face, these requirements do not appear particularly burdensome. However, the potential
for litigation and unfavorable judicial review of rules has prompted the
agencies to treat the APA's requirements copiously.

Agency notices regarding the substance of proposed rules have sometimes been found inadequate. Reviewing courts may want "to see what
major issues of policy were ventilated by the informal proceedings and
why the agency reacted to them as it did" (*Automotive Parts & Accessories
Association v. Boyd* 1968:338). A final rule may be invalidated if a significant issue addressed by it was not identified in the NPRM or if it is not a
logical outgrowth of the proposed rule. After receiving comments, an
agency can write a substantially different rule. However, the original notice must always enable the parties potentially affected by a final rule to
know that their interests were involved. An agency's notice cannot be so
cryptic that interested parties are unable to comment upon it meaning-
fully. This was the problem with the FDA's failure to disclose the scientific basis for its proposed rule in *Nova Scotia*. Additionally, as *Nova Scotia*

illustrates, an agency's concise statement of purpose may be defective. Finally, although the APA does not require rulemakers to respond to individual comments, agencies routinely docket them with some kind of assessment in order to build a record that will convince a court that its final rule is reasonable. Rules can have huge effects on the economy, environment, and the public. Courts often take a *hard look* at their logic and rationality (see Chapter 6 on judicial review of agency actions).

Assessments of informal rulemaking vary. Notice and comment was intended to be straightforward, not straitjacketing. In practice, however, agencies tend to use more elaborate procedures than those outlined in the APA itself. As noted above, this is partly because they need to build a satisfactory record for judicial review. But as discussed later in this chapter, it is also due to additional requirements imposed by statutes and executive orders. Rulemaking has become laborious enough for agencies to use a variety of techniques to obtain input from interested publics before writing, or deciding to write, proposed rules. In fact, as a means of exercising influence, informal contacts with the agency both before and after publication of an NPRM may be equally or more effective than submitting written comments or attending hearings, if any are held (Kerwin 1999:195).

Formal Rulemaking

Also known as *rulemaking on the record*, formal rulemaking is very elaborate. It is so elaborate, in fact, that it may be counterproductive in terms of timeliness and efficiency. This is why the 1981 Model State Administrative Procedure Act avoids it (Bonfield 1986:186). Federal agencies are also apt to dispense with it whenever possible, which is often. The APA sets forth the structure for formal rulemaking but does not require agencies to engage in it. Formal rulemaking is mandated by separate statutes when Congress considers it appropriate, as in some sections of the FDA's Food, Drug, and Cosmetic Act.

Formal rulemaking is a quasijudicial, trial-like process. Hearings, which are central to congressional lawmaking, are mandatory for formal rulemaking. A panel or specific officer, who can be an administrative law judge or similar hearing examiner, presides. The presiding officer or panel regulates the course of the hearing; administers oaths; decides on the information that may be offered as evidence; tries to arrange for agreement among the parties; and, failing that, issues a decision. The parties to the hearing submit evidence and may engage in cross-examination (section 556). The APA places the burden of persuasion on the proponent of the rule, which may be the agency or an outside interest. Ex parte (one-sided) contacts between the decisionmaker and a participant in the hearing in the absence of any other are prohibited. The agency maintains a complete transcript, and its decision must be supported by substantial evidence on the record as a whole. The presiding officer or panel can issue an initial or recommended decision. Initial decisions become final unless they are appealed; recommended decisions are automatically subject to review by the agency head or governing board or commission. The final rule, if any, is published in the *Federal Register* and takes effect as specified after at least thirty days have elapsed to enable those affected to comply. In unusual cases, the agency, board, or commission may issue a tentative decision for comment by the parties and possible revision. These provisions may be modified by whatever statute requires the agency to use formal rulemaking.

The weight of opinion among administrative law scholars, legislators, and judges is that "the formal rulemaking procedure normally 'does not work'" or at least works so badly that it ought to be avoided (Warren 1996:253). The courts, including the U.S. Supreme Court, seem to agree. They are unlikely to force agencies to use it unless "(1) a specific statute clearly requires formal rule-making; (2) an oral, evidentiary hearing is mandated by a statute; and (3) adjudicative facts specific to an individual involving 'property' or 'liberty' interests must be resolved through a [constitutional] due process, formal rule-making agency hearing" (Warren 1996:254; *United States v. Florida East Coast Railway Co.* 1973).

Hybrid and Negotiated Rulemaking Processes

Two additional general rulemaking approaches have gained currency since enactment of the APA in 1946.

Hybrid Rulemaking

Hybrid rulemaking was developed by some federal agencies, promoted by Congress, and, until 1978, sometimes imposed on administrators by the courts. Hybrid rulemaking follows a Goldilocks-type principle. As a means of making public policy, formal rulemaking is informational and procedural overkill, whereas informal rulemaking is potentially inadequate in providing agencies with the comprehensive data and perspectives they need to formulate sound rules. The APA allows the agencies to search for a middle ground that is just right. Most notably, they can hold public hearings in conjunction with notice and comment rulemaking and invite interested parties to participate or solicit their views in some other fashion. With wider information, the agency can build a more complete record and, presumably, a stronger rationale for its final rule.

Hybrid rulemaking is related to a shift toward greater public and public interest group participation in administrative policymaking (Stewart 1975). Prior to the 1960s or 1970s, individual agencies were often considered "captives" of specific, narrow-based economic interest groups (Bernstein 1955). In a classic case, the Interstate Commerce Commission was once considered a ward of the railroad industry. The same interest group capturing the agency would have considerable influence with the congressional (sub)committees that formulated legislation in the particular policy area and exercised oversight of the agencies involved. Relations among the group, committee, and agency tended to be harmonious—and nearly impervious to influence from outsiders. The terms "iron triangle" and "cozy triangle" (or "subsystems," as some political scientists call them) were used to describe these policymaking arrangements.

In the 1960s and 1970s, political demands for wider group representation and greater attention to the public's interest in administrative policymaking reached a crescendo. The period witnessed the enactment of the Freedom of Information Act (1966) and the Government in the Sunshine Act (1976) (see Chapter 5 on transparency), as well as the Federal Advisory Committee Act (1972), which is discussed later in this chapter. As the agencies responded to both the new statutes and political mood, the iron triangle image gave way to one portraying far more open, participatory *issue networks* or *policy networks* (Heclo 1978). These are made up of groups and individuals who share technical knowledge and interest in policy areas but not necessarily the same political perspectives. For instance, whereas energy policy may once have been dominated by economic interests, such as oil and electric power companies, issue networks bring environmental and conservation groups into the policymaking (rulemaking) process.

The growth of hybrid rulemaking was instrumental in the shift from iron triangles to issue networks. By expanding participation in rulemaking, "agency personnel give shape to the heretofore formless issue networks" and, importantly, may serve as "arbiters" of their perspectives (Golden 1998:12). This frees the agencies from captivity, or at least inordinate influence by a single interest, and brings rulemaking closer to the idealized legislative model. Airing competing perspectives in the rulemaking process should enhance rationality and also enable agencies to compile better explanations of the basis for their final rules. It should also lend more political legitimacy to rulemaking.

Hybrid rulemaking was boosted by the federal courts in the late 1960s and early 1970s. As litigation became a staple of the administrative process, judges were looking for better agency records upon which to review the legality of final rules. In particular, they might require the agencies to grant greater participation to environmental or other public interest groups. Judicially imposed hybrid rulemaking came to a dead end with the Supreme Court's unanimous decision in *Vermont Yankee Nuclear Power Corporation v. Natural Resources Defense Council, Inc.* (1978). In no uncertain terms, the Court held that the judiciary should not graft additional procedural requirements onto informal rulemaking. The agencies need only meet the minimal APA requirements, period. Otherwise, rulemaking requirements would be unpredictable, and from a practical perspective, the agencies would have to make the informal procedure much more like the laborious formal one. However, nothing in *Vermont Yankee* prohibited the agencies from using hybrid rulemaking on their own.

Negotiated Rulemaking

Negotiated rulemaking was developed in the 1980s, also as a means of bringing rulemaking closer to the idealized legislative model. It relies on face-to-face negotiation among interested parties, including agencies, to formulate rules. Also known as *regulatory negotiation* (Reg-Neg) it gained full legitimacy via the federal Negotiated Rulemaking Act of 1990, which amends the APA's rulemaking procedures. Reg-Neg is considered appropriate when only a limited number of identifiable interests will be affected by a rule. The general procedure is for agencies to establish rulemaking committees after notice and comment in the *Federal Register*. Committees will typically be composed of up to twenty-five members drawn from the agency, regulated entities, trade associations, unions, citizen groups, and other relevant interests. The committee should adequately represent all the affected interests. Its meetings are open to the public. A facilitator or mediator can be used to steer the proceedings in search of a consensus. Unanimity is required for a rule to be successfully negotiated, though members who are opposed to the majority can withdraw from the committee rather than block its efforts. If consensus is reached, the agency writes up the rule and publishes it in the *Federal Register* for notice and comment (and possible revision). Although the agencies are treated as any other participant in the negotiations, they retain ultimate control of whether a final rule will be issued and, if so, what its text will be.

The premise behind Reg-Neg is that it can improve on "the poor quality of rules produced, the burdensome nature of the rulemaking process, the length of time it takes to promulgate rules, and the frequency of litigation that follows" (U.S. Senate 1989:2). Compared with informal rulemaking, Reg-Neg is thought to be less adversarial, more creative, supported by better information and perspective, and more educational for the parties (Strauss et al. 1995:405). The Negotiated Rulemaking Act was permanently reauthorized in the 1996 Administrative Dispute Resolution Act.

Critics of Reg-Neg contend that it fails to deliver on its promise and "has the tendency to obscure, if not pervert, the public interest to the benefit of private interests" (Funk 1987:57; quoted in Strauss et al. 1995:405). Only a very small percentage of all final federal rules have been negotiated (Coglianese 1997:1277). Timeliness and litigation rates do not seem to have been dramatically affected by Reg-Neg, though the data are not conclusive (Coglianese 1997; Kerwin and Furlong 1992). By one count, the EPA's Farmworker Protection Standards rule took 2,528 days, or nearly seven years, to complete, whereas the U.S. Coast Guard took only 179 days to negotiate a rule regarding drawbridges on the Chicago River (Coglianese 1997:1279). Negotiated rules, both before and after the 1990 act, include such matters as residential woodstoves; nondiscrimination in air travel; asbestos in public schools; handicapped parking; clean fuels; wood furniture coatings; direct student loans; disadvantaged students; and Indian self-determination.

Additional Features of the Idealized Legislative Model for Rulemaking

Several other elements of the legislative rulemaking model are noteworthy.

Representation: Advisory Committees

Federal agencies have long used quasigovernmental advisory committees to guide them in setting rulemaking agendas, writing proposed rules, and other policymaking activities. Many of these committees have a relatively narrow focus, dealing, for instance, with a single geographic region, crop, animal, food, disease, chemical, or technology. The advisory committee system is fluid—committees come and go—but the following titles indicate their nature: Cascade Head Scenic Research Area Advisory

Council; National Advisory Council on Safety in Agriculture; National Cotton Marketing Study Committee; Cattle Industry Advisory Committee; National Advisory Council on Child Nutrition; Advisory Committee on Hog Cholera Eradication; Expert Panel on Nitrates and Nitrosamines; National Peanut Advisory Committee; and Raisin Advisory Board (Leahy 1976). Congress as well as agencies establish such committees, which are a valued resource in bringing greater expertise, perspective, and legitimacy to administrative policymaking. They also promote the democratic-constitutional values of participation and representation in agency decisionmaking (Steck 1984). The system is quite active: In 1998, fifty-five federal departments and agencies supported 892 advisory committees totaling 41,259 members who held 5,852 meetings and issued 973 reports (U.S. General Services Administration 1999).

Advisory committees have sometimes been considered a powerful "fifth branch" of the government (the agencies being the fourth; U.S. Senate 1978:48, 217, 293, 299–300). Despite their acknowledged value, there is always concern that they will be skewed in favor of some interests at the expense of others, generate conflicts of interest, or exercise untoward influence over the agencies.

The Federal Advisory Committee Act of 1972 seeks to reduce the potential for abuse. It requires that the membership of advisory committees be "fairly balanced in terms of the points of view represented and the functions to be performed" (section 5). It also specifies that the committees "will not be inappropriately influenced by the appointing authority or by any special interest" (section 5). The act promotes transparency through a number of public notice, open meetings, and reporting requirements (see Chapter 5 in this book). It does not apply to committees composed entirely of federal employees.

The Federal Advisory Committee Act contemplates joint congressional and executive management of the advisory committee system. Congressional committees are charged with reviewing the activities of those advisory committees under their jurisdictions and determining whether they should be merged with others, abolished altogether, or have their responsibilities revised. OMB also has a role in reviewing the status of advisory committees and issuing guidelines to improve their effectiveness.

Protecting Specific Interests and Values

The use of advisory committees is premised on the belief that many interests are well defined and coherent enough to be represented through direct participation in agency policymaking, including establishing rule-making agendas. But what about interests and values that are so diffuse in the economy and society that they are not readily amenable to such direct representation? The federal government's answer has been to protect them through impact assessments or analyses in notice and comment rulemaking. The Regulatory Flexibility Act of 1980 is a good example.

That statute requires agencies to analyze the effects of their rulemaking on small entities, which include small governmental jurisdictions, not-for-profits, and, most notably, businesses. Such entities often face a problem in that they are exceptionally burdened by the compliance costs associated with across-the-board regulations for clean air and water, worker safety, and other matters. Overall, small business has very strong support in Congress. But specific small enterprises, such as mom-and-pop outfits, are likely to be less effective than large firms in using their own resources and/or relying on trade associations to protect their interests through daily monitoring of the *Federal Register* for notices of proposed rulemaking and subsequent submission of comments to the agencies.

The Regulatory Flexibility Act also seeks to reduce small entities' vulnerability to unduly burdensome, prohibitively expensive, and impractical regulations by requiring the agencies to provide *regulatory flexibility* (Reg-Flex) analyses, when relevant in notice and comment rulemaking, along with their proposed and final rules. Reg-Flex analyses focus on the impact the rules will have on small entities and potential alternatives, if any, that would be less burdensome. Enforcement is through the Small Business Administration, with limited opportunity for judicial review (Sargentich 1997:124–126).

The Small Business Regulatory Enforcement Fairness Act of 1996 amended the 1980 act and strengthened the Reg-Flex process in a number of ways. It broadens the scope of judicial review for aggrieved small entities. It also contains provisions requiring EPA and OSHA actively to seek input from representatives of small entities. The act continues to apply primarily to informal legislative rulemaking but also covers some Internal Revenue Service interpretive rules.

The precedent set by the Regulatory Flexibility Act gained a foothold in executive orders as well. President Ronald Reagan issued two such orders in 1987: No. 12,606 required agencies to engage in assessments of the impact of their proposed rules on "family values," and No. 12,612 required "federalism impact assessments." Clinton followed suit in 1994 with a similar order for environmental justice (No. 12,898). In 1998, Congress strengthened the family values emphasis through the Assessment of Federal Regulations and Policies on Families Act, which requires the agencies to engage in "family policymaking assessments." The act particularly addresses measures that might strengthen or erode marital commitments, the authority and rights of parents, and the overall performance of family functions. The executive orders on rulemaking are not binding on the independent regulatory commissions, such as the Federal Communications Commission and the Federal Trade Commission, which nevertheless may comply voluntarily. Although it is not without controversy as a matter of constitutional law, "the President . . . lacks distinct constitutional power to manage these organizations [i.e., independent regulatory commissions]" (Moreno 1994:512). However, the orders do apply to EPA, OSHA, and similar executive-branch units.

The Paperwork Reduction Acts of 1980 and 1995 also bear mention. They seek to control and reduce the enormous paperwork burden that federal rules and requirements thrust on society. In 1980, the OMB estimated the overall burden at 1.5 billion hours (Skrzycki 1998:G2). By 1994, it had apparently reached 6.5 billion hours and may have cost as much as 9 percent of GDP (Strauss et al. 1995:872). The Paperwork Reduction Acts require agencies to publish notices of their intent to collect information in the *Federal Register* for public comment. They must also estimate the burden their forms and related instruments impose. After completing these steps, if the agencies decide to proceed, they must submit their proposals for collecting information to OMB's Office of Information and Regulatory Affairs. Their submissions must include considerations of whether the information sought is duplicative or burdensome, creates special hardships for small entities, and is clearly identified or defined. OIRA's role is to prevent the collection of unnecessary information by monitoring and coordinating the agencies' use of forms and other devices. It has sixty days to clear requests, which are approved for one year by default if it fails to meet this deadline. OIRA's disapproval is binding with two exceptions: It is subject to judicial review if challenged as arbitrary and capricious, and independent regulatory commissions can override OIRA's rejection by a majority vote of their commission or board members (Lubbers 1997:116). A public-protection provision prohibits penalizing anyone for failing to respond to a federal information collection instrument that was not properly subjected to the required clearance process.

The paperwork reduction process seems straightforward enough, if not wholly adequate, in limiting the agencies' appetite for information. However, like many administrative law procedures, it can be used (or abused) politically to achieve public policy objectives. In 2001, a Republican congressional aide, working in concert with the head of OIRA, convened key business lobbyists in an effort to "use obscure paperwork guidelines as a back-door mechanism to gut long-established regulations" for air and water quality, lead paint, truck safety, reporting the release of toxic substances, and family and medical leaves. In short, "paperwork technicalities [are] an excuse to review otherwise untouchable rules" (Grunwald 2001).

This experience with paperwork reduction makes the idealized legislative model look less ideal. As suggested earlier, there are apt to be important value trade-offs in rulemaking processes. The Federal Advisory Committee Act's reporting and transparency provisions encumber the use of such committees, albeit in an effort to promote democratic-constitutional values. Efforts to protect particular interests and values through impact assessments and paperwork review consume time and effort. Some scholars wonder whether, in the aggregate, the addition of so many administrative law requirements to the APA's basic process for informal rulemaking has such an inhibiting effect that a "'regulatory impact analysis' impact analysis would be useful in deciding whether to undertake any further such requirements"! (Strauss et al. 1995:217.) Yet rulemaking has been further complicated by presidents.

Executive Efforts to Influence Federal Agency Rulemaking

Legislative rulemaking by administrators occupies a somewhat uncomfortable place in the constitutional structure. When Congress exercises its legislative powers by enacting laws, the president has a veto. This gives the chief executive considerable bargaining power with Congress, which needs a two-thirds majority in both chambers to override vetoes. When Congress delegates its legislative authority to the agencies, the president has no formal veto power over their rules. The 1981 Model State Administrative Procedure Act provides that a governor may "rescind or suspend all or a severable portion of a rule of an agency," and some states authorize their attorney general to review rules (section 3–202; Bonfield 1993:180). However, the federal APA has no equivalent provisions. Presidents need other means of promoting their policy agendas and coordinating executive branch activity. To a large extent, they rely on their political appointees for these purposes. Beginning in earnest during President Richard Nixon's administration, they have also turned to administrative law devices.

Nixon established a lasting precedent by authorizing the Office of Management and Budget to undertake quality-of-life reviews of proposed administrative regulations. The reviews focused on the regulatory objectives, costs and benefits, and plausible alternatives to proposed measures. President Gerald Ford followed Nixon's precedent by requiring the agencies to send *inflation impact statements* to OMB along with their proposed regulations. But it was President Jimmy Carter who ratcheted up presidential control of agency rulemaking toward contemporary standards.

Carter established the Regulatory Analysis Review Group to review agency rulemaking proposals likely to cost industries at least $100 million per year. Among its purposes were to improve the analysis supporting proposed regulations and assure consideration of the least costly alternatives (Kerwin 1999:123). Carter's Executive Order 12,044 (1978) established the Regulatory Council, composed of the heads of the agencies most active in regulation, to coordinate administrative rulemaking and assess the cumulative effect of regulations. The order also called on the agencies to publish a regulatory agenda twice a year; write regulations in plain and simple language; increase outside participation in the development of regulations; prepare economic impact analyses for all significant regulations; and periodically review the efficacy of existing regulations. OMB was responsible for agency compliance, though actual review was typically by the review group.

President Reagan followed Carter's lead and put OMB at the center of much federal rulemaking. Executive Orders 12,291 (1981) and 12,498 (1985) centralized executive control of covered rulemaking in OIRA. Under the orders' combined provisions, agencies had to submit draft and final regulatory analyses, regulatory agendas, as well as major proposed and final rules to OIRA for review. Unless prohibited by a specific statute affecting a policy area, rulemaking had to incorporate cost-benefit analysis. Agency heads retained final authority to proceed with rulemaking but were required to explain any noncompliance with OIRA's recommendations (Warren 1996:279). Although compliance was the norm, this arrangement stuck to the letter of constitutional precedent, which allows Congress to vest legal authority specifically and directly in the agencies rather than in the president for subdelegation to them (*Kendall v. United States* 1838).

Observers agree that Reagan's approach had a permanent impact on presidential direction and control of federal rulemaking (Warren 1996:279; Kerwin 1999:126). President George H.W. Bush (Bush I) (1989–1993) retained

Reagan's initiatives and also appointed a Council on Competitiveness to review selected major rules. President Clinton revoked the Reagan orders but adhered to their general direction regarding OMB review, though with more transparency in OIRA's operations (Executive Order 12,866 [1993]).

President George W. Bush (Bush II) is likely to strengthen the role of cost-benefit analysis in OIRA review and the emphasis on searching for less costly alternatives (Skrzycki 2001a; Nakashima 2001a). His efforts to control rulemaking began in controversy on the very day of his inauguration (January 20, 2001), when his White House chief of staff, Andrew Card Jr., issued a memorandum asking the agencies to postpone the effective date of final rules for sixty days. The new administration wanted to review what many viewed as last-minute efforts to write final rules before the presidential transition. Bush II was building on a precedent set by Reagan in Executive Order 12,291, which imposed a sixty-day moratorium on new rules. Upon taking office, Bill Clinton also slowed "regulations that were underway, including those on the verge of becoming final, without touching any completed rules about to take effect" (Goldstein 2001:A6). George W. Bush's action affected forty published final rules, fifty-one proposed and final rules not yet published in the *Federal Register*, and thirty-three additional rules elsewhere in the process. Whether it was legal remains in dispute. As a general principle, "Any decision to repeal, withdraw, defer or amend . . . regulations should be accomplished with the same degree of study, analysis and deliberation that went into the promulgation of those regulations" (Skrzycki 2001b:E6). Moreover, "many argue that to delay an effective date, you have to go through notice and comment. An effective date is a substantive component of the rule" (Skrzycki 2001b:E6). If a rule can be delayed by sixty days, why not 120, or 180, or indefinitely? The matter may take years for the courts to sort out, if anyone brings suit.

The Bush II administration also sought to strengthen OMB review in five main ways. First, it favored more openness through use of the Internet to enable "the public to scrutinize how [OMB] use[s] science and economics to stop bad rules and help agencies craft better ones" (Graham 2002). Second, OIRA intended to hire more scientists and engineers to join its statisticians, economists, and information technologists in analyzing agency rulemaking proposals. Third, OIRA planned to cajole the agencies into doing higher quality regulatory analyses. Fourth, OMB took a proactive role in rulemaking by issuing "prompt letters" "to identify publicly areas where agencies might improve regulatory policies" (Graham 2002). For example, one such letter speeded up the FDA's work on a food labeling rule for transfatty acids. Finally, OMB initiated a broad effort to require that the data on which rulemaking is based are "reproducible, or at least highly transparent, about research design, data sources and analytical methods" (Graham 2002).

The logic behind presidential efforts to coordinate agency rulemaking and improve the quality of rules is clear. But the Card memo's uncertain legality illustrates the inherent ambiguities and limits of presidential influence on rulemaking. Administrative law scholar Kenneth Warren (1996:279–281) reminds us, with specific reference to Reagan, that controlling rulemaking presents presidential administrations with monumental challenges. Warren identifies the following limits:

1. The independent regulatory commissions "promulgate thousands of major rules profoundly affecting public policy areas," but their rulemaking is largely unaffected by executive orders (see also Moreno 1994). Requests that they voluntarily comply tend to be ignored.
2. Reagan's executive orders did not apply to formal rulemaking, and, more generally, executive orders cannot override statutory or constitutional requirements affecting such rulemaking.
3. Bureaucratic inertia along with legal obstacles (and, one might add, agency support in Congress) make centralized control of the rulemaking process very difficult.
4. Reagan's deregulatory agenda faced a substantial number of setbacks in court. Essentially it takes informal rulemaking, or at least a cogently reasoned analysis, to rescind final rules. A new administration cannot simply terminate rules promulgated by its predecessors (*Motor Vehicles Manufacturers Association of the United States, Inc. v. State Farm Mutual Automobile Insurance Co.* 1983; see Chapter 6).

Despite such obstacles, the decades-old presidential effort to gain greater control over administrative rulemaking is likely to continue—often contentiously—through the current administration and beyond.

Conclusion: The Philosopher's Stone Versus the Bubble Effect

During congressional debate on the APA in 1946, Senator Homer Ferguson, a Michigan Republican, predicted that "there will be fewer complaints because of the activities of governmental agencies if they will attempt to live within the rules and regulations laid down by Congress" (U.S. Congress 1946:2205). Maybe, but complaints about federal rulemaking still abound. Finding the "best" process is like searching for the philosopher's stone. Rulemaking procedures are not neutral. They inevitably involve important value trade-offs. They also advantage some interests and participants while disadvantaging others. Members of Congress, presidents, administrators, and interest groups will tend to support procedures that favor their policy preferences and contest those that hinder them. Pressure will be brought to bear wherever key policy decisions can be made, blocked, or reversed. Interests that are able to influence rulemaking agendas and criteria, such as the use of cost-benefit or Reg-Flex analysis, will do so; others, lacking the same avenues of influence, may turn to the courts to achieve their objectives. As a former OIRA official candidly summed up misuse of the Paperwork Reduction Acts for political gain—"The paperwork is a way in, you know?"—to gut rules opposed by favored lobbyists (Grunwald 2001). Both before and after 1946, changing federal rulemaking has been like trying to squeeze an air bubble in a clear plastic tube. Putting pressure on it in one place moves the point at which it can be squeezed to another.

Additional Reading

Kerwin, Cornelius. *Rulemaking: How Government Agencies Write Law and Make Policy*, 2nd ed. Washington, DC: CQ Press, 1999.

Lubbers, Jeffrey. *A Guide to Federal Agency Rulemaking*, 3rd ed. Chicago: American Bar Association, 1998.

4

Evidentiary Adjudication
and Enforcement

Adjudicating Cinderella:
A Case of Deceit, Abuse, and Due Process

The Federal Trade Commission has legal authority to initiate and decide cases against firms it believes are engaging in unfair and deceptive business practices. In the late 1960s, the FTC charged Cinderella Career College and Finishing Schools, Inc. (Cinderella) with thirteen counts of false advertising and deception. These included Cinderella's questionable claims that:

- Miss USA 1965 owed her success to Cinderella's program;
- Cinderella's courses qualified students to become retail buyers and airline hostesses and to assume executive positions;
- Cinderella was the official Washington, D.C., headquarters for the Miss Universe beauty pageant;
- Cinderella was a college; and
- Cinderella's placement services rarely failed.

The FTC also accused Cinderella of applying high-pressure and misleading sales tactics to prospective students. In short, to the FTC Cinderella was a cheat that should be exposed and forced to stop preying on naive teenage girls.

The FTC prosecuted Cinderella at a hearing within the FTC itself, presided over by an independent hearing examiner. The hearing took sixteen days, during which 247 exhibits were introduced, fifty-two witnesses appeared, and 1,810 pages of testimony were taken. The hearing examiner's ninety-three-page initial decision absolved Cinderella of all charges. The FTC had "failed to prove by a preponderance of reliable, probative and substantial evidence" that Cinderella deceived.

The FTC's prosecutor (the complaint counsel) appealed the initial decision to the full commission, that is, to the five FTC commissioners. In this type of proceeding, the commissioners may substitute their own decision for that of the hearing examiner. The commission was chaired by Paul Rand Dixon, who had no love for Cinderella. In a well-reported speech to members of the National Newspaper Association, he cited Cinderella's ads as exemplars of deception and urged his audience to stop printing such material: "Granted that newspapers are not in the advertising policing business, their advertising managers are savvy enough to smell deception when the odor is strong enough." He specifically mentioned "carrying ads that offer college educations in five weeks, fortunes by raising mushrooms in the basement, getting rid of pimples with a magic lotion, or becoming an airline's hostess by attending a charm school." Dixon's remarks were made *after* FTC staff had given notice that the hearing examiner's initial decision would be appealed to Dixon and the other commissioners.

With Dixon in charge, Cinderella fared poorly at the commission level. The commissioners sustained six of the FTC's original charges and ordered Cinderella to cease and desist from engaging in the illegal practices they covered. It reached this decision with scant attention to the transcript and outcome of the earlier proceeding. Instead of wading through the voluminous record before them, the commissioners decided "to independently analyze—and without assistance from consumer or other witnesses—the challenged advertisements and their impact." Consequently, it became "unnecessary" for the commissioners "to review the testimony of . . . expert witnesses and consumer witnesses." Believing that the commissioners knew deception when they saw it, ". . . the Commission [relied] on its own reading and study of the advertisements to determine whether the questioned representation has the capacity to deceive."

Cinderella went to court on the grounds that the FTC had egregiously violated constitutional due process by (1) making its decision without reference to the record produced by the hearing; and (2) allowing Dixon to participate in deciding the appeal. The Court of Appeals for the District of Columbia Circuit agreed that it was "preposterous for the Commission to claim a right to ignore [the hearing examiner's] evidence and, with more daring than prudence, to decide a case de novo [anew]" as it did with Cinderella. In plain English, " the Commissioners are not free to boil over in aggression and completely dismiss [the hearing] proceedings either because they are dissatisfied with the outcome, or for any other reason."

The court also had some choice words for chairman Dixon, who, in its view, was no Prince Charming. He had failed to recuse (disqualify) himself in other cases, and with obvious frustration the court found "it hard to believe that . . . Chairman Dixon is so indifferent to the dictates of the Courts of Appeals that he has chosen once again to put his personal determination of what the law requires ahead of what the courts have time and again told him the law requires." It rebuked him for exercising "questionable discretion and very poor judgment indeed," being "sensitive to theory but insensitive to reality," and distorting the law "beyond all reasonable interpretation" or just ignoring it altogether.

In reiterating the fundamental legal principle requiring recusal, the court noted that "it requires no superior olfactory powers to recognize that the danger of unfairness through prejudgment is not diminished by a cloak of self-righteousness." Disqualification is necessary when "a disinterested observer may conclude that [the agency] has in some measure adjudged the facts as well as the law of a particular case in advance of hearing it." Moreover, agency adjudications "must be attended, not only with every element of fairness but with the very appearance of complete fairness."

The court held that the FTC violated Cinderella's constitutional due process. The commissioners should have taken the whole record into account and also excluded Dixon from the appeal. Some seventeen months after the commission issued its final order, Cinderella won a reprieve (*Cinderella Career and Finishing Schools, Inc., v. Federal Trade Commission* 1970:584–586, 588, 591–592).

What Is Evidentiary Administrative Adjudication?

The violations of due process in *Cinderella* are atypical, but otherwise the case provides a good illustration of *evidentiary administrative adjudication*. An evidentiary adjudication is a proceeding—typically a hearing of some kind—in which evidence is adduced and law applied in determining the rights and obligations of individuals, corporations, and other entities. Evidentiary adjudication is used in a very wide variety of administrative decision making, including the following:

1. determining individuals' eligibility for benefits;
2. resolving charges of unfair or illegal personnel and labor relations practices;

3. granting or denying licenses;
4. challenging the award of a government contract; and
5. enforcing laws and agency regulations to protect the public, the environment, businesses, and other entities against harmful practices, threats, and dangers.

The product of an evidentiary hearing is an *order*.

The structure and process of agency evidentiary adjudication is broadly controlled by procedural due process under the U.S. Constitution's Fifth and Fourteenth Amendments as well as by administrative law provisions. As in *Cinderella*, adjudication may involve an elaborate hearing, with personal appearances and live testimony, as well as an appeals process. However, it may also be confined to written submissions and very limited opportunity for review. Unlike notice and comment rulemaking, where the model seeks to replicate an idealized version of how legislatures in the United States make law, administrative evidentiary adjudication is not intended to match courtroom procedure. Rather, the objectives are fourfold: (1) to achieve fundamental fairness; (2) to adjudicate cases competently; (3) to resolve conflicts efficiently; and (4) to accomplish all of the foregoing while enhancing, or at least not impeding, organizational performance.

Fairness is usually gauged in terms of how the parties to an adjudication believe they were treated. *Competence* is measured by the extent to which hearing examiners and agencies' decisions are upheld on appeal. *Efficiency* is essentially timeliness. *Organizational performance* can involve any number of factors, including the impact of adjudication on resources, coherent decisionmaking, and personnel systems. In practice, it is difficult for adjudicatory systems to excel on all four dimensions simultaneously.

Discussions of adjudication are often confusing. First, under the Administrative Procedure Act of 1946, there is overlap in the provisions for formal rulemaking and evidentiary adjudication. Formal rulemaking is an adjudicatory procedure. However, it is apt to focus on *legislative facts* or general policy concerns, such as whether a proposed rule is necessary or cost-beneficial. Legislative facts may involve empirical or scientific matters, like how to eliminate botulism in smoked whitefish. However, they do not pertain to the conduct of specific individuals or entities like Cinderella. Evidentiary adjudication, by contrast, focuses on *adjudicative facts*, which are concerned with individual motive, intent, and behavior. Whether individuals should have a right to cancel a contract with a school like Cinderella within a day or two of signing it is a legislative fact; whether Cinderella engaged in deceptive advertising is an adjudicative fact.

Evidentiary adjudication also differs from formal rulemaking in that it is retrospective rather than prospective. It deals with past and/or continuing conduct. By contrast, rulemaking—both formal and informal—addresses matters in the future. Another distinction is that evidentiary adjudication deals with specific parties, whereas rulemaking has general applicability. A rule prohibiting false advertising applies broadly throughout the economy; an evidentiary adjudication to determine whether a firm has violated the rule is specific, as in *Cinderella*.

A second source of confusion is that although evidentiary adjudication and rulemaking are analytically distinct, as just described, in practice sometimes they may be used interchangeably to achieve identical policy outcomes. The main problem is that although evidentiary adjudication applies directly only to the parties to a case and is retrospective, the decision reached will presumably apply to others in the future. For example, the National Labor Relations Board (NLRB) adjudicates charges of unfair labor practices by unions and businesses. Many cases are repetitive, and the evidentiary adjudication merely determines the facts, for example, did the union organize an employee "sickout," or did a large number of bargaining unit employees catch the flu at once? However, some cases will raise altogether new issues (called cases of first impression). When this occurs, the evidentiary adjudication will necessarily deal with legislative facts—is the practice unfair under the governing statute? It will also address adjudicative facts—did the union or business engage in it? When adjudication of a case of first impression by the NLRB determines that the labor practice at issue is unfair, the immediate and direct effect is on the parties to the dispute (i.e., the union and the company). Nevertheless, if the board is consistent, then the unfair practice in question will be prohibited in the future just as surely as if it had been outlawed through rulemaking. And the prohibition will apply to all other firms and unions under the NLRB's jurisdiction. Many believe that in such circumstances adjudication should be avoided because it is inferior to rulemaking as a vehicle for administrative policymaking.

Criticisms of Adjudication

Administrative adjudication is frequently criticized from two perspectives: legal and administrative.

Legal Perspectives

Administrative law scholars generally disfavor policymaking through agency adjudication in cases of first impression. First, it is a kind of "dog law" because notice is inadequate. Like a dog being trained, parties to an adjudication find out after the fact that they have done something wrong. The retroactive quality of such decisions fits uncomfortably with due process and other principles of U.S. law. Unless specifically constrained by law, agencies usually have the choice of proceeding by adjudication or rule-making. However, when adjudication results in a new regulation of general applicability, a court may sometimes direct an agency to engage in rule-making instead (*Ford Motor Company v. FTC* 1981; see Warren 1996:304).

Second, regulations and legal principles established through adjudication may be buried in hundreds or thousands of adjudicatory decisions. These form a kind of agency-specific case law that is difficult to master and far less accessible than agency rules. One may have to analyze a large number of agency adjudicatory decisions to know what is prohibited and why. Even then, it will sometimes be unclear whether a more recent decision has effectively overruled or modified an earlier one.

Third, evidentiary adjudication is not a participatory problem-solving exercise. The APA provides that in adjudication and other matters, "so far as orderly conduct of public business permits, an interested person may appear before an agency" (section 555[b]). In terms of adjudication, the word "interested" may be interpreted broadly. It may also be restricted to those potentially so adversely affected by an agency's adjudicatory decision as to have standing to challenge it in court (see Chapter 6). The *appearance* may be in the form of a written statement or legal brief, as well as live testimony and other direct participation in the hearing. However, in many instances participation will be limited to the parties directly involved and the experts and witnesses who testify. When controversial policy choices are involved, greater participation is apt to be generated through rulemaking than by adjudication. Less participation can limit the amount of information and range of perspectives available to the agency decisionmakers. This problem is compounded by adversary procedure, which inhibits the parties from volunteering anything that may weaken their cases. The agency decision must be supported by the record, but what goes into the record may be less than sufficient for making complex policy decisions.

Fourth, agency adjudicatory decisions may be inconsistent with one another because different hearing examiners, administrative law judges, and other decisionmakers come to disparate conclusions in similar cases.

This can be frustrating not only for the parties involved but also for reviewing courts. For instance, in a case involving the Federal Labor Relations Authority (FLRA), a court complained: "In the two cases at hand, the effects of the FLRA's failure adequately to set forth its governing rule are clear. With respect to the identical violation, one ALJ awarded back pay; the other did not. . . . The confusion and inconsistency within the Authority is abundantly evident" (*Professional Airways Systems Specialists, MEBA, AFL-CIO v. FLRA* 1987:860).

Finally, oversight of agency adjudication is difficult, especially compared to rulemaking. Congressional committees cannot engage in direct discussion with agency adjudicators about pending cases or those being heard. If Congress is dissatisfied with the policy direction of an agency's adjudicatory ordermaking, its primary recourse is to rewrite the pertinent statutes. Neither can an executive unit like the federal OMB do much to steer or coordinate agency adjudicatory decisionmaking. Political executives—and hence the governors and presidents who appoint them—have limited controls over ALJs and other hearing examiners. The ability of elected chief executives to direct agency adjudication is also weakened by the fixed and staggered terms and bipartisan composition of many boards and commissions.

Administrative Perspectives

A second set of criticisms of evidentiary adjudication focuses more on the administrative difficulties of achieving high levels of the values mentioned earlier: fairness, efficiency, competence, and neutral or positive effect on administrative performance. The federal personnel system, which uses evidentiary adjudication in its equal employment opportunity, labor relations, and merit system protection programs, is illustrative.

Federal equal employment opportunity (EEO) adjudication has been particularly problematic. Despite decades of adjudicating EEO complaints, only a few hundred (or less) of the thousands of cases filed annually result in clear findings of discrimination. About 40 percent of the federal employees who take the first step in the adjudicatory process by contacting EEO counselors never file formal complaints. Oversight is so difficult that no one knows why this is the case—the issues may be resolved, or the complainants may be dissuaded, both for good and bad reasons. According to the American Federation of Government Employees, agency EEO investigations are a sham—"almost a complete waste of time" (Shafritz et al. 2001:537–541).

Other data make it difficult to believe that potential EEO complainants and those who actually file cases are a disgruntled lot, out of touch in a personnel system that operates fairly. In 1996, only a minority of all federal employees agreed that their agencies "have no problem, or a minor one, in providing fair and equitable treatment" (U.S. Merit Systems Protection Board [MSPB] 1997:90). Only 21 percent of African Americans could say that about their agencies, as could about 30 percent of Hispanic, Asian Pacific Americans, and Native Americans. Among non-Hispanic whites, less than half—43 percent—subscribed to it (MSPB 1997:90). In 2000, 54 percent of African-American civilian federal employees thought their group was extensively or moderately subject to "flagrant or obviously discriminatory practices." Thirty-one percent of Hispanic employees, 27 percent of Native American employees, and 23 percent of Asian Pacific American employees thought the same with regard to their groups (MSPB 2002a:3).

Additional evidence that the EEO adjudicatory system fails to achieve fairness is found in data regarding sexual harassment. Surveys in the late 1980s and mid-1990s indicate that more than 40 percent of all female and about 19 percent of all male civilian employees are likely to be sexually harassed during any given two-year period. Of these, only 6 percent take formal action. Why? Many give one or more of the following reasons for not filing formal charges: The harassment was not serious enough (50 percent); it would make the work situation unpleasant (29 percent); nothing would be done about it (20 percent); confidentiality would be breached (19 percent); and it would have adverse career ramifications (17 percent). Eight percent thought the victim would be blamed (MSPB 1995: figure 1, tables 7, 10, 11).

The EEO complaint system scores low on efficiency as well. It frequently takes agencies a year or longer to close complaints. In the 1990s, it took the Equal Employment Opportunity Commission, the nation's chief EEO agency, 707 days to close complaints from its own workforce! The EEOC frequently has had a huge backlog of cases brought by federal employees throughout the government. In 1997, 58 percent of the cases in its inventory had been there for more than 200 days (Shafritz et al. 2001:537; Rivenbark 1998:3).

The handling of EEO complaints weakens the federal personnel system's adjudicatory performance on the dimensions of fairness and efficiency. The difficulty of establishing competence was best illustrated by the FLRA. Although its record has since improved, between 1979 (when it was created) and 1987 the FLRA was overruled in slightly more than half the reported cases in which the federal courts reviewed its decisions on substantive legal issues (as opposed to procedural matters). In one case, the court sent the case back to FLRA with instructions to "address and resolve the conflict [in its decisions] candidly and in a manner that persons affected by the Authority's decisions can comprehend" (*American Federation of Government Employees, Local 32 v. FLRA* 1985:506). In another, the court would not say FLRA's interpretation was wrong, only that "it was assuredly not right for the reasons stated" (*National Association of Government Employees v. FLRA* 1985:1227). FLRA's problem was not bias against unions or management but an inability to adjudicate coherently (Rosenbloom 1992).

The federal government's adverse action system exemplifies how adjudication that works well in terms of fairness, efficiency, and competence may have a substantial detrimental impact on administrative performance. The adverse action system is used to ensure that employee discipline, including dismissals, comports with merit system requirements. Agency decisions may be appealed to the MSPB, whose adjudicatory decisions form a major component of federal personnel policy. The MSPB generally receives high marks for fairness, efficiency, and competence (Vaughn 1992). In 1997, a remarkable 96 percent of the 444 MSPB decisions appealed to federal court were upheld without modification (MSPB 1998:4). However, it is generally believed that merit system adjudication dampens agency performance. In 1996, 28 percent of federal supervisors were unwilling to take adverse actions against employees, even though they considered them warranted. Among the multiple reasons cited were: the time required to go through the adverse action process (67 percent); lack of support by upper management (62 percent); impact on the work group (48 percent); prospect of facing an EEO complaint (40 percent); lack of familiarity with procedures (25 percent); and cost to the agency if the employee appealed (18 percent) (MSPB 1998:4). At the same time, a majority of supervisors (59 percent) *and* employees (51 percent) agreed that "their agencies have a major problem . . . separating employees who cannot or will not improve their performance to meet required standards" (MSPB 1997:7).

The legal and administrative problems with adjudication reviewed above are inherent and substantial. As a policymaking format in cases of first impression, adjudication has intrinsic shortcomings. The difficulties illustrated by evidentiary adjudication in the federal personnel system are also endemic. They cannot be attributed to the newness of systems, inexperience, or the federal government's inability to provide adequate human and financial resources. Where underfunding exists, it may be due to inadequate agency performance as much as to a lack of congressional support for a particular adjudicatory program. If adjudication is so problematic, then why use it?

Why Adjudicate?

Adjudication is used primarily for five overlapping reasons: (1) agency convenience; (2) incrementalism may be advantageous; (3) suitability for resolving conduct and application cases; (4) equity and compassion; and (5) to satisfy constitutional procedural due process.

Agency Convenience

Despite its costs and difficulties, adjudication has several advantages for agencies. It generally affords them considerable flexibility in enforcing policy. This is especially true when agencies have the discretion to initiate cases. They can invest their enforcement resources wherever they deem most appropriate. In *Cinderella*, the court chided chairman Dixon for "pouncing on the most convenient victim" (*Cinderella Career and Finishing Schools, Inc. v. FTC* 1970:591). Such an enforcement strategy may or may not be less efficacious than tackling a more substantial and visible firm. Picking easy cases that can be adjudicated relatively quickly may help an agency recruit high-quality, newly minted lawyers who want to gain experience and build winning records before moving to the private sector. Cases against large, prominent firms may have a great impact, but they can also consume an inordinate share of agency resources. The key point is that whatever the court thought about the efficacy of FTC's move on Cinderella, the choice of where to invest enforcement resources ordinarily lies with the agency unless its actions violate statutory or constitutional restrictions.

When agencies have broad discretion because there is no clear law to apply, they may find it easier to change policy by adjudicating than by rulemaking. Rulemaking and rule rescission are publicized through the *Federal Register*. They can prompt comments from any person, group, or entity that cares to offer them. Broad participation, coupled with requirements for cost-benefit or various impact analyses, can make establishing a satisfactory rulemaking record arduous. Adjudication generally attracts less public attention. As noted earlier, participation can be restricted, and adjudication is subject to weaker legislative and executive oversight than rulemaking. Agency adjudicators are not required to consider the impact of their decisions on sets of specific values that are extraneous to their missions, such as environmental justice, families, protecting small business, and federalism.

Adjudication also affords agencies flexibility in that it is difficult to win legal challenges against incremental—or even abrupt—policy changes introduced in individual adjudicatory decisions. An agency can usually distinguish the basis of a new adjudicatory order from an earlier precedent in terms of the specific facts; changes in public policy or economic concerns; technological developments; and other considerations that a rational decisionmaker should take into account. As Supreme Court Justice Felix Frankfurter once said, adherence to precedent "is not, to be sure, an imprisonment of reason" (*United States v. International Boxing Club of New York, Inc.* 1955:249). Moreover, the parties to whom a policy is first applied through adjudication may assume that it will bind others in the future. They may therefore decline to challenge the agency for being inconsistent or discriminatory. It may take years to see if the assumption is correct. Using adjudication, in 1969 the Federal Communications Commission required the Boston *Herald-Traveler* newspaper to divest itself of Boston TV station 5 on the grounds that "it is important in a free society to prevent a concentration of control of the sources of news and opinion" (Woll 1977:81). The reviewing court held that the decision was within the FCC's discretion. However, the FCC's decision turned out to be anomalous: "In case after case, the FCC has permitted media concentration that directly contradicts its Boston *Herald-Traveler* decision, and the Court of Appeals has upheld the Commission in every case" (Woll 1977:83). By the time it was clear that the *Herald-Traveler* had been singled out, it was too late for the newspaper to take effective legal action against the FCC.

Multiheaded boards and commissions may especially prefer adjudication to rulemaking when they have highly fragmented policy preferences or are uncertain about the direction in which an agency should move. Adjudication provides board members and commissioners with a forum to resolve their policy differences and arrive at compromises, often in an incremental fashion. Each can explain why he or she would decide the case in a certain way and what the policy and other advantages would be. A board or commission that would become deadlocked in a rulemaking might nevertheless be able to carry out its functions through case-by-case adjudication.

Incrementalism Is Advantageous

When an agency is charged with regulating and implementing law in a new or uncertain field of public policy, incrementalism may be advantageous. This is especially true when a legislative delegation is particularly vague or a technology is new and in flux. For instance, an agency might find the task of defining the "public interest" or "unfair" practices daunting, especially when it is just beginning to deal with a policy area. The meaning of such terms is not self-evident. If it were easy, the legislature probably would have defined key terms in the relevant statute. It is often precisely because terms like "public interest," "convenience," "necessity," " just cause," "reasonable," and "adequate" gain meaning only in specific contexts that the task of interpreting them is delegated to administrative agencies. Adjudication allows for incremental definition on a case-by-case basis. When the NLRB started out in 1935, how could it write a rule identifying the full range of possible unfair labor practices, or even a relatively complete set of principles distinguishing "fair" from "unfair"? In time, through sufficient adjudication, what is in the public interest, reasonable, unfair, and so forth might be comprehensively established in an agency's adjudicatory decisions. At that point, an agency could (many would say *should*) write a rule essentially codifying the principles in its adjudicatory case law.

Adjudication is also helpful in regulating new and rapidly changing technologies where there are significant hazards and unknowns. This is especially true if the number of cases is sufficient to promote substantial agency learning. Adjudication in the face of uncertainty may reduce the scope and cost of mistakes. If a new and potentially dangerous technology is not well understood, rulemaking may be more prone to error and resistant to correction than adjudication. For example, according to Kenneth Warren, the Nuclear Regulatory Commission should have regulated by order making rather than rulemaking: It "has been severely criticized for failing to prevent unnecessary and dangerous accidents in nuclear power plants because the commission irresponsibly promulgated rules not based on a thorough collection and evaluation of crucial scientific facts and questions concerning the safety of nuclear power plant operations, including the disposal of nuclear waste" (Warren 1996:305).

Conduct and Application Cases

Broadly construed, conduct and application cases encompass a very wide range of administrative decisions. They include matters such as:

sanctioning firms like Cinderella; retention of benefits; governmental licensing; and dealing with unfair or illegal labor and other personnel practices. Adjudication is desirable in conduct and application cases because they turn on specific facts or individual motives. By allowing affected parties to present their claims and challenge those raised against them, adjudication guards against arbitrary governmental action. This is true whether the matter involves an individual's retention of welfare benefits or a multimillion-dollar false advertising action. Adjudication is so preferred as a means of making such decisions that it is often required by constitutional procedural due process (as discussed below).

Unless there is no factual or legal dispute at all, adjudication is usually the safest approach in significant conduct cases. For example, the *Cinderella* court explained,

> While it may be true that some advertisements are so glaringly misleading that anyone can recognize that fact, we think it could only benefit the ultimate determination if the Commissioners had before them the testimony both of experts on youth and of teenage girls themselves, in addition to their own reading of the statements alleged to be misleading. While they might initially decide that a given statement had the capacity to mislead, perhaps testimony of experts and consumers would reveal that the group at which the statements were directed was in fact more knowledgeable and sophisticated than the Commissioners had originally anticipated. In any event, we think it can only help, and certainly it will not hurt, to have the testimony before the reviewing Commissioners. (*Cinderella Career and Finishing Schools, Inc. v. FTC* 1970:586)

In other words, things are not always as they may appear to administrators. Adjudication helps to ensure that agency decisions are based on correct factual premises. Congress fashioned the APA's adjudicatory requirements against a background in which it was widely believed that "the rights of individual citizens have been arrogantly disregarded" in administrative decisionmaking (U.S. Congress 1940:4649).

Equity and Compassion

Adjudication may be particularly favored in cases involving individuals' eligibility for welfare and other safety net–type governmental benefits because it has the capacity to promote equity and compassion. Welfare and safety-net decisions are a subset of conduct and application cases that are set apart by involving individuals only, rather than firms or other entities, and being nonadversarial. The governments administering welfare and safety-net programs and the claimants seeking benefits share a common interest. Both want the benefits to be available to those in need. These programs sometimes contain regulatory aspects, such as requiring individuals seeking unemployment compensation payments to be actively job-hunting. However, deserving claimants are not in an adversary relationship with government or in competition with one another, as the parties to licensing decisions for TV stations and other types of mutually exclusive public benefits might be.

Equity and compassion may be important factors in promoting the policy objective of helping people who need welfare and safety-net programs to deal effectively with their economic and other problems. In this context, equity is the ability to make principled exceptions to general regulations when they serve the interests of both the government and the individual. The phrase "I feel your pain" has become a cliché. But compassion may sometimes be a necessary component of successful rehabilitation or sociotherapy, as in some aspects of public health administration and social work. It may also encourage equity.

The advantages of adjudication over rulemaking in providing equity and compassion were illustrated in *Heckler v. Campbell* (1983). That case dealt with social security disability benefits. Eligibility is established in a two-stage process. First, a medical assessment is made to determine the level of work, if any, a physically or mentally impaired applicant can perform. Second, applicants who are capable of some level of work are eligible for benefits only when there are few or no jobs in the national economy that they could handle. Until 1978, ALJs from the Social Security Administration (SSA) relied on the testimony of vocational experts to gauge whether jobs might exist for individual claimants. The vocational experts' testimony was often inconsistent, perhaps being swayed by equity and compassion, but leading to contradictory outcomes. In 1978, the SSA decided to replace the vocational experts, who were personally familiar with the claimants' impairments, with rules known as *grid regulations* (grid-regs or grids).

Grid-regs are individual rules that use age, education, and work experience to specify whether jobs exist for claimants who can perform certain levels of work. Individuals can receive benefits only if they are considered disabled under the grids. The following are examples:

1. For individuals whose impairment permits them to perform light work:

Rule	Age	Education	Previous Work Experience	Decision
202.02	55 & over	Limited or less	Skilled/semi-skilled, not transferable	Disabled
202.03	55 & over	Limited or less	Skilled/semi-skilled, transferable	Not disabled

2. For individuals whose impairment permits them to perform medium work:

Rule	Age	Education	Previous Work Experience	Decision
203.10	55 & over	Limited or less	None	Disabled
203.11	55 & over	Limited or less	Unskilled	Not disabled

Overall, there were more than thirty such sequentially numbered individual rules for light and medium work (U.S. Department of Health and Human Services 1978). They acted to severely constrain the ALJs' discretion and ability to bring considerations of equity and compassion into their decisionmaking.

Carmen Campbell applied for disability benefits when a back condition and hypertension forced her to stop working as a hotel maid. She was fifty-two years old, had limited education, and was classified as unskilled. She was also from Panama, and although she could read and understand English fairly well, she had difficulty speaking and writing it. Her initial application was denied. She then requested a hearing, which was held before an ALJ who determined that she was capable of light work. Based on the grid-regs, the ALJ also found that she was not disabled (i.e., jobs that she could perform existed). After the ALJ's decision was upheld by the Social Security Appeals Council, Campbell sued the SSA.

The district court ruled against Campbell, who then pressed on to the court of appeals. That court found the grid-regs defective. It reasoned that the SSA was required to "identify specific alternative occupations available in the national economy that would be suitable for the claimant," to provide descriptions of such jobs, and to demonstrate that they do "'not require' exertion or skills not possessed by the claimant." The court reasoned that without this information "the claimant is deprived of any real chance to present evidence showing that she cannot in fact perform the types of jobs that are administratively noticed by the guidelines [i.e., the grid-regs]." In short, the determination based on the grids was defective, and therefore the ALJ's decision was not supported by substantial evidence.

The Supreme Court reversed the court of appeals. It noted that the Social Security Act "contemplates that disability hearings will be individualized determinations based on evidence adduced at a hearing." However, this did not preclude the SSA from using rules (i.e., the grid-regs) to provide ALJs and other decisionmakers with a factual determination regarding the existence of jobs in the national economy. Two justices raised a cautionary note regarding the desirability of building equity and compassion into disability determinations.

Justice William Brennan concurred with the majority but admonished that ALJs should exercise a "duty of inquiry" "in these nonadversarial proceedings to develop a full and fair record" and "scrupulously and conscientiously explore for all the relevant facts." "In a case decided under the grids," this includes inquiry "into possible nonexertional impairments and into exertional limitations that prevent a full range of work." In plain English, the ALJ ought "to inquire whether factors besides strength, age, or education combined with her other impairments, rendered [Campbell] disabled." What is her mental state, energy level, threshold for pain?

Justice Thurgood Marshall concurred and dissented in part. In his view, the hearing was defective because Campbell never had the opportunity to show that she was unable to perform light work, which under the grid-regs was the "central issue." Additionally, the ALJ was ill-prepared to exercise equity or compassion because "he conducted little inquiry into the effect of her medical problems on her capacity to perform work. Yet reasonably complete questioning concerning the claimant's ability to function in her daily activity was essential to resolving this question in a fair manner."

Although the grid-regs were valid and Campbell lost the case, the different perspectives raised by the court of appeals and Justices Brennan and Marshall illuminate some of the concerns for equity and compassion in welfare and safety-net adjudication. Campbell and other claimants would be clearly better off with more elaborate and probing hearings in which their status was determined by individualized factors, rather than boxes on the grid-regs. The Supreme Court's majority was unwilling to require a different hearing process, because compelling the SSA "to relitigate the existence of jobs in the national economy at each hearing would hinder needlessly an already overburdened agency" (*Heckler v. Campbell*, 1983:464, 467, 468, 471, 474–475). Its opinion speaks to the immediate needs of efficiency rather than the desirability of individualized and compassionate treatment in the abstract.

Procedural Due Process

The Fifth and Fourteenth Amendments prohibit the federal, state, and local governments from depriving individuals of "life, liberty, or property, without due process of law." *Procedural due process* does not have a fixed meaning. It requires fundamental fairness when a government decision dealing with one or a few individuals creates a deprivation of life, liberty, or property. It does not apply to legislation or decisionmaking that affects the population generally, such as raising taxes. Neither does it apply when the deprivation is unintentional, being caused by governmental negligence. Its overall structure and application was explained in Chapter 2. For the most part, its requirements are incorporated into the adjudicatory provisions of the APA and state administrative law statutes. When these statutes apply and are properly followed, a violation of due process is unlikely. The greater problem is determining what procedural due process requires in an adjudication that is not regulated by administrative law.

In some administrative contexts, it will be uncertain whether a property or liberty interest protected by procedural due process exists. This is because the due process clause does not create property or liberty interests; it only protects those that are established independently by other constitutional provisions, statutes, administrative rules, or governmental practices. Procedural due process is implicated in the termination and/or revocation of welfare benefits, parole, drivers and occupational licenses, and civil service and tenured public university employment, as well as in public school expulsions and suspensions, some forms of prison discipline, and deportations. But this list by no means exhausts the range of interests to which procedural due process might apply (Fox 2000:133–137; Gellhorn and Levin 1997: chapter 6). The levying of significant governmental sanctions, as in

Cinderella, also engages procedural due process, as does the termination of service by a municipal electric, gas, and water utility (*Memphis Light, Gas & Water Division v. Craft* 1978). As a general rule, the more harm the governmental deprivation of liberty or property interest causes an individual, the greater the likelihood that procedural due process will apply. If welfare, other benefits, or licenses terminate automatically or according to a legislative scheme, there is no right to procedural due process. For example, civil service employees have no due process protection when their jobs are eliminated by reductions in force. Neither will procedural due process be required when there is no factual dispute.

When procedural due process applies, what it requires is also an issue. *Goldberg v. Kelly* (1970) outlined the maximal protection for individuals being deprived of a benefit by administrative action. The case involved the termination of a means-tested welfare benefit, which Kelly presumably needed in order to survive. The Supreme Court held that he was entitled to a pretermination hearing with the following safeguards: (1) notice of the government's intent and reasons for terminating the benefit; (2) an oral hearing before an impartial decisionmaker; (3) confrontation and cross-examination; (4) representation by counsel (though not the right to have counsel provided by the government); (5) the maintenance of a record of the proceedings; (6) a decision based exclusively on the record; and (7) a statement of reasons for the decision (*Goldberg v. Kelly* 1970).

By contrast, *Goss v. Lopez* (1975) set forth the apparent minimal requirements when procedural due process applies at all. There, the Supreme Court held that procedural due process is satisfied in a one-day suspension from public school by "at least an informal give-and-take between the student and the disciplinarian, preferably prior to the suspension" (*Goss v. Lopez* 1975:584). Many cases lie in between these extremes. Sometimes notice and opportunity to respond prior to the administrative action are coupled with more elaborate due process afterward. In other cases, a posttermination or deprivation process with varying due process elements is sufficient. By following the case law, or consulting an attorney or someone else who does, one can determine what, if anything, procedural due process requires in circumstances that have been previously litigated. In other situations, precedents can serve only as an uncertain guide. For instance, whether applicants for welfare benefits are entitled to procedural due process has yet to be definitively determined (Fox 2000:137).

Caveat Estoppel

As it applies to governmental benefits, the *law of estoppel* negates the application of procedural due process when individuals receive misinformation from the government that causes them to forego something to which they are actually entitled. To "estop" means to stop, prevent, preclude, or impede. The problem of estoppel is well illustrated in *Schweiker v. Hansen* (1981). Ann Hansen met for about fifteen minutes with an SSA field representative who incorrectly told her she was ineligible for "mother's insurance benefits." The SSA rep also violated the SSA's thirteen-volume *Claims Manual* by failing to tell her to file a written application anyway. About a year later, Hansen learned she was eligible for the benefits and received them after filing a written application. Under the relevant statute, Hansen was also entitled for twelve months' retroactive benefits, which she received. However, she wanted retroactive benefits for the twelve months prior to her initial meeting with the field representative, whose mistakes cost her about a year's worth of benefits in the first place. The question for the Supreme Court was whether the SSA was estopped (i.e., prevented) from withholding those retroactive payments. Put positively, did the field representative's errors compel the SSA to give Hansen the retroactive benefits she sought? The Court's answer was that the SSA was not estopped; legally it could withhold the benefits.

The law of estoppel is far from crystal-clear. Justices Marshall and Brennan charged that it amounts to the Court saying, "We will know an estoppel when we see one." However, to win an estoppel Hansen had to satisfy two requirements. First, she had to be harmed by the agency's misinformation. Hansen was clearly harmed, though the Court questioned whether the injury was sufficient for an estoppel. Second, there must be no other way in which the individual can obtain the correct information. The two requirements are related. Because correct information was available, Hansen could have undone the harm at any time.

The general principle of the law of estoppel is that agency heads should not be bound by the mistakes of subordinate employees. Making estoppel easy in cases like Hansen's would undercut hierarchical control and could drain the agency's budget. Marshall was joined by Brennan in a dissent that emphasized the unfairness of estoppel doctrine: "It is quite clear that [Hansen] provided [the field representative] with sufficient information on which to make a correct judgment, had he been so inclined. . . . Such preliminary advice is inevitably accorded great weight by applicants who—like [Hansen]—are totally uneducated in the intricacies of the Social Security laws. . . . The fault for [Hansen's] failure to file a timely application for benefits that she was entitled to must rest squarely with the Government" (*Schweiker v. Hansen* 1981:789, 792, 794–5). The bottom line: their fault, her loss, no remedy unless the SSA would voluntarily pay the retroactive benefits.

Adjudicatory Hearings

The APA provides for elaborate adjudicatory hearings, which are triggered by separate statutes or constitutional due process. Coverage does not extend to decisions based entirely on inspections, tests, or elections, military and foreign affairs, and some additional matters (section 554[a]). When adjudication is required, "Persons entitled to notice of an agency hearing shall be timely informed of: (1) the time, place and nature of the hearing; (2) the legal authority and jurisdiction under which the hearing is to be held; and (3) the matters of fact and law asserted" (section 554[b]). Hearings are to be scheduled with regard to the "convenience and necessity of the parties or their representatives." The agency must provide the parties the opportunity for the "submission and consideration of facts, arguments, offers of settlement, or proposals of adjustment when time, the nature of the proceeding, and the public interest permit" (section 554[c]). Additional provisions include:

1. The right to be represented by retained (not agency provided) counsel;
2. the conclusion of hearings within "a reasonable time";
3. prompt notification of the outcome of the hearing, as well as a brief explanatory statement of the grounds for the denial of an application or other request;
4. a decision based on substantial evidence in the record;
5. the appointment of impartial ALJs (originally, "hearing examiners") or other employees to preside over hearings when the agency itself does not do so;
6. an opportunity for parties to present their "case or defense by oral or documentary evidence, . . . submit rebuttal evidence, and . . . conduct such cross-examination as may be required for a full and true disclosure of the facts";
7. maintenance of a complete and exclusive record, including a transcript of testimony;

8. a statement of the "findings and conclusions, and the reasons or basis therefor, on all the material issues of fact, law, or discretion presented on the record"; and
9. judicial review of final agency action (sections 555, 556, and 557; chapter 7).

The APA also contemplates the potential to appeal initial ALJ decisions within the agencies, but the opportunities and procedures available depend on agency rules. As substantial as the APA's adjudicatory requirements are, they differ in significant ways from judicial trials, primarily in the interests of more flexibility and less formality.

Presiding Officers

The federal employees who preside over adjudications have several different titles and levels of skill and independence. For the sake of convenience, they can be considered under two headings: ALJs, and all others.

Administrative Law Judges. The title "administrative law judge" replaced that of "hearing examiner" in 1972. Whatever the name, the main concerns with ALJs have always been impartiality, competence, and efficiency. Prior to enactment of the APA in 1946, hearing examiners were subject to discipline by the agencies in which they worked. They might combine investigatory, prosecutorial, and judicial functions. The APA requires a separation of functions and prohibits ALJs from hearing from one party, in the absence of the other, about matters under adjudication (that is, they cannot engage in ex parte [one-sided] contacts). Although discipline is now by the Merit Systems Protection Board, the ALJs are still employed by the individual agencies. The vast majority are in the SSA, though significant numbers also work for the Department of Labor and NLRB. The federal ALJs perform the following functions:

1. Administer oaths and affirmations
2. Issue subpoenas
3. Rule on offers of proof and receive relevant evidence
4. Handle depositions
5. Manage the hearings
6. Hold conferences, which the parties are required to attend, for consideration of the settlement or simplification of cases

7. Encourage the parties to engage in alternative means of resolving the case (discussed below)
8. Dispose of procedural requests
9. Make initial or recommended decisions
10. Take other actions consistent with APA procedures (APA section 556[c]; see Lubbers 1994:293–294).

This list makes it clear that ALJ performance is a major component of administrative adjudicatory systems.

The problem of ALJ impartiality is complicated. Despite their independence from agency hierarchies, ALJs are part of the organizations in which they work. They are likely to share many organizational goals and values. Their responses to political and media criticisms of their agencies may be identical to those of other employees. Their association with an agency, especially over a long period of time, is likely to have an impact on their worldview and judgment. Even if this were not the case, the whole arrangement of allowing an agency to employ a judge who rules on its own enforcement efforts creates an appearance of bias. The Federal Communications Commission openly recognizes this by physically separating its ALJs from other agency personnel (Fox 2000:246). Another approach to maintaining impartiality is to place ALJs in a special corps to be assigned on a rotational basis to the various agencies by a central agency, such as the Office of Personnel Management or the MSPB. Several states, including Florida and New Jersey, use such a system, with apparent success (Fox 2000:245). The idea has been discussed at the federal level for years but never adopted. The flip-side concern is that federal adjudication is too specialized and complex to make rotation practicable (Lubbers 1994).

Administrative law is tolerant of the appearance of bias in another context as well. Prehearing bias does not automatically disqualify agency adjudicators, including ALJs, from participating in adjudicatory decision-making. If the bias involves legislative facts, adjudicators are excluded only if they have an "unalterably" or "irrevocably closed" mind on the matter under consideration (*Housing Study Group v. Kemp* 1990:332; *FTC v. Cement Institute* 1948:701; Warren 1996:318–319). The rationale for this standard is that FTC, FCC, and other commissioners advocate and promote policies as part of their jobs, often indicating a preference for enforcement in one area or another. If such statements precluded them from participating in adjudication, essentially they would have to give up one function or the other. Either way, they would be less effective in implementing their agencies' missions. Moreover, in drafting the APA, Congress clearly gave broad adjudicatory authority to boards, commissions, and agency heads.

By contrast, if the prehearing bias involves adjudicative facts, it is highly likely that the adjudication will be unfair, and the ALJ or other decisionmaker should be disqualified. The *Cinderella* court emphasized that chairman Dixon's conclusive public statement of adjudicative facts was particularly offensive. Essentially he had prejudged Cinderella's fate. Any adjudication with his participation would be poisoned. Even though Dixon's vote was not necessary for a majority of the commissioners to condemn Cinderella, "Litigants are entitled to an impartial tribunal whether it consists of one man or twenty and there is no way which we know of whereby the influence of one upon the others can be quantitatively measured" (*Cinderella Career and Finishing Schools, Inc. v. FTC* 1970:592).

Personal bias, which sometimes manifests itself during hearings, can also lead to disqualification. ALJs and other adjudicators are, after all, human beings with a variety of personal preferences and prejudices. Personal bias may be displayed in open derogatory statements about a participant in the adjudication. At other times, it is derived from an adjudicator's overall record of favoring one set of interests over another (e.g., management over labor).

An exception to disqualification for any of these biases may be made under the *rule of necessity*. This occurs when enforcement would be impossible because there are no impartial adjudicators who can hear the case. The point is that from a public policy perspective biased enforcement is better than none at all, and it can be subsequently checked by judicial review.

ALJs' competence and efficiency are also of concern, though perhaps more so to the agencies than private parties. Federal ALJs are not subject to performance appraisals, but they can be disciplined or fired for *good cause*. Consequently, their performance can be evaluated. During the 1980s, the SSA embarked on controversial initiatives to encourage better and quicker ALJ decisionmaking. One effort dealt with competence by tracking the rate at which individual ALJs ruled in favor of disability claimants (so-called allowance rates). Those with the highest rates had all their decisions reviewed by the SSA Appeals Counsel, presumably on the assumption that many were incorrect. The SSA also developed, but never implemented, a plan to counsel ALJs with the highest allowance rates. The agency also set allowance-rate goals for the ALJs in an attempt to rein in the disability budget. These practices were challenged in court but changed before a definitive decision was handed down (Lubbers 1994:295–296).

In addition, the SSA created monthly production goals for the ALJs in order to increase their efficiency. The goals established the minimum number of dispositions expected. The ALJs charged that the goals infringed on their independent decisionmaking. However, the courts disagreed and found no violation of the APA (Lubbers 1994:296). Additionally, the SSA tried to fire several ALJs for low productivity. It was successful in getting the MSPB to agree that this constituted good cause, though it was unable to carry the heavy burden of persuasion required. In the MSPB's view, the productivity rate by itself was an inadequate indicator of poor performance because cases are not "fungible." Some are more difficult than others and take more time to resolve. Perhaps the SSA's greatest victory was promoting agreement that guidelines could feasibly be used to maintain or improve the quality and efficiency of ALJ decisionmaking (Lubbers 1994:296–297).

Other Presiding Officers.   Neither the APA nor procedural due process requires that ALJs preside over all types of adjudications and hearings. For instance, the adjudication of veteran benefit claims and many federal personnel matters takes place before non-ALJ presiding officers. Overall, there are more non-ALJ presiding officers than ALJs. Many of these are not insulated from the agencies' hierarchical authority. They may be hired and fired like other federal employees. Most do not work solely as adjudicators. Their performance has not been systematically tracked, and they may be considered "the real 'invisible' judiciary" (Lubbers 1994:306). On occasion, an agency commission or board may preside over the hearing stage of a case, though usually their role is to hear appeals or review recommended decisions.

Decisions and Appeals

Under the APA, ALJs and other hearing officers make initial and recommended decisions. Initial decisions are generally issued in ordinary cases and become final unless they are appealed within the agency. Recommended decisions are more likely to involve unsettled policy questions. They have no legal effect until reviewed by the agency's reviewing authority, be it the head, commission, board, or a designated unit. In licensing and formal rulemaking, the reviewing authority sometimes issues a tentative decision after receiving a record (without a decision or recommendation) from an ALJ. Tentative decisions are submitted to the parties for comment and may subsequently be revised by the reviewing authority (Gellhorn and Levin 1997:264).

Evidentiary adjudicatory decisions must be based on acceptable evidence and include findings and conclusions with regard to facts and law. Agencies are not required to use the same rules of evidence that would apply in judicial trials. The evidence should be relevant, reliable, probative (tending to prove), and substantial. However, such terms lack precision, and the extent to which presiding officers rely on evidence that would be inadmissible in court varies. It was once settled doctrine that decisions had to be supported by a "residuum" of evidence that could be used in a judicial trial. However, since the Supreme Court's decision in *Richardson v. Perales* (1971), the status of the residuum rule has been uncertain. According to one interpretation, *Perales* retained the rule but required the federal courts to apply it more flexibly. Others contend that the rule is no longer applicable. Some thirty states follow it; only a few have clearly rejected it (see Warren 1996:327–334).

The APA does not include a standard of proof for adjudicatory decisions. Its requirement that decisions be supported by "substantial evidence" is taken as referring to the *quantity* of evidence in the record. This is somewhat confusing, because when the term is used in the context of judicial review of an agency action, it essentially means "reasonable" (see Chapter 6). The Supreme Court has ruled that "preponderance of evidence" is the minimum standard for APA evidentiary adjudications (*Steadman v. Securities and Exchange Commission* 1981). This means that the evidence in the record as a whole must make the presiding officer's decision more likely correct than incorrect. In some types of cases, a higher standard, "clear and convincing evidence," is imposed by statute, court decisions, or perhaps agency policy. This requires a substantially higher level of likelihood that the decision is correct (roughly, a 75–80 percent or greater probability). These standards are, of course, significantly lower than "beyond a reasonable doubt," which applies in criminal trials (almost 100 percent probability).

Before the presiding officer issues the initial or recommended decision, the parties may submit proposed findings and conclusions, with explanations, to guide his or her judgment. Agencies use a variety of approaches for internal appellate review. In multiheaded agencies, commissioners or board members may perform this function or delegate it to subordinate boards. Single-headed agencies are likely to use review boards. However, appeals and reviews may also be decided by agency heads, who are not required to go through the entire record, but only to be briefed on it by subordinates who have. OSHA follows a "split enforcement" process in which ALJ hearings and review are within a separate body, the Occupational Safety and Health Review Commission (Funk, Shapiro, and Weaver 1997:206).

The APA specifies that when dealing with appeals the "agency has all the powers which it would have in making the initial decision." In theory, this protects hierarchical authority and allows great flexibility. However, the Supreme Court has cautioned appellate decisionmakers to give great weight to the presiding officer's decision when it is largely based on his or her assessment of the witness' credibility (*Universal Camera Corp. v. NLRB* 1951). As in *Cinderella*, the appellate decisionmakers must also take the hearing record into account (*Morgan v. United States* 1936; *Morgan v. United States* 1938). Presumably an agency will have good reasons for overturning a presiding officer's decision, as the matter may be appealed to court.

Alternative Dispute Resolution

The APA was intended to make administrative evidentiary adjudication fair, competent, efficient, and workable. It envisioned adjudicatory hearings that were far less formal than judicial trials. Over the years, the initial level of informality has given way to greater formality in response to judicial decisions, the establishment and evolution of the ALJ position, and the accretion of precedent. Hearings and appeals became less timely and more cumbersome, arduous, and expensive. In 1990, Congress enacted the Administrative Dispute Resolution Act (ADRA) to counter this trend. The act was strengthened by the 1996 Administrative Dispute Resolution Act.

The ADRA is premised on the belief that "administrative proceedings have become increasingly formal, costly and lengthy resulting in unnecessary expenditures of time and in a decreased likelihood of achieving consensual resolution of disputes" (section 2[2]). Congress also noted that alternative dispute resolution (ADR) "can lead to more creative, efficient, and sensible outcomes" (section 2[4]). The APA specifically calls on agencies to try to settle disputes without adjudicatory hearings, and ADR was used by several federal agencies prior to 1990. The main purpose of the ADRA was to provide comprehensive regulations for ADR and resolve some of the legal questions associated with it.

ADR is a mutually acceptable way of resolving a dispute by means other than a formal hearing or trial (Hawes and Rieke 1998). The most common approaches are:

1. The use of ombudsmen and ombudswomen (ombuds) in the agencies, who can be contacted by aggrieved parties or otherwise called upon to resolve administrative errors or disputes.
2. Mediation by a third party who helps the parties resolve the dispute by suggesting "win-win" or otherwise acceptable solutions. Mediators often meet independently with each of the parties in an effort to determine what would be acceptable to them.
3. Facilitation by a third party who coordinates meetings and discussions to aid the parties in finding a resolution. Facilitators are less involved than mediators in the actual effort to resolve or settle the dispute.
4. Fact-finding is used when the dispute is over some factual issue that can be resolved through empirical investigation or, possibly, expert opinion. For example, fact-finding could determine whether Cinderella's ads had a significant propensity to deceive.
5. Arbitration by a third party who offers a resolution of the dispute. Arbitration, which is frequently used in public-sector labor relations, can take several forms. First, entrance into it can be voluntary or compulsory. Voluntary arbitration allows the parties to leave a dispute unresolved; compulsory requires that an unresolved dispute be settled through arbitration. Second, arbitration can be binding or advisory. A binding arbitration award has the same effect as a final adjudicatory order. It decides the dispute, though under limited circumstances it may be challenged in court. Advisory arbitration ("nonbinding" arbitration) offers the parties a resolution and can create pressure for one or both to end the dispute. However, it has no legal force.

    Third, arbitration can be conventional, or "final-offer." In the conventional format, the arbitrator hears the dispute and questions the parties. He or she then writes up an award based on the proceedings. Final-offer (also called "last best offer") arbitration requires each party to make a final offer for settling the dispute and limits the arbitrator's decision to accepting one or the other. There are two variants: "whole package," and "issue-by-issue." In whole package, the arbitrator cannot modify the favored final offer. In issue-by-issue, he or she can choose, without modification, the final offer of one side on a particular issue and the other side on a different issue. The rationale for final-offer arbitration is that it prods the parties to make reasonable offers lest the other side's becomes the arbitrator's award. Logically, it must be binding to function as anticipated, as well as to bring finality to the dispute.

Fourth, arbitration can be combined with mediation (so-called med-arb). Here the third party first mediates the dispute to reduce the issues on which there is disagreement and then he or she arbitrates any remaining ones. The ADRA provides for voluntary arbitration only; the parties cannot be compelled to submit to it. (However, federal agencies and unions do negotiate labor grievance resolution procedures that rely on compulsory binding arbitration.) Agency decisions to use arbitration are not subject to judicial review, except when an arbitral award adversely affects a third party. The 1996 ADRA requires the agencies to specify the maximum amount of money that can be included in an arbitral award in each case.

6. Minitrials are structured to enable the parties to present the core of their cases to one another before personnel from each side who are authorized to reach a settlement. A neutral third party may be present to orchestrate the proceeding and/or to offer an advisory resolution.

7. Mock trials with advisory resolution by mock juries may also be used to avoid formal hearings and trials (Funk, Lubbers, and Pou 2000:299–300).

The 1990 ADRA instructs agencies to consider ADR in a very wide range of activities, including anything for which adjudication might be used. However, it also cautions them to consider avoiding ADR when (1) it would be better to resolve the matter in a fashion that establishes an authoritative precedent; (2) policy issues are involved; (3) consistency is important; (4) outside parties would be significantly affected; (5) a comprehensive record of the proceedings is important; or (6) "the agency must maintain continuing jurisdiction over the matter with authority to alter the disposition . . . in light of changed circumstances" (section 572[b]). The act also instructs each agency to designate a high level dispute resolution specialist. The 1996 act protects the confidentiality of ADR proceedings.

Satisfaction with ADR is bound to vary among agencies, programs, and parties. It should always be measured against the alternative, which is adjudication. The MSPB listed ADR's major virtues as improving timeliness, reducing costs, fashioning win-win outcomes, giving the parties "ownership for the solution," revealing the underlying causes of conflicts, and increasing managers' willingness to take necessary disciplinary action (MSPB 2002b:3). A comprehensive study of ADR in the Environmental Protection Agency also found highly favorable views in general but pointed to the need for better education of managers about ADR; higher-quality mediators; continuing evaluation by the agency; and greater integration of ADR into the dominant administrative culture. It also called for independent evaluation of ADR by the EPA's ALJs (O'Leary and Raines 2001).

Enforcement

Agencies can impose a wide variety of civil sanctions on individuals, firms, and other entities that violate laws or administrative rules. Ordinarily, sanctions are levied after notice and the opportunity to adjudicate the matter. Exceptions may occur in emergency situations, that is, where there is an imminent specific danger to the public's health or welfare. Civil sanctions include cease-and-desist orders; financial penalties; forfeitures; product seizures and recalls; and the revocation and/or suspension of licenses. At the federal level, the authority to take such actions must be delegated to an agency by Congress. Frequently, these penalties are negotiated rather than imposed in a strict sense. Without admitting guilt, violators agree to stop or remedy a practice and perhaps pay a financial penalty. In return, the agency takes no further action. Agencies do not have the power to impose criminal penalties, though the Immigration and Naturalization Service can physically confine individuals. Criminal wrongdoing may be brought to the attention of the Department of Justice for prosecution. In some cases, financial penalties require civil lawsuits. Although not technically a sanction, adverse publicity can have a harsh impact on a violator, and the threat of it may be enough to change behavior.

Agencies use several common means to detect violators and pursue sanctions:

First, there are *informational requirements*. As the discussion of paperwork reduction in Chapter 3 suggests, agencies require regulated entities to provide them with a great deal of information. They also impose record-keeping requirements on the regulated, including taxpayers. Additionally, many agencies have the power to subpoena individuals and records. The APA regulates, but does not convey, the subpoena power, which must be "authorized by law" (section 555[c]). Aside from the possibility that an agency will be acting ultra vires (outside the scope of its authority), limits on the subpoena power require that the information sought be relevant and specific, not unduly burdensome, and not subject to attorney-client or other privilege. The Fifth Amendment's protection against self-incrimination can sometimes be invoked to defeat the subpoena's utility. However, the amendment does not apply to civil matters and is available only to individuals, not firms and other entities. Even in criminal matters, individuals can be compelled to testify under a grant of immunity from prosecution (Gellhorn and Levin 1997:127–138).

Second, there are *inspections*. Physical inspections of businesses and other entities are a staple of regulatory enforcement. Inspectors play a variety of roles. They deter violations, help educate the regulated about what compliance requires, and try to persuade them that cooperation with the agency is the best approach for the long term (Scholz 1994:425–426). Insofar as agencies have statutory authority to undertake inspections, legal issues are likely to arise only with respect to the Fourth Amendment.

The Fourth Amendment applies directly to the federal government and to the states through incorporation into the Fourteenth Amendment. It affords individuals, other entities, and some physical facilities protection against unreasonable governmental searches and seizures. It applies to administrative as well as criminal searches. Inspectors sometimes need to obtain warrants in order to do their jobs. These are generally easier to obtain in the administrative context than in criminal investigations. They are likely to be issued by judges or other judicial officers when the inspection is part of a reasonable, systematic administrative enforcement strategy or is based on specific information regarding violations. In several circumstances, warrants are not required at all.

As noted in Chapter 2, the Fourth Amendment applies only when one has a reasonable expectation of privacy. If someone voluntarily consents to a search, then that person no longer has such an expectation. Similarly, there is no reasonable expectation of privacy when something is in plain view. An open field or smokestack that can be seen from the air is fair game for an airborne EPA or other inspector. If a facility is open to the public, an inspector can enter it and look for violations. Searches in emergency situations, such as fire fighting or dealing with hazardous materials, are likely to be considered reasonable (*Michigan v. Tyler* 1978). Customs agents have broad authority to search individuals, containers, and vehicles at ports of entry. Under relatively narrow circumstances, the homes of welfare recipients may be subject to inspections by social workers (*Wyman v. James* 1971; Fox 2000:106–108).

Pervasively or closely regulated entities may also be subject to an administrative search without a warrant. They are considered to have reduced expectations of privacy. But what constitutes such an entity? The leading Supreme Court decision, *New York v. Burger* (1987), involved a junkyard believed to be engaged in "chop shop" automobile theft. The Court identified three factors that permit warrantless searches: (1) There was a substantial governmental interest in the regulatory scheme; (2) the warrantless inspections were necessary under that scheme; and (3) the certainty and regularity of the inspections "provides a constitutionally adequate substitute for a warrant" by (a) notifying the business that inspections will occur, and (b) placing "appropriate restraints upon the inspecting officers' discretion" (*New York v. Burger* 1987:691–692; Schwartz 1994:209).

Third, there are *tests*. Agencies rely on tests to ensure that products meet regulatory standards. Testing may take place before a product can be marketed or afterward. Premarket testing is common for drugs, food additives, and other substances for human consumption. The Food and Drug Administration relies heavily on testing but primarily by evaluating the tests done by the drug companies and others. New drug applications have contained as many as 200 volumes of information (Quirk 1980:207). Postmarket tests may be initiated in response to consumer complaints, accidents, illnesses, and other indicators that a product or service is not performing properly. Safety testing is common, but tests can also be used to ensure that products live up to required performance standards and/or satisfy advertising and labeling claims. The Fourth Amendment is relevant when tests occur within the producer's facility and when product seizures are required. The APA specifically provides that hearings are unnecessary in "proceedings in which decisions rest solely on inspections, tests, or elections" (section 554[a][3]).

Contemporary administrative thinking favors alternatives to traditional "ruthless and efficient investigation and enforcement capability" as a means of deterring violations (Sparrow 1994:ix). In a movement that parallels substituting ADR for formal adjudication, regulators may now seek cooperation and partnership as alternatives to the standard enforcement tools of the past. Although agencies retain the capacity to deal forcefully with the worst offenders, they also try to conserve resources and reduce hassles by treating regulatees as customers and by focusing on genuine problems and serious violations rather than on writing up countless minor infractions (Sparrow 1994:ix, xxiii–xxiv). Today, a great deal of administrative enforcement is consensual, albeit with legal sanctions available as a backup. If the partnership approach proves successful, it will reduce agency adjudication, both internally and in court.

Conclusion: Should Adjudication Be Reformed?

Improving federal agencies' evidentiary adjudication was one of the APA's core objectives. Prior to 1946, adjudicatory processes varied among the agencies, and many practices were viewed by Congress and others as patently unfair. If 1946 is used as a baseline, there is no doubt that federal evidentiary adjudication has advanced vastly in terms of fairness. Presumably, it is more competent today as well. In addition to the APA's specific provisions, the establishment and professionalization of the ALJ position have been major contributors to improvement. However, the ALJs have also promoted greater formality and the growth of courtlike procedure in hearings. Some ALJs wear judicial robes. The ALJs have their own professional advocacy associations, which weigh in on proposed reforms and agency practices affecting adjudication. The SSA's ALJ Association took the SSA to court to prevent the imposition of allowance-rate goals (Lubbers 1994:296). In several agencies, there are now chief ALJs who have administrative and managerial responsibilities for the operation of adjudicatory systems.

The increasing formalization of administrative evidentiary adjudication is often referred to as "judicialization." It promotes fairness and competence but, as enactment of the ADRA indicates, also inefficiency and adverse effects on organizational performance. The act's section on congressional findings concludes that "the availability of a wide range of dispute resolution procedures, and an increased understanding of the most effective use of such procedures, will enhance the operation of the Government and better serve the public" (section 2[8]). Congress's expectation was that in time ADR would supplant adjudication as a means of resolving many disputes.

But some adjudication will always remain. What can be done to improve it further? Administrative law scholar Jeffrey Lubbers offers an important reform agenda for consideration. The following are among his key proposals:

1. Develop guidelines "on when to choose to require administrative law judges or non-ALJ hearing officers, formal adjudication or informal adjudication, split-enforcement adjudication, or traditional single-agency adjudication."
2. Reduce delay by improving statistics on case processing and identifying and removing bottlenecks. "Time limits and case tracking should be institutionalized at agencies."
3. "Model or uniform rules of practice and procedure (including rules of evidence) should be explored." Presumably, standard rules and practices would reduce procedural errors and disputes about the quality of evidence used in decisionmaking.
4. Improve ALJ performance by giving ALJs more authority to control hearings, using productivity guidelines, developing better recruiting, training, and continuing legal education, and by finding better ways of handling complaints of ALJ bias or abuse.
5. "Agency heads should delegate more final decisional authority to ALJs."
6. Customer service initiatives to make it easier for outside parties to participate without lawyers and by telephone and video hearings (Lubbers 1994:307–308).

Many would agree that such incremental reforms would be of considerable value. Yet none has been systematically adopted governmentwide. On the macro level, Lubbers offers a truly daunting challenge: "The current landscape needs to be remapped and reordered" (Lubbers 1994:307). Not everyone would agree. However, just thinking about how politically and conceptually difficult the prospect would be reminds us that the APA, with all its limitations and problems, has been remarkably durable and effective.

5

Transparency

Introduction: The Central Intelligence Agency's Budget? What Budget?

The U.S. Constitution seemingly requires that "a regular Statement and Account of the Receipts and Expenditures of *all* public Money shall be published from time to time" (Article I, section 9, clause 7; emphasis added). Now suppose you want to know how much the Central Intelligence Agency (CIA) spends and on what. Suppose further that you suspect the CIA is spending your hard-earned tax dollars wastefully or on illegal domestic surveillance. A logical first step would be to take a look at the CIA's budget—the account of receipts and expenditures mentioned in the Constitution. However, one would look in vain. The CIA's budget is secret, and under the Central Intelligence Act of 1949 it accounts to the Treasury for its expenditures by a nonpublic "certificate."

William Richardson, a member of the electorate, loyal citizen, and taxpayer sued to have the CIA Act declared unconstitutional. A lawyer with a background in military intelligence, he was apparently incensed by the CIA's secretive domestic spending (Wharton 1995). He had a dual constitutional complaint. On the one hand, he could not obtain the CIA's budget; on the other, without the CIA's budget numbers, the Treasury's published "Combined Statements of Receipts, Expenditures, and Balances of the United States" was "a fraudulent document" (*United States v. Richardson* 1974:169). How could Richardson be an informed citizen and voter if the government was withholding some budget information from him and putting out disinformation in its constitutionally mandated account of receipts and expenditures?

Richardson never received an answer. When the case reached the Supreme Court, a slim majority of five justices decided not to give him one. Instead they found that he lacked standing to bring the suit in the first place. He had no concrete personal injury, only a generalized grievance, perhaps shared with millions of others (see Chapter 6 on standing). The four dissenting justices would have granted standing for a variety of reasons. One justice, William O. Douglas, had a good deal of sympathy for Richardson's cause:

> The sovereign of this Nation is the people, not the bureaucracy. The statement of accounts of public expenditures goes to the heart of the problem of sovereignty. If taxpayers may not ask that rudimentary question, their sovereignty becomes an empty symbol and a secret bureaucracy is allowed to run our affairs. . . .
>
> The public cannot intelligently know how to exercise the franchise unless it has a basic knowledge concerning at least the generality of the accounts under every head of government. No greater crisis in confidence can be generated than today's decision. Its consequences are grave because it relegates to secrecy vast operations of government and keeps the public from knowing what secret plans concerning this Nation or other nations are afoot. (*United States v. Richardson* 1974:201–202)

Douglas was in the minority, but his views succinctly capture the chief concerns that frame administrative law's requirements for open government.

The Administrative Law
Framework for Transparent Government

As Douglas argues, open government is a prerequisite for government by the people. The Constitution's Framers were acutely aware that the system they designed, without a good measure of transparency, would fail. James Madison, author of the Bill of Rights and chief architect of the separation of powers, ranked openness alongside other fundamental constitutional values: "A popular Government, without popular information, or the means of acquiring it, is but a Prologue to a Farce or a Tragedy; or, perhaps both. Knowledge will forever govern ignorance: And a people who mean to be their own Governors, must arm themselves with the power which knowledge gives" (Madison 1999:790; see also U.S. House 2001:1; U.S. Senate 1974:37–38). In addition to the Receipts and Expenditure Clause, the Constitution requires that "Each

House [of Congress] shall keep a Journal of its Proceedings, and from time to time publish the same" (Article I, section 5, clause 3). It also requires a record of presidential vetoes and publication of the names of those members of Congress voting to override or sustain them (Article I, section 7, clause 2).

Nevertheless, the Framers recognized that some matters would have to be secret. Constitutionally, whatever material Congress wants to keep secret may be omitted from its journal (Article I, section 5, clause 3). The Constitution itself was framed under a veil of strict secrecy.

American constitutional democracy relies heavily on administrative law to determine what should be open, what should be secret, and how decisions regarding governmental transparency should be made, challenged, and reviewed. Since adoption of the Administrative Procedure Act of 1946, five main approaches to regulating openness have become widely used: public reporting, freedom of information, protection against invasions of privacy, open meetings, and whistle-blowing.

Public Reporting

As amended, section 552 of the Administrative Procedure Act of 1946 requires all covered agencies to publish the following in the *Federal Register*: (1) descriptions of their organization and location along with whom to contact for information, making submittals or requests, or obtaining decisions; (2) explanations of their operations and procedural requirements; (3) procedural rules, descriptions of forms and where to obtain them, and information regarding the content of papers, reports, and examinations; (4) substantive and interpretive rules and policy statements; and (5) amendments, revisions, and repeals of any of the above. A public protection clause provides that no person may be held responsible for noncompliance with an agency requirement in any of these categories that was not properly published.

The agencies are also required to make some documents available for public inspection and copying, unless they are published. These include the final adjudicatory opinions, concurrences, and dissents; adopted policies and interpretations that are not available in the *Federal Register*; and staff manuals and instructions that affect the public. These materials must be indexed for public inspection or sale. Anything in one of the documents that creates a "clearly unwarranted invasion of personal privacy" should be deleted.

These requirements are important. They go a very long way toward overcoming what Congress perceived as excessive administrative secrecy in the 1930s and 1940s. However, they are really just the tip of the iceberg. Agencies face myriad reporting requirements. Along with special reports mandated by Congress, they routinely publish annual reports on their performance and finances. The General Accounting Office publishes reports on virtually every significant aspect of administration, including personnel practices, organizational design, budgets and financial management, performance, and the implementation of specific statutes. In total, these reports would probably overwhelm any citizen diligently trying to assess federal administration.

Agencies also issue news releases and public relations material. As electronic government continues to catch on in the digital age, more and more agencies at all levels are maintaining websites. The federal government maintains a portal (FirstGov) to a massive amount of online information, so much, in fact, that after the terrorist attacks on September 11, 2001, many agencies removed information about water resources, chemicals, nuclear energy, and other potentially dangerous topics (Ombwatch 2001).

Government reports are sometimes criticized for blurring the distinction between factual reporting and spinning information for favorable public relations. Reading *The United States Government Manual*, one would assume that the federal government houses the most benevolent, caring, rights-protecting, and efficient agencies imaginable. Never mind that they are routinely denounced by politicians and the media, largely distrusted by the public, and routinely sued. Two particularly sweet mission statements belong to the Department of Health and Human Services and the Botanic Garden. The former is "the Cabinet-level department of the Federal executive branch most involved in the Nation's human concerns. In one way or another, it touches the lives of more Americans than any other Federal agency. It is literally a department of people serving people, from newborn infants to persons requiring health services to our most elderly citizens." The Botanic Garden "informs visitors about the aesthetic, cultural, economic, therapeutic, and ecological importance of plants to the well-being of humankind." Not to be outdone, the Department of Justice, a usually no-nonsense law enforcement agency that includes the Federal Bureau of Investigation and Bureau of Prisons, presents itself as "the largest law firm in the Nation [serving] as counsel for its citizens" (Office of the Federal Register 1999: 271, 45, 323).

Freedom of Information

Freedom of information is aptly defined as regulations and laws "that provide members of the community with a legally enforceable right of access to information in the possession of government" (Zifcak 1998:941–942). The first freedom of information law was apparently introduced in Sweden in 1766, but contemporary U.S. federal freedom of information did not begin to develop until enactment of the APA in 1946. The APA's provisions were rudimentary, perhaps naive, and they largely failed. The act provided: "Save as otherwise required by statute, matters of official record shall in accordance with published rule be made available to persons properly and directly concerned except information held confidential for good cause found" (section 3[c]). Between a citizen's need to show that he or she was "properly and directly concerned" and an agency's ability to withhold information for undefined "good cause," the APA became "a basis for withholding information" despite "the clear intent of the Congress to promote disclosure" (U.S. Senate 1974:6–7). The Freedom of Information Act of 1966 (FOIA) amended the APA in an effort to fix these problems. The Presidential Records Act of 1978 later applied the basic principle of open government to presidential materials.

The Freedom of Information Act

After its initial enactment in 1966, FOIA was significantly amended in 1974, 1986, and 1996. From its inception, the act sought to balance four concerns: open access, privacy, necessary secrecy, and the government's ability to obtain information. FOIA promotes access by giving *all* individuals a right to information. There is no requirement that they be properly and directly concerned with the information sought. Anyone can ask for anything, though the fees an agency charges may vary with the purpose for which the information will be used. By itself, FOIA is a disclosure statute. It does not prohibit the release of any information. Rather, it permits agencies to withhold substantial categories of information at their discretion. These categories are called "exemptions," of which there are nine. They guard individuals' right to privacy and protect governmental secrecy in the interests of national security, effective decisionmaking, and administrative efficiency. Personal privacy is also protected by the Privacy Act of 1974, which is discussed further on in the chapter. The ability to collect information is crucial to contemporary governmental policymaking and regulatory enforcement. FOIA works in conjunction with the APA and other statutes, such as the Federal Trade Secrets Act (1948), to protect some types of commercial information, whether submitted voluntarily or under compulsion.

Basically, FOIA operates as follows. Activity is triggered by the submission of a FOIA request to an agency. Requests may be submitted by corporations and associations as well as by individuals. Foreigners may request information. Federal agencies cannot make FOIA requests of one another. There is no standard form, though the U.S. Department of Justice publishes the *FOIA Reference Guide*, which provides advice on how to request information (U.S. Department of Justice 2000). The requester is obligated to "reasonably describe" the agency records he/she is seeking, which is defined as being specific enough to enable a professional employee, familiar with the material, to locate it without undue effort. Only information in the form of records is covered. One could ask an agency for a record on John Lennon but should not request all the information it might have on him scattered throughout its documents or organized as records on other subjects (Weinberg 2000). If the information is electronic, the agency may create the requested record, depending on the circumstances. Requesters should indicate whether they want a record in electronic form. Agencies are responsible only for records under their control, generated within the agency or placed in its files, and used by the agency for some work purpose (*Bureau of National Affairs, Inc. v. U.S. Department of Justice* 1984). The agency bears the burden of persuasion in demonstrating that the requested information is not an agency record. Requests should be in accordance with the agency's published rules regarding time, place, fees, and procedures.

FOIA's coverage is very broad, applying to the CIA, Federal Bureau of Investigation, military, executive departments and agencies, independent regulatory commissions, and government corporations. FOIA also covers those units in the Executive Office of the President that have statutory responsibilities, such as the Office of Management and Budget, but not those that are purely advisory (e.g., the Council of Economic Advisers) (Funk, Shapiro, and Weaver 1997:595). It does not apply to Congress, the judiciary, or the president.

Timeliness has been a longstanding FOIA problem. There has been far more FOIA activity than Congress foresaw in 1966, and amendments have been adopted to prod the agencies to process requests more promptly. Today, agencies have twenty days (up from the original ten) to tell a requester whether the information sought will be released. If the agency's response is positive, it still may take years to supply the information itself to the requester. Agencies are required to explain their denials of requests. These may be appealed within the agency, in which case the agency has another twenty days to decide whether to release the information. An additional ten days may be tacked on to these time limits under unusual circumstances, such as a particularly voluminous request or an agency's difficulty in obtaining the records from field offices or other facilities.

The agencies are often overwhelmed by requests and unable to meet these deadlines. The courts have largely let them off the hook when they are diligently processing requests as best they can. Prior to amendments taking effect in 1997, diligence generally meant that the agencies were responding on a first-come, first-served basis. Since 1997, they are authorized to guard against building large backlogs by answering easy requests first, rather than queuing them up indefinitely behind the more difficult ones. When asked, agencies may expedite the release of information of imminent importance to the life or physical safety of an individual or of "urgency to inform the public concerning actual or alleged Federal Government Activity" (section 552[a][6][E]).

Fees have also been an issue. When FOIA went into effect, some agencies levied exorbitant charges for reviewing, searching, and copying. Amendments adopted in 1974 limited these but had the effect of subsidizing searches initiated for commercial gain, as when a business seeks information on its competitors. Additional amendments in 1986 regulate fees according to how the information will be used. These are highly detailed, but their gist is that requests for information of value to scholarship, research, news reporting, and the public's understanding of government are billed for less than those seeking information for commercial purposes.

Although FOIA applies broadly across the federal executive branch, the nine exemptions exclude a considerable amount of information from mandatory release. These are:

1. National defense or foreign policy information that is properly classified for secrecy.
2. Information "related solely to the internal personnel rules and practices of an agency."
3. Information that is specifically prohibited from disclosure or regulated by another statute.
4. "Trade secrets and commercial or financial information obtained from a person and privileged or confidential."

5. Interagency or intra-agency memos or letters that would not be available by law to a party in litigation with the agency.
6. "Personnel and medical files and similar files the disclosure of which would constitute a clearly unwarranted invasion of personal privacy."
7. Law enforcement records, to the extent that release could reasonably be expected to constitute an unwarranted invasion of personal privacy or would interfere with enforcement proceedings, fair trials and hearings, confidential sources, investigations and prosecutions, or an individual's physical safety.
8. Information pertaining to the regulation of financial institutions.
9. "Geological and geophysical information and data, including maps, concerning wells." (section 552[b][1–9])

Two points about the exemptions should be borne in mind. First, information in these categories may be released at an agency's discretion unless it would violate some other law. In other words, the fact that requested information falls into one of the exemptions does not necessarily determine whether it will be released. Over the years, federal attorneys general have provided different guidance. Some, such as Janet Reno (1993–2001), promoted disclosure; others, including John Ashcroft (2001–), have sought to dampen it. Reno authorized the Department of Justice to defend the agencies in FOIA suits only when release of the information sought would create "foreseeable harm." Under Ashcroft, the department will defend agencies whenever they have a "sound legal basis" for withholding information (U.S. Department of Justice 2001).

Second, FOIA specifically provides that "any reasonably segregable portion of a record shall be provided to any person requesting such record after deletion of the portions which are exempt" from release (section 552[b]). To the extent technically feasible, the agencies should identify the places where deletions were made.

FOIA has engendered far more litigation than can be reviewed here. A great deal of it is incredibly detailed and fact-specific. This seems particularly true in suits over what constitutes a record. One example should be of particular interest to public managers. In *Bureau of National Affairs, Inc. v. U.S. Department of Justice* (1984), a U.S. court of appeals had to decide whether government officials' telephone message slips, daily agendas, and appointment calendars were agency records. It reached the following conclusions:

1. The telephone message slips "are not 'agency records' within the meaning of FOIA. No substantive information is contained in them. No one but the official for whom the messages were taken used the telephone slips in any way. And, in many cases, there might be no way for the official to segregate personal from business calls."

2. "The daily agendas are 'agency records' within the meaning of FOIA. They were created for the express purpose of facilitating the daily activities of the Antitrust Division. Even though the agendas reflected personal appointments, they were circulated to the staff for a business purpose." They were created "for the convenience of [the] staff in their conduct of official business."

3. "The appointment calendars are the most difficult to categorize. . . . We conclude, however, that *these particular* appointment calendars are not 'agency records.' They are distinguishable from the daily agendas in two important respects. First, they were not distributed to other employees, but were retained solely for the convenience of the individual officials. Second, . . . the appointment calendars were created for the personal convenience of individual officials so that they could organize both their personal and business appointments." (*Bureau of National Affairs, Inc. v. U.S. Department of Justice* 1984:1495–1496, emphasis added).

Public managers sometimes assume that *anything* work-related may be obtained under FOIA for all the world to see. *Bureau of National Affairs* suggests FOIA's operation is more complex and less governed by categorical rules. This also tends to be the case with regard to the specific exemptions. Although it is not possible to treat these in detail here, the following general points are important.

- Exemption 1, for national security, does not affect the government's ability to classify documents. Where an agency's very admission that it has or does not have a record could compromise national security or foreign policy, it may respond that it can neither confirm nor deny the existence of the record. For historical reasons, this is called a "Glomar denial" (Funk, Shapiro, and Weaver 1997:607).

- Exemption 2, for personnel rules and practices, covers less than its language suggests. The Supreme Court interpreted it to exempt only internal information that would be of no interest to the public. For example, records pertaining to the Air Force Academy's internal disciplinary system are not exempt (*Department of the Air Force v. Rose* 1976).

- Exemption 3: On occasion an issue of statutory interpretation may arise, but the principle is clear enough—agencies may withhold information when disclosure is prohibited or regulated by other statutes. As explained immediately below, releasing such information may violate the APA.
- Exemption 4, for confidential commercial information and trade secrets, has had a difficult history. In addition to definitional problems, FOIA by itself would allow the release of such information. To defend against this possibility, firms developed "reverse FOIA" suits. A business can file suit in a district court to block an agency from disclosing information requested on it. The firm's challenge takes the form of contending that release would be arbitrary, capricious, an abuse of discretion, or otherwise not in accordance with law as defined by section 706 of the APA (see Chapter 6). For example, all things being equal, releasing information protected by an act protecting trade secrets would violate section 706. Under a 1987 executive order, agencies are required to inform businesses that their commercial information is being sought.
- Exemption 5, dealing with inter- and intra-agency memos, is interpreted to privilege (i.e., shield them from disclosure) two types of information. One is information generated by an attorney-client relationship that would not be available in litigation. The other is information covered by executive privilege. This is a somewhat more amorphous concept derived from judicial interpretation of the separation of powers (*Nixon v. Administrator of General Services* 1977; *United States v. Nixon* 1974). The general principle is that predecisional information is privileged to protect the free flow of ideas within and among agencies. In other words, before a decision is made, participants should be able to engage in uninhibited brainstorming and feel free to bounce half-baked ideas off one another. Who would start a thought with, "This may sound crazy, but . . ." if the rest might be on the front page of a newspaper someday? The predecisional exemption applies to private parties who participate in a decision as well as to agency

employees. Predecisional material is not privileged if it becomes specifically incorporated into the final decision.

- Exemption 6 protects only against "unwarranted" invasions of personal privacy. It should be considered in conjunction with the Privacy Act, which is discussed below. It applies only to human beings, not to corporations or associations. Under some circumstances, its coverage is broad enough to allow withholding information to protect the privacy of the relatives of an individual on whom information is being sought.

- Exemptions 7, 8, and 9, dealing with law enforcement, financial institutions, and oil wells, are of less importance to public managers generally. Nine was included to assuage oil industry concerns that information about potential oil and natural gas fields, developed at great expense through exploration, would be released to competitors or speculators.

Enforcement of FOIA depends heavily on the federal district courts. The act places the burden of persuasion on the agency to show that nondisclosure was legal. The district court makes its determination de novo (afresh) rather than being bound by the agency record. It may review the records at issue in camera (i.e., privately in chambers). When requesters substantially prevail, agencies may have to pay their attorneys' fees and related costs. Theoretically, a court's finding that an agency acted arbitrarily and capriciously can result in a Merit Systems Protection Board disciplinary action against an official, though apparently there was by 1997 only one such finding and no actual discipline (Funk, Shapiro, and Weaver 1997:593). When a suit involves discovering what information actually exists, the agency is required to provide an index of its relevant records to both the court and the requester (known as a "Vaughn index"; see Funk, Shapiro, and Weaver 1997:607).

Evaluations of freedom of information radically differ. In principle, it is broadly accepted as necessary for representative government. Voters, like Richardson, need information to fulfill their roles as citizens. Access to public information, as Madison maintained, is a key to governmental accountability. Every U.S. state has a statutory-based freedom of information policy, as do most, if not all, democracies abroad. As early as 1946, the United Nations General Assembly resolved that "freedom of information is a fundamental human right and is the touchstone for all the freedoms to which the United Nations is consecrated" (Zifcak 1998:942).

Nevertheless, there may still be some holdouts. In 1982, when he was still merely a law professor, Supreme Court Justice Antonin Scalia denounced the premise "that the first line of defense against an arbitrary executive is do-it-yourself oversight by the public and its surrogate, the press" (quoted in Strauss et al. 1995:909).

There is broad agreement that implementation of FOIA is costly, litigious, and time-consuming. Explanations vary with respect to why the act has not worked better. Clearly, the volume and expense were unanticipated. In fiscal year 2000, the Department of Justice alone received more than 235,000 requests and 4,500 appeals. It spent more than $69 million on FOIA activities (Piotrowski and Rosenbloom 2002). No doubt many requests are frivolous, and most may be for commercial information that has no immediate value to the public. However, requesters' ardor for information is not the sole problem. The federal government's administrative culture has been slow to change from valuing secrecy to embracing openness (Warren 1996:187). The vast majority of agencies pay no attention to FOIA activities in their annual performance plans (Piotrowski and Rosenbloom 2002). Professor Robert Vaughn, for whom the Vaughn index is named, maintains that "the Founding Fathers would be proud of the act—unless they could see how the people['s] government often frustrates its purpose" (Mashaw, Merrill, and Shane 1992:697). Federal Judge Patricia Wald's summary may be best: "Something like [FOIA] had to be invented to prevent a 'curtain of fog and iron' from falling between the American public and its government" but "FOIA, like all basic freedoms, sometimes hurts the worthy and sometimes helps the unworthy" (Strauss et al. 1995:909).

The Presidential Records Act

The Presidential Records Act was adopted to resolve an issue simmering in the demise of Richard M. Nixon's presidency. Who has control over the release of presidential papers, tapes, and related materials? A former president, claiming executive privilege, or the federal government? The act placed presidential materials in the custody of the Archivist of the United States, with the "affirmative duty" to make them public "as rapidly and completely as possible" (section 2203[f][1]). It allows former presidents to prevent access to some records for twelve years after leaving office. Most of the FOIA exemptions apply to disclosure by the archivist. However, papers and so forth should not be withheld simply because they reveal internal White House deliberations or staff advice. The act allows a former president to sue the archivist to prevent access to specific documents. The act is considered of great value to historians, public interest groups, the media, and, ultimately, the American people.

Its first (and so far only) application has been to President Ronald Reagan, whose papers became eligible in 2001. But implementation was frustrated by President George W. Bush, whose father, President George H.W. Bush, was Reagan's vice president and might figure prominently in the released documents. Bush II issued Executive Order 13,233 (2001), which blocks the archivist from permitting access to any papers that either a former or *incumbent* president wants withheld. In some cases the order would allow the family members of incapacitated or deceased former presidents to prevent access. It also increased the control of vice presidents over their papers. Bush's order is broadly based on claims of constitutional executive privilege. It flips the legal process regarding access. Under its terms, the burden is on those seeking access, not former presidents seeking to prevent it. Individuals and associations suing for access to blocked material would have to demonstrate a specific need for the records involved (U.S. House of Representatives 2001; Allen and Lardner Jr. 2001).

Bush's order provoked criticism in Congress and at least one lawsuit, brought by the American Historical Association, the Reporters Committee for Freedom of the Press, Public Citizen, and independent historians (Miller 2001; Lardner Jr. 2001). Eventually, the conflict between Bush's order and the provisions of the act or any successor statute may be resolved by the Supreme Court in a decision that clarifies the scope of executive privilege at constitutional law.

Privacy

The federal Privacy Act of 1974 reflects the APA's broad interest in protecting individual rights against administrative encroachment. Its coverage within the executive branch is similar to FOIA, though somewhat broader because it extends to advisory units in the Executive Office of the President. The act was a congressional response to a variety of issues that crystallized in the Watergate years (1972–1974), especially concern about the abuse of agency information on private individuals. There was also a sense that the federal government was collecting too much personal information and that it was poorly safeguarded. For example, during the 1960s some federal agencies used personality tests and privacy-invading questionnaires that contained items such as the following true-false questions:

"My sex life is satisfactory" and "There is little love and companionship in my family as compared to other homes" (Westin 1967:256–268). A congressional investigation concluded that there was a high potential for misuse of such information because "confidentiality of government files is a myth. Such files float from agency to agency. Federal investigators in some instances are given access to information far removed from the subject of their inquiry" (U.S. Congress 1966:398). At one point, some nondefense agencies were routinely requiring their employees to fill out a questionnaire that was originally designed for use by patients in government hospitals. The form asked numerous detailed questions about physical and mental health symptoms, including bed-wetting and nightmares (see Rosenbloom 1971:213.)

The Privacy Act is primarily concerned with regulating the collection, management, and release of information regarding individual citizens and permanent residents. It does not apply to corporations, associations, and other organizations. The following are its main features:

1. Access to records: Individuals have a right to review agency records on them. If they find errors, they may request that the records be amended. If the agency refuses, the individual involved may file a statement of disagreement, which essentially becomes part of the record. A person may also request information about the purpose, nature, and date of agencies' disclosure of records on him/her. A general exemption prevents individual access to CIA and law enforcement agency records.

2. Management of records: Agencies are required to publish notices in the *Federal Register* explaining the nature of their record systems and policies regarding access, disposal, storage, and related matters. They must also develop safeguards against inaccuracies and misuse of information, including through computer matching. The information contained in an agency's records should be relevant to its mission.

3. Restrictions on disclosure: In principle, the act prohibits the disclosure of any record on an individual without his/her prior consent. However, there are twelve specific exceptions. The most important among these are that records may be disclosed to Congress, to law enforcement agencies at all levels of government, in response to a FOIA request, and in "compelling circumstances" regarding an individual's health or safety. Records may

also be released for "routine use," which is rather circularly defined as use "for a purpose which is compatible with the purpose for which it was collected." (section 552a[b][1–12]; [a][7])

In a case with odd protagonists, *U.S. Department of Defense v. Federal Labor Relations Authority* (1994), the Supreme Court noted that the relationship between FOIA and the Privacy Act is "convoluted." Information
protected by the Privacy Act may be disclosed under FOIA's sixth exemption unless it would "constitute a clearly unwarranted invasion of
personal privacy." How does one determine what is "unwarranted"?

In *Department of Defense*, two local unions were seeking the names and
home addresses of the employees in the bargaining units they represented, some of whom were not union members. The Department of Defense (DoD) supplied the employees' names and work stations, but, cit-
ing the Privacy Act, not their home addresses. The unions filed unfair
labor practice charges with the Federal Labor Relations Authority, which
ultimately ordered the DoD to supply the home addresses. The DoD refused, and the conflict went to court.

The Supreme Court applied the following framework for analyzing the
relationship between the Privacy Act and FOIA. First, "in evaluating
whether a request for information lies within the scope of an exemption
that bars disclosure when it would amount to an unwarranted invasion
of privacy, a court must balance the public interest in the disclosure
against the interest Congress intended the exemption to protect." Second,
and the key point, "the only relevant public interest to be weighed in this
balance is the extent to which disclosure would serve FOIA's core purpose of contributing significantly to public understanding of the Government's operations or activities." Third, "whether an invasion of privacy
is warranted cannot turn on the purposes for which the information request is made."

In applying this three-step analysis to the facts, the Court had no trouble finding that the home addresses were protected by the Privacy Act.
The *public interest* in disclosure was "negligible, at best"—"virtually
nonexistent." This interest must be defined in terms of what the public
might learn from disclosure, not whether releasing the home addresses
would improve collective bargaining in the federal government. Consequently, "a very slight privacy interest would suffice to outweigh the relevant public interest." The Court reasoned that even though home addresses are often available through phonebooks and other published

sources, "the employees' interest in nondisclosure is not insubstantial" because "many people simply do not want to be disturbed at home by work-related matters." It also noted that if the unions could obtain the addresses, they would likewise be available to commercial advertisers and solicitors (*U.S. Department of Defense v. Federal Labor Relations Authority* 1994:487–489, 497–501).

The Privacy Act is enforced through civil lawsuits and criminal prosecutions, though the latter is very rare (Funk, Lubbers, and Pou 2000:819). In recent years, there have been a few highly publicized allegations of violations of the act. During the 1992 election campaign, one Elizabeth Tamposi allegedly went rummaging through the State Department's passport files on candidate Bill Clinton and his mother, Virginia Dell. Toward the end of Clinton's presidency, agency information on Linda Tripp, a key figure in the Monica Lewinsky scandal, was improperly released. However, enforcement for anything other than an agency's failure to provide access or correct its records is difficult. Suits for money damages require a showing of actual damages and that the violation at issue was intentional.

The Privacy Act has not produced a great deal of litigation, perhaps because its exceptions are broad and winning damages is so difficult (Bonfield and Asimow 1989:560). Every state has a counterpart of the federal act.

Open Meetings

The federal government and all fifty states promote transparency through open meetings laws. Their purpose is to place agencies' oral policymaking in full public view in order to obtain better decisions, promote greater understanding of government, and generate more trust and confidence in it. Open meetings laws complement freedom of information by creating public access to verbal decisionmaking, where there may be a relatively thin paper trail for subsequent retrieval. Such laws are based on two major premises. First, when agencies exercise delegated legislative authority orally in formulating and adopting binding public policy decisions, they ought to emulate legislatures by doing so in the open rather than behind closed doors. Second, openness combats political favoritism, corruption, and opportunities for special interests to wield undue influence.

Open meetings laws are often called "sunshine laws," presumably in the spirit of Supreme Court Justice Louis Brandeis's well-known statement that "sunlight is said to be the best of disinfectants; electric light the most efficient policeman" (quoted in *Buckley v. American Constitutional Law Foundation* 1999:223). However, despite their popularity, these laws are often criticized for being cumbersome, having a chilling effect on informal collegial discussions, and driving agency decisionmaking backstage, which leads to "scripted," "perfunctory" open meetings (May 1997:421; Coyle 1995:A12). At the federal level, the major open meetings laws are the Government in the Sunshine Act of 1976 and the Federal Advisory Committee Act of 1972.

The Sunshine Act applies to multiheaded federal boards and commissions to which a majority of the members are appointed by the president with the advice and consent of the Senate. There are about fifty such units, including the Security and Exchange Commission, the Federal Trade Commission, the Federal Communications Commission, and the Consumer Product Safety Commission. Covered agencies are required to give at least one week's advance notice of their meetings. In principle, all meetings of a quorum of the agency members necessary for official business should be open to the public. By majority vote, meetings or portions of them may be closed in the public interest for reasons that parallel the FOIA exemptions. However, a major difference is that a meeting cannot be closed simply to protect predecisional discussions from public scrutiny. The act's purpose is to force as much of the decisionmaking process into the open as possible. Meetings may also be closed when public decisionmaking would frustrate implementation of the proposed policy. A vote to close meetings must be made public. Depending on the reason for closure, the agency must keep either a transcript, recording, or set of minutes of the meeting. This record is available to the public, except for discussion that may be withheld under an exemption. The act contains a number of reporting requirements to Congress.

Enforcement is by civil lawsuit, though the Sunshine Act has not produced much significant litigation. The remedy for improper closure of a meeting is likely to be access to the agency's transcript. Under the federal act an agency action cannot be invalidated on the basis that a meeting should have been open. Some state laws do provide such a remedy (Bonfield and Asimow 1989:554). Litigation by Common Cause and Public Citizen established that meetings cannot be closed to shield budget decisions or simply to promote more candid discussions (Funk, Lubbers, and Pou 2000:542).

Several features of the Federal Advisory Committee Act were discussed in Chapter 3 on rulemaking. The whole thrust of the act was to bring the advisory committee system above-board. It seeks to make openness in advisory committee meetings the general rule (section 10). Notices of meetings must be published in the *Federal Register*, and "interested persons shall be permitted to attend, appear before, or file statements with any advisory committee" (section 10[a][3]). FACA requires that detailed minutes of meetings be kept and provides public access to these as well as to written materials supplied to advisory committees, including reports, working papers, and studies. These documents may be withheld under a FOIA exemption. Open meetings are the norm; exceptions may be made based on the same criteria as apply to agencies under the Sunshine Act. FACA does not apply to committees composed solely of federal employees, the CIA, the Federal Reserve System, and local civic groups.

FACA has produced considerable litigation, mostly over what constitutes an "advisory committee." Remedies for improper secrecy may include a court injunction against the use of an advisory committee report, but in some cases there may be no remedy even for clear violations—except to prevent their repetition (Strauss et al. 1995:957). Enforcement against presidential advisory committees raises constitutional questions involving the separation of powers and executive privilege. Perhaps the most publicized case to date is *Association of American Physicians and Surgeons, Inc. v. Hillary Rodham Clinton* (1993). The First Lady—is she or isn't she a federal employee for FACA purposes? If not, then the President's Task Force on National Health Care Reform was an advisory committee and its closed meetings violated FACA. Applying dexterous statutory interpretation "to the point of disingenuous evasion," as one judge put it, the court concluded that First Lady Clinton was a federal employee, at least in the FACA context. The court articulated some general principles that provide useful guidance:

1. A "group is a FACA advisory committee when it is asked to render advice or recommendations as a group, and not as a collection of individuals."
2. "In order to implicate FACA, the President, or his subordinates, must create an advisory group that has, in large measure, an organized structure, a fixed membership, and a specific purpose."
3. "When an advisory committee of wholly government officials brings in a 'consultant' for a one-time meeting, FACA is not triggered because the consultant is not really a member of the advisory committee."

4. "When we examine a particular group or committee to determine whether FACA applies, we must bear in mind that a range of variations exist in terms of the purpose, structure, and personnel of the group." Formal groups of private citizens "brought together to give publicized advice as a group" are clearly covered; "an unstructured arrangement in which the government seeks advice from what is only a collection of individuals who do not significantly interact with each other" is not regulated by the act. (*Association of American Physicians and Surgeons, Inc. v. Hillary Rodham Clinton* 1993:913–915)

FACA was back in the news in 2001–2002 in conjunction with Vice President Richard Cheney's refusal to release the records of the National Energy Policy Development Group, which he chaired. The George W. Bush administration claimed that the task force was not a government unit subject to FOIA. But it may have been an advisory group subject to FACA. The Natural Resources Defense Council sued for records on its membership and meetings, and in an unprecedented step the U.S. General Accounting Office took similar legal action (Nakashima 2001b; Milbank 2002).

It is difficult to predict the future of FACA. On the one hand, the law has significant implications for reinvented government, in which public-private partnerships are common. Some public-private partnership meetings may fall under the act. Hillary Clinton's case also drew attention to the potential for using the act to delay, if not upend, federal policymaking. On the other hand, remedies for violations have been tepid thus far.

Whistle-Blower Protection

Providing legal protection to whistle-blowers is another way to promote transparency. Public-sector whistle-blower protection regulations are intended to prevent reprisals against public employees, contractors, and others who expose wrongdoing observed in their relationships with government agencies. Exposure of maladministration can be internal to an inspector general or other agency official. It may also be external to some outside agency, a legislature, the media, or some other party. More broadly, whistle-blower protections seek to transform organizational cultures to view whistle-blowing as a civic obligation and public virtue rather than as insubordination, snitching, or tattling. The premise is that insiders are in an excellent position to reveal maladministration and protect the public from it. At the federal level, whistle-blowing is defined as disclosing violations of laws, rules, or regulations, mismanagement, "gross waste of funds," abuses of authority, or substantial and specific dangers to public safety or health (Civil Service Reform Act 1978, section 1206[b]). This covers a very broad array of activity encompassing everything from illegal handling of radioactive materials to run-of-the-mill violations of federal personnel law.

As noted in Chapter 2, all civilian public employees in the United States enjoy a measure of constitutionally protected free speech on matters of public concern, which includes whistle-blowing. However, such speech may legitimately provide a cause for discipline when it significantly harms a public employer's interests in confidentiality, performing ongoing operations, and similar concerns. Although whistle-blowing is a form of protecting the public interests, it can also create unnecessary public anxiety, disdain for government, or the inability of administrative agencies to implement their missions effectively. The free speech rights of government contractors parallel those of public employees, as may those of individuals who are engaged in preexisting commercial relationships with public agencies (*Board of County Commissioners, Wabaunsee County v. Umbehr* 1996; *O'Hare Truck Service, Inc. v. City of Northlake* 1996).

A problem for whistle-blowers is that vindicating these rights may involve a tortuous path of litigation. The public employee, contractor, or supplier of goods or services to a government has the initial burden of persuasion in showing that his/her protected speech triggered a reprisal. The burden then shifts to the agency involved to show that its action served a substantial governmental purpose *or* that it would have taken the action based on other factors even if the speech had not occurred. An agency may also prevail if it can show that the action is justified based on information it gained *after* disciplining an employee or terminating an economic relationship with a contractor or other party. Statutory whistle-blower protection regulations are intended to afford an easier—though sometimes still difficult—route for combating reprisals.

The 1978 federal Civil Service Reform Act prohibited taking any personnel action as a reprisal against a federal employee's whistle-blowing. The Merit Systems Protection Board and the Office of the Special Counsel were charged with enforcement. These provisions were strengthened by the Whistleblower Protection Act of 1989, which (1) extends protection to threats of retaliation; (2) provides protection if an employee can show that retaliation was a factor, rather than the dominant factor, in an adverse action; (3) raises the government's burden of persuasion in showing that the action was taken for reasons other than retaliation; and (4) permits employees to initiate action for redress before the Merit Systems Protection Board when the Special Counsel does not act on the matter (Warren 1996:401). Under current interpretation by the Court of Appeals for the Federal Circuit, which some consider misguided, federal employees are not protected if they initially report their concerns to coworkers or supervisors. They must also offer very strong proof that their allegations are credible (Miller 2002b).

At least thirty-five states offer legal protection to some category of whistle-blowers (Dworkin 1992:260–273; Taylor 1993:37). Every statute covers public employees; some provide protection to government contractors; eleven apply to private employees as well (Taylor 1993:37). Substantive protection varies widely. As of 1992, California, Delaware, Hawaii, Kansas, Michigan, Minnesota, New Hampshire, New Jersey, Rhode Island, and Texas protected public employees' whistle-blowing only when it reported violations of law. Louisiana limited protection to disclosures of violations of federal, state, and local environmental laws or regulations. By contrast, Colorado's law extended to activities that were not in the public interest. Pennsylvania appears to be the only state that specifically protects whistle-blowers who reveal breaches of ethical codes (Dworkin 1992:260–273; Goldman and Rosenbloom 1998:2399).

A whistle-blower's charges will not be protected if he/she knows they are false or, depending on the specifics of the law, makes them with disregard of their truth or falsity. Claims that turn out to be false may be protected if they were made in good faith, that is, the whistle-blower reasonably believed them to be true. Under some laws, individuals seeking personal gain by whistle-blowing may be afforded less protection.

Whistle-blower protection statutes vary in their procedural requirements. Some require that the first effort to expose wrongdoing be made internally within the organization in which it is occurring. Others allow disclosure directly to an external state agency, such as the federal Special Counsel, a personnel board, an auditor's office, or a law enforcement authority.

Remedies for retaliation against protected whistle-blowing also vary. Public employees are generally made whole through reinstatement and back pay, benefits, and seniority. They may also recoup attorneys fees. Punitive damages may be awarded in California, Alaska, and Texas (Taylor 1993:37). Treble damages are available in North Carolina (Taylor 1993:37). In South Carolina, whistle-blowers can keep 25 percent of the savings gained through their disclosures, up to a limit of $2,000 in any given year. Penalties for public employees who violate whistle-blowers' rights range from one year imprisonment and five-year debarment from public service (in Oregon) to negligible (in other jurisdictions; Dworkin 1992:271; Goldman and Rosenbloom 1998:2399).

Laws may offer financial gain as an inducement for private individuals to expose fraud and cheating against the government. The federal False Claims Act of 1863, revised in 1986, authorizes *qui tam* actions against federal contractors. *Qui tam* means "who as well." The legal action is brought by the private individual on behalf of the government as well as him/herself. He/she can collect up to 30 percent of the judgment, if the Department of Justice does not join the suit, and a maximum of 25 percent if it does. By some estimates, in the aggregate, *qui tam* actions can recover billions of dollars (Dworkin 1992:247).

The overall effectiveness of whistle-blower protection statutes is difficult to gauge. Certainly, whistleblowers have more protection with them than under the Constitution alone. Equally certain, perhaps, the whistle-blower's lot is still generally an unhappy one. Laws can reduce and punish overt retaliation but not ostracism and subtle measures that result in dead-ended careers (Soeken 2002). Whistle-blower protection appears to be an area in which American culture has yet to catch up with the law.

Conclusion: An Opaque Fishbowl?

Here is a snippet from a brief conversation between a *USA Today* reporter and the author sometime in the mid-1990s:

> Reporter: "Can government operate like a business?"
> Author: "Which one? Tobacco? Silicone implants?"
> Reporter: "What?"
> Author: "Did you ever try to 'foia' Phillip Morris or Dow-Corning?"
> Reporter: Laughter.

Of course, the reporter might have had the same response if asked whether she ever tried to foia the CIA for its budget numbers. Many contend that public administrators operate in a fishbowl; many others say government has a strong penchant for secrecy. For some, the water in the fishbowl is too clear; for others it is too murky. And many feel quite passionate about how open government should be. But as one of the twentieth century's leading public administrative thinkers, Dwight Waldo, was fond of asking, "Compared to what?"

If the comparison is to the private sector, many executives with experience in both government and business would undoubtedly agree that "governmental management tends to be exposed to public scrutiny and to be more open, while private business management is more private and its processes more internal and less exposed to public review" (Allison 1979:136).

If the comparison is to public administration before and after the development of regulations for transparency, there would be broad agreement that freedom of information, sunshine, and whistle-blower protection have advanced, though not fully achieved, their purposes.

It is worth keeping Waldo's question in mind when assessing transparency policy. If criticism alone could make for perfection, freedom of information in particular might be among the most perfect of all public policies. The job of improving transparency policy is more difficult than diagnosing what is wrong; it requires prescribing what will be better. Open government necessarily involves trade-offs and balances among competing concerns of fundamental importance to U.S. democratic constitutionalism. The exemptions in FOIA and open meetings laws, exceptions in the Privacy Act, crafting of whistle-blower protection, and the judicial decisions dealing with transparency inescapably provide an ever-evolving, applied political theory of openness in contemporary U.S. government. The tensions among openness, security, administrative effectiveness and efficiency, access, privacy, and confidentiality may be irresolvable yet manageable through continual adjustments to transparency policy. And clearly, the long-term trend has been toward better implementation of FOIA and other transparency provisions.

Additional Reading

Foerstel, Herbert N. *Freedom of Information and the Right to Know.* Westport, CT: Greenwood Press, 1999.

6

Judicial and Legislative
Review of Administrative Action

Introduction: The Drug Companies'
Acetaminophen, Salicylic Acid, and Caffeine Headache

In 1962, Congress amended the Food, Drug, and Cosmetic Act of 1938 to require pharmaceutical companies to print a drug's generic name "prominently and in type at least half as large" when using the drug's trade name on labels and advertising. The point was to familiarize doctors and the public with the availability of identical generic versions of many proprietary drugs. Identical, that is, in everything but price.

The FDA commissioner undertook notice and comment rulemaking to develop rules for efficient enforcement of the amendment. The final regulations mandated that the labels and advertisements for prescription drugs include the generic name *every time* the trade name appeared. Thirty-seven individual drug companies and the Pharmaceutical Manufacturers Association found the commissioner's action hard to swallow. To them, the rules were a prescription for lower profits. They brought suit to block enforcement on the grounds that the 1962 amendment did not authorize the every-time requirement.

When *Abbott Laboratories v. Gardner* (1967) reached the Supreme Court, the issue was whether the drug companies were entitled to *preenforcement* review of the legality of the FDA commissioner's final rules. The Court split 5-3 in favor of such review (one justice did not participate). The majority reasoned that precedent and the Administrative Procedure Act of 1946 created a strong presumption in favor of judicial review for anyone legally wronged, adversely affected, or aggrieved by agency action. In their view, the regulations clearly put the drug companies in an aggravating bind:

> If [they] wish to comply they must change all their labels, advertisements, and promotional materials; they must destroy stocks of printed matter, and they must invest heavily in new printing type and new supplies. The alternative to compliance—continued use of the material which they believe in good faith meets the statutory requirements, but which clearly does not meet the regulation of the Commissioner—may be even more costly. That course would risk serious criminal and civil penalties for the unlawful distribution of "misbranded" drugs.

Moreover, enforcement could harm the companies' public image even if it ultimately turned out the commissioner, not they, had acted illegally. So, better for the courts to review the regulations before the commissioner enforced them.

Sensible? Not according to the three dissenters. They argued that "established principles of jurisprudence, solidly rooted in the constitutional structure of our Government, require that the courts should not intervene in the administrative process at this stage, under these facts and in this gross, shotgun fashion." In litigious America, a precedent favoring preenforcement review would insidiously "threaten programs of vast importance to the public welfare" in order to assuage "the cries of anguish and distress" raised by regulated industries. A potential flood of litigation would forestall the implementation of untold congressional mandates. The dissenters adamantly warned against accepting "the invitation to abandon the traditional insistence of the courts upon specific, concrete facts, and instead entertain this massive onslaught in which it will be utterly impossible to make the kind of discrete judgments which are within judicial competence." Preenforcement judicial review would "permit the administration of a law of the Congress to be disrupted by [a] nonadjudicable mass assault" (*Abbott Laboratories v. Gardner* 1967:152–153, 175–176, 200–201).

Sensible as well. These opinions speak to the large questions of judicial review of administrative action. Under what conditions should the courts rule on the legality or constitutionality of administrative action? What are the consequences of taking a case too soon or too late? Should the courts entertain cases only after a concrete factual record is developed through an agency's enforcement of a regulation? Should the courts decide matters, as in *Abbott Labs*, when there are genuine legal issues and either preenforcement compliance or noncompliance would be expensive? What are the effects of such choices on the relationships between courts and agencies? How might they affect the role of the courts in an institutional sense? The doctrines and case law regarding judicial review address these and related questions. They focus on determining what is judicially reviewable as well as the timing and scope of review.

Legislative review of agency action raises a companion set of issues. Who is in a better position than Congress to determine whether the commissioner's every-time regulation was in keeping with legislative intent? Justice Tom Clark joined the dissenters in *Abbott Labs* but also added a few choice words of his own. He hoped "that the Congress will not delay in amending the Act to close this judicial exition [*sic*] that the Court has unwisely opened up for the pharmaceutical companies." Why? Well, in nonjudicious language, the companies "have deceitfully and exorbitantly extorted high prices . . . from the sick and the infirm. Indeed, I was so gouged myself just recently when I purchased some ordinary eyewash drops and later learned that I paid 10 times the price the drops should have cost." "Rather than crying over the plight that the laboratories have brought on themselves, the Court should think more of the poor ailing folks who suffer" because the drug companies "mislead the public by passing off ordinary medicines as fancy cures." According to Clark, because the Court's majority got it wrong, Congress should step in and make it right (*Abbott Laboratories v. Gardner* 1967:201).

Sensible? Of course, but thousands of federal rules are promulgated annually. How can Congress deal with them all? What if the sentiment of a legislature changes faster than an agency can write a rule? What form should congressional action take, if and when it occurs? More generally, how can a legislature ensure that administrators' exercise of delegated legislative authority is in keeping with its intent?

Judicial Review of Administrative Action

The courts are generally viewed as essential to subordinating administrative action to the rule of law. They provide a check against abuse of administrative discretion and unconstitutional, illegal, irrational, or procedurally irregular decisionmaking and enforcement. They are a full-fledged part of public administration and often considered partners or, more likely, senior partners with administrators (Bazelon 1976).

However, the precise shape that the partnership should take is inherently debatable. As suggested by the colliding opinions in *Abbott Labs*, the key questions are what should be reviewable, when, and how deeply. Over the years, the courts have developed complex—some might say convoluted—legal doctrines in an effort to supply answers. Judicial review of administrative action is an area of the law in which there are exceptions to everything—including, no doubt, this statement. One can even write law-review articles on "Judicial Review of Non-reviewable Administrative Action" (Morris 1977). This chapter provides an overview of the main principles and considerations that define contemporary judicial review of public administration. It then focuses on the tools for legislative review of agency activity.

The Court System

Judicial review takes place within federal and state court systems. These generally have a well-defined division of labor among trial courts, appellate courts, and specialized courts. The federal court system is illustrative.

The district courts are the workhorses of the federal judiciary. There are eighty-nine district courts in the states (one to four per state, depending on size), plus one each in the District of Columbia and Commonwealth of Puerto Rico. They are trial courts and hear criminal as well as civil cases. Litigation at this stage of the process is aimed at establishing the relevant facts, applying the law to them, and resolving disputed legal issues. The judge determines matters of law; the jury, if one is sitting, determines the facts. In bench trials, there is no jury; the judge decides whether the plaintiff's or the defendant's version of facts is more credible, as well as the legal outcome. When there is no factual dispute, the case may be decided efficiently by summary judgment, in which the judge rules on the legal questions presented. A single judge presides over most district court cases, though sometimes a three-judge panel is used. The district courts are usually the first judicial level to deal with administrative law cases, as in *Abbott Labs* and *Nova Scotia* (see Chapter 3).

The district courts can resolve administrative law cases in several ways. They can rule that an administrative action is legal (e.g., that the FDA commissioner had legal authority to write the every-time rule and that it was properly promulgated). Alternatively, they can find that the administrative action was illegal or unconstitutional. When ruling against the government, the district courts can block further enforcement of an administrative rule or order. They can also remand cases (send them back) to the agency for further rulemaking, clarification, or adjudication. Short of resolution, the courts can also issue temporary restraining orders to prohibit the continuation of a challenged activity while a trial is held or a final decision reached.

Judges explain the legal and logical basis for their decisions in written opinions. Though these are not necessarily published or widely circulated, written opinions are central to judicial accountability and the evolution of U.S. legal doctrines. Future cases are decided by weighing the applicability, reasoning, and conclusions of past decisions—that is, precedents—to them. Precedents can be modified or even discarded, but they are rarely disregarded altogether. Most federal cases, including administrative law cases, begin and end in the district courts (Warren 1996:42).

Appeals from district court decisions usually go to a court of appeals, though decisions in a three-judge case may be appealed directly to the Supreme Court. The courts of appeals are organized by circuits. There are eleven numbered territorial circuits, such as the Second Circuit (Vermont, Connecticut, New York) and the Seventh Circuit (Indiana, Illinois, Wisconsin), as well as a District of Columbia Circuit. There is also a Court of Appeals for the Federal Circuit, which has nationwide geographic jurisdiction but specialized legal jurisdiction involving patents, federal contracts, trade, veterans' claims, and some administrative actions by the Merit Systems Protection Board, the Department of Veterans Affairs, and other agencies. Appeals court cases are usually heard by three judges. Sometimes all the judges in a circuit will sit as a full panel, which is called a hearing *en banc*.

Appeals courts serve as a check on the district courts. Even though only a limited proportion of cases are appealed, the possibility of review probably enhances the quality of district court decisions. Appeals overwhelmingly deal with matters of law. The appellate courts ordinarily accept the factual record as it comes from the district court. In nonjury cases, the lower court's factual findings may be rejected if they are clearly erroneous. In jury cases a more difficult standard is applied: Essentially the evidence or the inferences drawn from it must be so faulty that the jury's verdict is completely implausible (Strauss et al. 1995:522–523).

As with the district courts, appeals court decisions are written in the form of opinions. They can create a number of outcomes. The district court's decision may be affirmed or reversed or, occasionally, affirmed in part and reversed in part (in other words, an appellate ruling may agree/disagree with separate parts of the lower court's opinion). The appeals court may remand the case to the district court for further proceedings. A district court's decision may also be vacated—that is, entirely voided—which may mean a new trial will be held if the dispute is not settled in some other way. In addition, sometimes a specific legal question is sent by a district court to an appeals court for certification, that is, to be answered one way or another so that the lower court can proceed. Appeals court decisions apply directly only within their particular circuits. Consequently, an agency that loses a case in one territorial circuit is not required to change its practices in the others. When two or more circuits are at odds with one another, agency operations must comport with the law governing the geographic area where they take place. As a result, the administration of a single federal program may vary significantly from circuit to circuit unless or until the Supreme Court definitively resolves the issues involved.

Judge Patricia Wald of the Court of Appeals for the District of Columbia Circuit described what may be a fairly typical array of appeals court outcomes in cases involving administrative rules:

> Between July 1, 1992 and July 1, 1993, panels of our circuit sat on thirty-five cases involving . . . rules (plus one en banc proceeding).
>
> . . .
>
> Out of the thirty-six cases, the agency's judgment was upheld in its entirety nineteen times or more than fifty percent. In the remaining seventeen cases, a portion of the rule or rules was remanded; although in most of those cases the key portions of the rule survived. In four of these cases parts of the rule went back for failure to provide the required APA notice and comment, the agency having unsuccessfully argued in court that they were only "clarifications" not "amendments" of existing rules, or that there was "good cause" for waiving notice and comment. The court sent the rule or parts thereof back for failure of the agency adequately to explain its rationale in six cases; in seven cases, it thought the agency had interpreted the statute in a way that contradicted the clear intent of Congress; in a few cases it was a combination of these two reasons that doomed the rules. It must also be noted that in many of these cases the rule was left in place [rather than nullified] while on remand. (Wald 1994:632, 636–638; quoted in Strauss et al. 1995:650–651)

The Supreme Court sits at the top of the federal court system. Its most important jurisdiction is appellate—that is, it hears cases brought from the lower federal courts, primarily the appeals courts, and from the state supreme courts or their equivalents. It possesses *original jurisdiction* to act as a trial court only in a limited range of cases, such as controversies between two or more states (e.g., over disputed boundaries). The Court has very broad discretion to pick and choose among the roughly 6,000 petitions for review it receives annually. Nowadays, it will end up writing full decisions in perhaps eighty to 120 cases each year. Most cases come to the Supreme Court via writ of certiorari (i.e., review); cases are accepted when four or more justices favor granting review. Administrative law cases are not typically a large part of the Court's docket. The justices are likely to take them in order to resolve significant differences among the circuits or because they raise issues of national importance. Cases involving some federally protected civil rights and voting rights, antitrust, and a few other matters may be brought on appeal, rather than via certiorari, which increases the likelihood that the Court will give them full attention.

Original jurisdiction aside, the outcomes of Supreme Court cases parallel those of the appeals courts. The Court can affirm or reverse the lower court; dismiss cases, vacate judgments, remand for further action, and certify legal questions. Its decisions are by majority vote of the justices who hear a case, which is usually the full body of nine. When a majority of those voting subscribe to a single written opinion, it becomes the opinion of the Court. If a majority of the justices agree on the specific holding (e.g., to affirm) but not the reasons for doing so, there is a judgment—but no opinion—of the Court. In such instances, the written opinion supported by the largest number of justices favoring the judgment is called a plurality opinion. When the chief justice is in the majority, then he assigns the task of writing the Court's opinion to himself or another justice in the majority. When the chief justice is in the minority, the most senior justice in the majority determines who will write majority opinion. Any justice is free to write a separate concurring or dissenting opinion. In future decisions, concurrences and dissents are given whatever weight their reasoning commands. Only opinions of the Court are true precedents, which generally serve as significant—though not necessarily binding—guides to resolving subsequent cases.

The federal court system also includes a number of specialized courts and functionaries that do not fit neatly into the three tiers described above. These include the Court of Federal Claims (hearing money claims against the United States), the Court of Appeals for the Armed Forces, the Tax Court, the Court of Appeals for Veterans Claims, courts with local jurisdiction in the District of Columbia, territorial courts (Guam, Virgin Islands), and the Court of International Trade (dealing with import transactions). There are also special courts and judges for bankruptcy cases, as well as federal magistrates, who are supervised by district courts and preside over some civil and misdemeanor trials.

Supreme Court justices as well as district and appeals court judges are appointed by the president with the advice and consent of the Senate. They hold office during good behavior and are removable only through impeachment and conviction. These are called Article III judges because their authority and appointments are governed directly by the Constitution's third article, dealing with the federal judiciary. This is true even though the district and appeals courts are established by legislation rather than the Constitution itself. By contrast, Article I courts (e.g., the Claims Court and Tax Court), which are also established by law, have limited subject-matter jurisdiction and authority rather than Article III's full judicial power. The terms of Article I judges are fixed by law. As noted earlier, state court systems more or less parallel the federal model, though many state judges are elected.

The federal courts are a powerful component of government and a major institutional force in administrative law. Chapter 2 explained how federal court decisions have brought the Constitution to bear directly on administrators' relationships with clients, customers, fellow government workers, contractors, and individuals involved in street-level regulatory encounters, as well as on the management of prisoners and individuals confined to public mental health facilities. Agency rulemaking, adjudication, and transparency have also been substantially affected by court decisions. Yet like all U.S. political institutions, the judiciary operates within a system of checks and balances.

One obvious limitation on judicial power is that court decisions are not necessarily self-enforcing. Many a judge has become frustrated at the slow pace of court-ordered public school desegregation, prison reform, and other changes in government operations. There are writs and powers, such as holding individuals in contempt of court, that judges can use in an effort to compel compliance. In the end, though, as Alexander Hamilton pointed out more than two centuries ago, the judiciary "may truly be said to have neither FORCE nor WILL but merely judgment; and must ultimately depend upon the aid of the executive arm even for the efficacy of its judgments" (Hamilton 1788:465).

Another institutional limitation is the judiciary's inability to reach out to initiate cases. Courts can decide only matters that are brought to them in appropriate form. Under Article III, the federal judiciary's power is limited to deciding *cases and controversies* arising under the Constitution and federal laws or involving diplomats, admiralty, the United States, and, in some situations, one or more of the states as a party. Not every dispute, even when framed in legal terms, qualifies as a case or controversy within the Constitution's meaning. This is the matter of reviewability.

Reviewability

Judicial review in the United States has at least two meanings. One is the power to declare governmental actions unconstitutional (and therefore null and void). For instance, a federal court can declare the whole or part of an act of Congress, treaty, presidential executive order, lower court action, or agency rule, practice, or decision, and their equivalents at the state or local levels, unconstitutional. State courts exercise similar powers within their jurisdictions. Judicial review in this sense is not found in the text of the U.S. Constitution. It was established for the federal courts by the Supreme Court's decision in *Marbury v. Madison* (1803), and it is well accepted as necessary if the Constitution is to remain the supreme law of the land.

Another meaning of judicial review concerns what it is that the courts will review, when, and how. Article III courts cannot give advisory opinions because, constitutionally, their power is confined to resolving legal cases and controversies. These are genuine only when the parties have an adversarial relationship with some substantial concrete interest at stake, such as liberty or property. The adversary legal system works best when there are true adversaries working hard to adduce evidence and legal argument that may convince a court of the correctness of their own claims and the weaknesses of their opponent's. In part, the dissenters in *Abbott Labs* did not want to grant preenforcement review because the full parameters of the adversarial relationship between the FDA commissioner and the pharmaceutical interests had yet to be established.

Over the years, the courts have developed several tests to determine whether a dispute is judicially reviewable, that is, whether it is a case or controversy suitable for judicial resolution. Reviewability in this context is known as *justiciability*. It is broadly rooted in the limits Article III places on judicial authority and the constitutional separation of legislative and judicial powers. Its main components follow.

Standing to Sue. *Standing to sue* means that one has a sufficient stake to bring a case against another party to court. Perhaps Supreme Court Justice Antonin Scalia explained standing most succinctly:

> Over the years, our cases have established that the irreducible constitutional
> minimum of standing contains three elements. First, the plaintiff must have
> suffered an "injury in fact"—an invasion of a legally protected interest
> which is (a) concrete and particularized, . . . and (b) "actual or imminent, not
> 'conjectural' or 'hypothetical.'" Second, there must be a causal connection
> between the injury and the conduct complained of—the injury has to be
> "fairly . . . trace[able] to the challenged action of the defendant, and not . . .
> th[e] result [of] the independent action of some third party not before the
> court." . . . Third, it must be "likely," as opposed to merely "speculative,"
> that the injury will be "redressed by a favorable decision." (*Lujan v. Defend-
> ers of Wildlife* 1992:560–561)

Each of these components has been defined through litigation.

"Injury" is treated broadly as a "zone of interest" that may include economic, aesthetic, conservational, recreational, and other such cognizable
concerns as well as harm to one's constitutional or legal rights or status.
Under the APA an injury includes "suffering legal wrong" or being "adversely affected or aggrieved" by agency action (section 702). "In fact"
creates a strong presumption that the party seeking standing be personally among those injured. Generally, the injured is a group or individual
who is directly regulated by governmental action. However, sometimes
the injury will be to an adversely affected third party. For example, in
Craig v. Boren (1976), a licensed vendor of 3.2 percent "nonintoxicating"
beer had standing to bring an equal protection challenge against an Okla-
homa statute allowing females to purchase the brew upon reaching age
eighteen but males only at twenty-one. The beer-seller had an injury in
fact because she "must obey the statutory provisions and incur economic
injury or disobey the statute and suffer sanctions" (*Craig v. Boren*
1976:190). An association or organization meets the "in fact" requirement
when its members would individually have standing; it seeks to protect
interests of importance to its purpose; and the nature of the suit does not
require personal participation by its members (Strauss et al. 1995:1144).

The injury must also be "concrete and particularized." It is easier to say
what is not such an injury than what it is. The grievance a citizen feels
when he or she believes a statute or agency rule is unconstitutional, illegal,
or bad public policy is neither concrete nor particularized. It is a generalized complaint that may be shared with many other citizens. Consequently, at the federal level, citizens do not have standing as citizens per se
to bring suits against the government. This was Richardson's problem in
United States v. Richardson (1974), discussed in Chapter 5. In most instances,

being a taxpayer is also insufficient to create standing to bring cases in federal court. The effect of a national public policy on one's income tax bill is a generalized injury that is widely shared with other individuals (*Frothingham v. Mellon* 1923). An exception occurs when a taxpayer is challenging the federal taxing and spending power to fund a policy that is specifically forbidden by the Constitution, such as government spending for the purpose of establishing religion (*Flast v. Cohen* 1968).

The requirement that the injury be "actual or imminent" rather than "conjectural" or "hypothetical" is also central to the adversary process. The courts prefer that "the legal questions presented . . . will be resolved, not in the rarefied atmosphere of a debating society, but in a concrete factual context conducive to a realistic appreciation of the consequences of judicial action" (*Valley Forge Christian College v. Americans United for Separation of Church and State, Inc.* 1982:472). When the harm is actual, the courts and parties to the case can evaluate it and weigh the government's countervailing interests. When it is imminent, its character and scope can be assessed. But when it is merely conjectural or hypothetical, the adversary process operates uncomfortably like legislative decisionmaking. The courts are not well positioned, relative to elected legislatures and expert administrators, to deal with the speculative costs and benefits of one policy option over another.

The requirement that the plaintiff demonstrate that the injury was fairly traceable to a governmental action may be easily met, as when one is directly regulated by an agency rule. However, sometimes it will be alleged that a policy creates an injury in the zone of interest of a third party who is not directly regulated but more like an innocent bystander who incidentally suffers harm. An obvious chain of causality, as in *Craig v. Boren*, satisfies the traceability requirement. Some cases are more difficult. In *Allen v. Wright* (1984), the parents of African-American public school students challenged the U.S. Internal Revenue Service's lax enforcement of a legal provision disallowing tax-exempt status to racially discriminatory private schools. The parents' argument was that the racially discriminatory schools were using tax-deductible contributions to expand their attractiveness to white students, which frustrated efforts to desegregate the public schools. The Supreme Court found the alleged causal chain far too weak to convey standing. The more speculative or convoluted the purported connection between cause and effect, the less likely traceability will be accepted.

The final standing requirement is that the injury is likely to be redressed by a favorable court decision. All other components of standing being met, good lawyering should prevent this from being an issue. Before filing suit, one ought to know whether victory will appropriately remedy injuries. Remedies can be complex, as in prison reform and public school desegregation cases, or straightforward, as when a rule is nullified, a practice stopped, a new hearing held, a plaintiff compensated, and so on. But they should be clearly connected to the injury.

The main problem arises when there is an uncertain relationship between the requested relief and the course of action a defendant may take upon losing the case. For instance, in 1969 the Internal Revenue Service dropped a ruling allowing charitable nonprofit hospitals to receive beneficial tax status by providing services to indigents below cost. A welfare rights organization brought suit to have the ruling reinstated. It argued that the inducement of favorable tax treatment was necessary to encourage the hospitals to care for indigents. The Supreme Court found it insufficiently likely that the relief sought would redress the injury. The Court thought that the hospitals might just as plausibly forfeit their tax status as bear the costs of treating indigents (*Simon v. Eastern Kentucky Welfare Rights Organization* 1976). In a more recent case, an obviously frustrated Supreme Court found the requested relief "worthless"—not only to the plaintiffs—but "seemingly worthless to all the world" (*Steel Co. v. Citizens for a Better Environment* 1998:106).

Mootness. A case is not reviewable if it is *moot*, meaning that a judicial decision will have no practical effect because the specific legal dispute has disappeared or already been resolved in some other way. For instance, in *Craig v. Boren*, one of the plaintiffs, Craig, had sought prospective relief—to be legally eligible to buy 3.2 beer at age eighteen. By the time the case was decided he was twenty-one, and the Court's ruling could have no effect on his purchase of beer. His case was moot. The suit proceeded because the other plaintiff, the beer-seller, was suffering an ongoing injury. In another example, a condemned prisoner's challenge to electrocution as cruel and unusual punishment was mooted when the state offered death-row inmates a choice between lethal injection and the electric chair (*Bryan v. Moore* 2000).

An exception to mootness may occur when the issue is "capable of repetition and yet evading review" (Barron and Dienes 1999:51). *Roe v. Wade* (1973), which protected the right to have an abortion, is a classic example. It would be next to impossible for a pregnant woman to have such a case decided with finality by the Supreme Court within nine months. Yet at any given time millions of women were pregnant, and some were prohibited by the states from having abortions. There are two ways around this problem. Most simply, the case can proceed if the plaintiff is capable of repeating the behavior, that is, Roe could have conceived again and sought an abortion. The other is to file the suit as a class action, that is, representing a large number of parties in the same situation.

Another exception is that a case will not necessarily be moot because one of the parties voluntarily changes his, her, or its behavior. For instance, after the city of Erie, Pennsylvania, made it an offense to "knowingly or intentionally appear in public in a 'state of nudity,'" Pap's A.M., a corporation operating the nude dancing establishment Kandyland, challenged the ordinance as a violation of freedom of expression under the First and Fourteenth Amendments. The city lost at the trial level, won on appeal, lost in the Pennsylvania Supreme Court, and then petitioned the U.S. Supreme Court for review. In the meantime, Pap's stopped the nudity at Kandyland and operated no other business falling under Erie's prohibition. Pap's wanted the Supreme Court to dismiss the case as moot. The Court refused because Erie was still bound by the Pennsylvania high court decision and, therefore, could not enforce its ordinance. Pap's might also go nude again in the future and would be free to do so if the Pennsylvania court's ruling stood. Finding Pap's apparent strategy in pleading for mootness too transparent, the U.S. Supreme Court noted that its own "interest in preventing litigants from attempting to manipulate its jurisdiction to insulate a favorable decision from review further counsels against a finding of mootness" (*City of Erie v. Pap's A.M.* 2000:277, 278). The Court went on to reverse the Pennsylvania Supreme Court.

Ripeness. *Ripeness* focuses on whether the matters involved in a case have developed sufficiently to make it ready for judicial review. As explained in *Abbott Labs,* the basic rationale for demanding that a case be ripe

> is to prevent the courts, through avoidance of premature adjudication, from entangling themselves in abstract disagreements over administrative policies, and also to protect the agencies from judicial interference until an administrative decision has been formalized and its effects felt in a concrete way by the challenging parties. The problem is best seen in a two-fold aspect, requiring us to evaluate both the fitness of the issues for judicial decision and the hardship to the parties of withholding court consideration. (*Abbott Laboratories v. Gardner* 1967:148–149)

Abbott Labs was a difficult ripeness case that split the Court. The majority found the issues sufficiently clear and the potential harm to the drug companies great enough to warrant preenforcement review. The minority argued that the case was not ripe and would not be until enforcement occurred or perhaps was imminent.

The Supreme Court's decision in a companion case to *Abbott Labs* illustrates how ripeness analysis works. *Toilet Goods Association, Inc. v. Gardner* (1967) dealt with coloring additives in cosmetics, which are regulated by the Food and Drug Administration. In order to facilitate enforcement, the FDA commissioner issued a regulation authorizing immediate suspension of FDA certification service to anyone who denied the agency's employees access "to all manufacturing facilities, processes, and formulae involved in the manufacture of color additives." The Toilet Goods Association's members were manufacturers whose products accounted for 90 percent of all domestic cosmetic sales annually. It challenged the regulation as exceeding the commissioner's authority under the relevant statutes. The association viewed the commissioner's action as a circumvention of legislative intent, noting that the FDA had long asked Congress to authorize the kind of access the commissioner sought and that Congress had always refused, except with respect to prescription drugs. The cosmetic manufacturers were particularly concerned that free access could compromise valuable trade secrets.

The Supreme Court reasoned that *Toilet Goods*, unlike *Abbott Labs*, was not ripe for judicial resolution. On the one hand, the issues were speculative. Until the commissioner implemented the regulation, the courts could not understand what kind of enforcement problems the FDA faced and how these might be resolved within the agency's statutory authority and with appropriate attention to safeguarding trade secrets. On the other hand, refusal to decide the case at this stage placed minimal hardships on the cosmetic companies. In the Court's words, "a refusal to admit an inspector here would at most lead only to suspension of certification services to the particular party, a determination that can then be promptly challenged through an administrative procedure, which in turn is reviewable by a court" (*Toilet Goods Association, Inc. v. Gardner* 1967:161, 165). Although ripeness is subjective, the contrast between *Abbott Labs* and *Toilet Goods* well illustrates how the underlying theory is applied.

Political Questions.   *Political questions* are not justiciable. These are defined by three considerations: (1) The matter is committed by the Constitution's text to the legislature or executive branch or both; (2) the courts would lack "discoverable and manageable standards for resolving" the issues; and (3) no other provision of the Constitution would be defeated by the judiciary's refusal to adjudicate the issues (*Nixon v. United States* 1993:224–225). *Nixon v. United States* (1993) may be the best illustration. Walter L. Nixon Jr. was convicted of federal crimes and sentenced to prison. He was also chief judge of a federal district court, holding tenure during good behavior and drawing pay. He was impeached by the House of Representatives. A Senate committee took testimony from him and reported to the whole Senate, which voted to convict. Nixon claimed that the Senate's action violated the Constitution's Impeachment Clause, which provides that the "Senate shall have the sole Power to try all Impeachments" (Article I, section 3, clause 6).

Did the Senate *try* Nixon? The Supreme Court held that the question was political rather than legal and therefore not justiciable. First, the Constitution's text unarguably commits impeachment trials to the Senate. Second, the word "try" is too vague in this context to yield standards that would be judicially manageable on review. Nixon's protection against arbitrary decisionmaking lay primarily in the requirement that conviction be by a two-thirds majority vote. Finally, failure to review has no effect on the constitutional system.

Nixon has some relevance to administrative law because the Court's decision would apply to the impeachment of executive officers as well. However, political questions are likely to arise far less frequently in the administrative context than concerns about standing, mootness, and ripeness.

Timing

Reviewability analysis is infused with constitutional considerations driven by the scope of judicial authority under Article III and the separation of powers. Timing concerns are primarily policy decisions about when judicial review of administrative action should take place. These are embodied in the principles of primary jurisdiction, exhaustion, finality, and doctrines regarding federal judicial deference to state courts.

Primary Jurisdiction. *Primary jurisdiction* is relevant when a case is brought to court that could also be decided, at least initially, by an administrative agency. The court may essentially tell the parties to take the case to the agency for resolution. The agency may have greater expertise in the subject matter than the court. A decision at the administrative level, where regulations are enforced, may also promote the application of uniform standards. A decision that an agency has primary jurisdiction also helps relieve pressure on the courts' heavy dockets.

In fact, from an administrative law standpoint there seem to be only three good reasons why a court should not place primary jurisdiction with an agency. First, the question may involve a matter of law in which the agency has no special expertise. One of the more remarkable illustrations grew out of Allegheny Airlines's incredibly bad judgment in bumping Ralph Nader from a flight. Nader charged that the airline's overbooking practices amounted to fraudulent misrepresentation. Looking for a friendly forum, the airline argued that the Civil Aeronautics Board (CAB) should have primary jurisdiction because it regulated unfair and deceptive practices in the industry. Ultimately, the Supreme Court ruled for Nader on the basis that the courts, rather than the CAB, have special expertise in the law of fraudulent misrepresentation (*Nader v. Allegheny Airlines, Inc.* 1976).

A court may also avoid placing primary jurisdiction with an agency when a challenged regulation, decision, or action appears completely unreasonable. In such circumstances, there is no point in prolonging the matter. Finally, the agency may have already ruled on the matter in a case involving other parties. If so, the court is not likely to learn much from another agency decision along the same lines. These exceptions notwithstanding, the basic premise with respect to the division of labor between courts and agencies is that the agencies should generally have primary jurisdiction (Warren 1996:437).

Exhaustion of Administrative Remedies.   As a rule, parties are required to *exhaust their administrative remedies* before turning to the courts for relief. From a jurisprudential policy perspective, exhaustion takes advantage of agency expertise, allows agencies to learn where their operations are causing problems and correct them, if possible, and it lightens the judiciary's load. However, as suggested in Chapter 4, from the nongovernmental party's perspective, such as Cinderella's, exhaustion may seem just that—exhaustion of time, energy, spirit, and resources. An individual, firm, or other entity may be required to deal with the issue at the agency level, and perhaps an appeal within it as well, in what may appear to be a futile effort at winning justice.

Not surprisingly, exhaustion is porous. The courts can often relieve parties of it at their discretion. This is most likely when: (1) the issue is purely legal, with no factual dispute; (2) the agency lacks the wherewithal to provide the remedy sought or any meaningful one; (3) the agency has clearly exceeded or misused its authority; (4) violations of constitutional procedural due process inhere in the agency's procedures; (5) the agency is responsible for unreasonable delays; or (6) the only step in the agency's process not exhausted is an optional one (Warren 1996:439–440; Gellhorn and Levin 1997:372–373).

Finality. *Finality* concerns are similar to those of exhaustion. The courts and agencies have strong interests in avoiding premature judicial review. The APA provides for review of "final agency action" (section 704) but does not define the phrase. When an agency issues a final rule or order, finality is clear enough. But what if it makes a policy decision that appears final but is not communicated as such? For instance, an agency might consider regulating something but ultimately decide not to do so without making any formal announcement. Under some circumstances, such inaction can be construed as final. Alternatively, an agency may take an interim or temporary step that burdens some as it proceeds toward its final action. Challenging such preliminary action may not be barred by the finality principle. Perhaps the best generalization is that when finality is unclear judicial analysis will be highly fact specific (Gellhorn and Levin 1997:378).

Deference to State Courts. Federal *judicial deference to state courts* is embodied in two main doctrines. First, under the doctrine of adequate and independent state grounds, the U.S. Supreme Court will not exercise jurisdiction over a case appealed from a state supreme court (or its equivalent) if the state court was able to decide it on the basis of state law, independently of whatever federal question may have been involved. For example, a state may afford individuals greater civil rights and liberties in some contexts than they would have under the U.S. Constitution or federal statutes. In such circumstances, a state court ruling in favor of an individual could be based on adequate and independent state grounds, without reference to the parallel federal provisions. Second, under the doctrine of abstention, the federal courts will temporarily abstain from hearing a constitutional claim when the case turns on an unsettled matter of state law. The doctrine also limits federal court involvement in state criminal proceedings and, sometimes, in administrative and civil proceedings when there is an important state interest at stake.

The Scope of Judicial Review

The *scope* of judicial review refers to the depth of the courts' probe of administrative action. It establishes the extent of judicial deference to administrators' expertise and their need for flexibility. It also defines the quality of the partnership between courts and agencies. The more deferential judges are, the greater discretion agencies have in formulating and implementing their policies and programs. A limited scope of review discourages litigation and reduces the judiciary's role in public administration.

Administrative law scholars are divided on the question of how deeply the courts should review various administrative activities. At times the discussion was posed in terms of whether the courts should be *passive* or *active* in reviewing agencies' actions. Passive judges were seen as essentially conservative, adhering to the Framers' original intent. Activist judges were considered to be results-oriented in their jurisprudence, that is, prone to legal interpretation that promoted their own policy preferences (which were usually liberal). However, the Rehnquist Court (1986–present) has drastically altered the terms of the debate. Its Commerce Clause and Tenth and Eleventh Amendment decisions clearly demonstrate that a court can be both activist and politically conservative at once (see Chapter 2). Regardless of the judiciary's political leanings, today the federal courts as a whole are far more active in reviewing administrative action than in the 1950s and 1960s. Arguments against judicial involvement (i.e., meddling) in administration are probably now more common in law-review articles than in court decisions (see Warren 1996:421–426).

To some extent, the debate over passive versus active jurisprudence obscured the reality that the scope of review has always been a variable. As discussed in Chapter 2, in constitutional law cases the scope of review varies from strict scrutiny to reasonableness to rational basis analysis depending on the specific rights and legal questions involved. It also varies in administrative law, though the terminology is different. Scrutiny is frequently conceived in terms of "looks," ranging from a most probing hard look through a soft one to essentially no look at all. These "looks" are really degrees of deference to the agencies. Which look the courts apply is guided by the APA's language, but the matter also depends heavily on judicial doctrines, practices, and discretion. It is best to think of the relationship between the scope of review and specific administrative activities as one of tendencies rather than inflexible rules. In a litigious nation with one-twentieth of the world's population and two-thirds of its lawyers, there are ample exceptions (Warren 1996:420).

Agency Rules. The substance of agency rules and their underlying logic tend to receive a hard look. Ever since the 1970s, the courts have shown strong interest in evaluating the legal basis and rationale for challenged rules. All rules must be in accordance with constitutional and statutory law. Under the APA, final rules made through formal rulemaking must be supported by "substantial evidence" (section 706[2][E]). Although this may sound like a high threshold, "substantial" basically means "reasonable" in this context (Warren 1996:448). Rules produced by informal rulemaking are subject to review under a standard requiring that they not be "arbitrary, capricious, an abuse of discretion, or otherwise not in accordance with law" (section 706[2][A]). In nuance, this standard is weaker. But the difference may be no greater than saying formally made rules must be supported by reasonable evidence, whereas informally promulgated rules must not be unreasonable. Arcane distinctions between the substantial evidence and arbitrary and capricious tests notwithstanding, in practice the federal courts are apt to apply a hard look to substantive rules. This is well illustrated by two Supreme Court decisions that helped define the hard look.

Industrial Union Department, AFL-CIO v. American Petroleum Institute (1980) involved OSHA standards for reducing benzene from ten parts per million to one part per million in the ambient atmosphere in a number of industries. The Occupational Safety and Health Act of 1970 directs OSHA to "set the standard [for toxic materials or harmful physical agents] which most adequately assures, to the extent feasible, on the basis of the best available evidence, that no employee will suffer material impairment of health or functional capacity." OSHA's policy was to assume that carcinogens like benzene had no safe limit and to regulate accordingly. It established the benzene standard after notice and comment, along with public hearings. There is no doubt that inhaling benzene can do awful damage to one's health. And there was also no doubt that the standard was expensive. The first-year costs per employee would be $82,000 in the petroleum industry, $39,675 in petrochemicals, and $1,390 in manufacturing rubber.

Using a hard look, the court of appeals held that the standard was invalid because it was not supported by the administrative record. The court "concluded that OSHA had exceeded its standard-setting authority because it had not been shown that the 1 ppm [part per million] exposure limit was 'reasonably necessary or appropriate to provide safe and healthful employment' . . . and that [the Occupational Safety and Health Act] did not give OSHA the unbridled discretion to adopt standards designed to create absolutely risk-free workplaces, regardless of cost."

The Supreme Court was badly divided. Five justices voted to affirm the lower court's invalidation of the rule. Three argued that "the burden was on OSHA to show, on the basis of substantial evidence, that it is at least more likely than not that long-term exposure to 10 ppm of benzene presents a significant risk of material health impairment. Here, OSHA did not even attempt to carry such burden of proof." One justice believed that under the act OSHA was obliged to explain "the method by which it determined that the benefits justified the costs and their economic effects." Justice William Rehnquist would have invalidated the standard on the basis that the section of the act involved was an unconstitutional delegation of legislative authority. In his view, it provided a "legislative mirage" rather than a constitutionally required "intelligible principle" to guide the agency and reviewing court. He also argued that Congress, not OSHA, should make the important social policy choice of what is feasible in terms of costs and benefits.

Four justices dissented. They contended that substantial evidence review of OSHA standards should be more deferential than the plurality's opinion claimed because: (1) judges are not trained or experienced in the highly complex technical issues linking toxic substances to diseases; (2) the factual issues in making such links sometimes defy definitive resolution; and (3) "the ultimate decision must necessarily be based on considerations of policy, as well as empirically verifiable facts," which is a job for an agency rather than a court. These are good reasons to give a softer look. The fact that they did not convince the other five justices suggested that the hard look approach, taken primarily by the lower courts in the late 1960s and 1970s, had become dominant (*Industrial Union Department, AFL-CIO v. American Petroleum Institute* 1980:607–610, 681, 685–686, 705–706).

If there had been any doubt about the ascendance of the hard look, it was dispelled three years later in *Motor Vehicle Manufacturers Association of the United States, Inc. v. State Farm Mutual Automobile Insurance Company* (1983). The case concerned the "complex and convoluted history" of the National Highway Traffic Safety Administration's (NHTSA) rules regarding safety restraints in automobiles. Between 1967 and 1982, the agency issued approximately sixty rulemaking notices leading to the imposing, amending, rescinding, reimposing, and re-rescinding of various requirements. At issue was the agency's decision to rescind a passive restraint rule requiring automobiles to be equipped with either automatic seatbelts or air bags. When NHTSA adopted the rule, it assumed automatic seatbelts would be installed in 40 percent of new cars and airbags in the other 60 percent. By 1981, it was clear 99 percent of new cars would have automatic seatbelts and only 1 percent would be equipped with airbags. Armed with this new information, the agency viewed the passive restraint rule as pointless. Conventional seatbelts were already standard equipment, and the large number of recalcitrant drivers and passengers who refused to buckle them would simply detach the automatic ones.

The Supreme Court ruled that the rescission was subject to the same arbitrary and capricious standard of review as would be used in dealing with a new rule. It then applied a hard look and concluded that NHTSA could not pass the test. First, the agency was mixing its apples and oranges: "The . . . most obvious reason for finding the rescission arbitrary and capricious is that NHTSA apparently gave no consideration whatever to modifying the Standard to require that air bag technology be utilized." Second, "the agency's explanation for rescission of the passive restraint requirement is not sufficient to enable us to conclude that the rescission was the product of reasoned decisionmaking." In sum, "the scope of review under the 'arbitrary and capricious' standard is narrow and a court is not to substitute its judgment for that of the agency. Nevertheless, the agency must examine the relevant data and articulate a satisfactory explanation for its action. . . . In reviewing that explanation, we must 'consider whether the decision was based on a consideration of the relevant factors and whether there has been a clear error of judgment'" (*Motor Vehicle Manufacturers Association of the United States, Inc. v. State Farm Mutual Automobile Insurance Co.* 1983:43, 46, 52).

FOIA Requests. Denials of freedom of information requests receive a hard look. Under the Freedom of Information Act (1966, as amended), the agency has the burden of persuasion in showing that an exemption or other legal provision permits it to withhold the requested information. In deciding cases, courts should not be deferential to the agency or confined to its records.

Rulemaking Procedures. Rulemaking procedures receive a soft look as long as they meet the minimum APA or other applicable statutory requirements. This was established in *Vermont Yankee Nuclear Power Corporation v.*

Natural Resources Defense Council, Inc. (1978). After engaging in hybrid rule-making, in which hearings were held, the federal Atomic Energy Commission (AEC) granted licenses to two power companies to operate nuclear plants for generating electricity and steam. The Natural Resources Defense Council challenged the action on the basis, in part, that the AEC's hearing procedures fell short of those used in formal rulemaking.

The Supreme Court unanimously upheld the AEC, noting that informal rulemaking does not require the agency to hold hearings at all and that, in drafting the APA, "Congress intended that the discretion of the *agencies* and not that of the courts be exercised in determining when extra procedural devices should be employed." The Court concluded that a soft look was necessary for three reasons. First, "if courts continually review agency proceedings to determine whether the agency employed procedures which were, in the court's opinion, perfectly tailored to reach what the court perceives to be the 'best' or 'correct' result, judicial review would be totally unpredictable." In self-defense, the agencies would have to hold full formal hearings, despite the fact that Congress deliberately avoided making them the only vehicle for rulemaking.

Second, the lower court "reviewed the agency's choice of procedures on the basis of the record actually produced at the hearing, . . . and not on the basis of the information available to the agency when it made the decision to structure the proceedings in a certain way." Allowing hindsight to determine what agencies might have done better would, again, virtually compel them "to conduct all rulemaking proceedings with the full panoply of procedural devices normally associated only with adjudicatory hearings."

Third, "and perhaps most importantly" in terms of the soft look, the lower court's decision "fundamentally misconceives the nature of the standard for judicial review of an agency rule." In informal rulemaking, the adequacy of the record depends on whether the agency has followed the APA or other relevant statutes, not on how much opportunity is given to interested parties to participate in the proceedings (*Vermont Yankee Nuclear Power Corp. v. Natural Resources Defense Council, Inc.* 1978:546–547; Justices Harry Blackmun and Lewis Powell did not participate).

Agencies' Statutory Interpretations. An agency's reasoned interpretation of the statutes it administers also receives a soft look. *Chevron U.S.A., Inc. v. Natural Resources Defense Council, Inc.* (1984) tested EPA's authority to define "stationary sources" of air pollution in two very different ways in different programs and also differently in the same program at different times. One definition was that such sources could be individual machines or pieces of equipment; the other was that they were entire plants or industrial groupings. The Supreme Court's landmark decision framed the application of a soft look for statutory interpretation as follows: (1) If Congress has directly spoken to the precise issue and its intent is clear, the agency has to implement the statute accordingly; (2) if the court determines that Congress has not clearly addressed the issue, then "the question for the court is whether the agency's [interpretation] is based on a permissible construction of the statute"; and (3) the agency's statutory interpretations will be permissible "unless they are arbitrary, capricious, or manifestly contrary to the statute." In short, the courts should be deferential to agencies' statutory interpretation. They should also recognize that "an initial agency interpretation is not instantly carved in stone" but rather flexible and subject to reasonable change. Two different definitions of the same two words in a single statute are permissible as long as both definitions are reasonable (*Chevron U.S.A., Inc. v. Natural Resources Defense Council, Inc.* 1984:843, 844, 863).

Chevron provides the agencies with great flexibility in defining the terms of vague delegations of legislative authority. However, the Supreme Court applied an important caveat in *United States v. Mead Corp.* (2001). *Chevron* deference applies only when "Congress delegated authority to the agency generally to make rules carrying the force of law, and . . . the agency interpretation claiming deference was promulgated in the exercise of that authority." But where an agency issues a number of ruling letters that do not have the force of law, such as a Customs Service classification of day planners as dutiable diaries (as in *Mead*), weaker deference is granted to its statutory interpretation (*United States v. Mead Corp.* 2001:2166). This is called *Skidmore* deference, which treats the agency's action with respect or courtesy but requires a harder look than under *Chevron* (*Skidmore v. Swift & Co.* 1944).

Agency Nonenforcement. An agency's discretion *not* to undertake an enforcement action, within constitutional and statutory limits, receives no look—or at least there is a very strong presumption against judicial review under the APA. In *Heckler v. Chaney* (1985), death-row prisoners challenged the FDA's failure either to approve the drugs used in lethal injection as "'safe and effective' for human execution" or to prohibit their use for that purpose.

The Supreme Court noted that under the APA judicial review is not available when another statute precludes it or if the agency action "is committed to agency discretion by law" (section 701[a][1][2]). The Court reasoned that these provisions were based on sound jurisprudential policy. Decisions not to take enforcement steps are generally unsuitable for judicial review for several reasons, as stated in *Heckler v. Chaney* 1985:831–832:

> First, an agency decision not to enforce often involves a complicated balancing of a number of factors which are peculiarly within its expertise. Thus, the agency must not only assess whether a violation has occurred, but whether agency resources are best spent on this violation or another, whether the agency is likely to succeed if it acts, whether the particular enforcement action requested best fits the agency's overall policies, and, indeed, whether the agency has enough resources to undertake the action at all. An agency generally cannot act against each technical violation of the statute it is charged with enforcing. The agency is far better equipped than the courts to deal with the many variables involved in the proper ordering of its priorities. Similar concerns animate the principles of administrative law that courts generally will defer to an agency's construction of the statute it is charged with implementing, and the procedures it adopts for implementing that statute. . . .
>
> In addition to these administrative concerns, we note that when an agency refuses to act it generally does not exercise its *coercive* power over an individual's liberty or property rights, and thus does not infringe upon areas that courts are often called upon to protect. Similarly, when an agency *does* act to enforce, that action itself provides a focus for judicial review, inasmuch as the agency must have exercised its power in some manner.

The Court went on to compare agency decisions not to enforce to those of prosecutors, whose discretion not to see indictment is regarded as part of the executive's constitutional responsibility to "take Care that the Laws be faithfully executed."

The Court's sweeping language triggered a concurring opinion by Justice William Brennan, who cautioned that the presumption of nonreviewability did not apply where an agency: (1) claims that it lacks enforcement authority; (2) "engages in a pattern of nonenforcement of clear statutory language"; (3) refuses "to enforce a regulation lawfully promulgated and still in effect"; and (4) violates constitutional rights through its nonenforcement (*Heckler v. Chaney* 1985:839).

Discretionary Actions.   By contrast, discretionary *actions* on substantial matters tend to receive a hard look. These are a residual catch-all of agency activities, other than nonenforcement, that are not precluded from judicial review by the APA or another statute and do not fall into some regulated category of agency action, such as rulemaking, adjudication, or freedom of information. In *Citizens to Preserve Overton Park, Inc. v. Volpe* (1971), the Supreme Court held that judicially reviewable administrative discretion should be assessed under a somewhat generalized APA standard, which requires "the reviewing court to engage in a substantial inquiry." This includes attention to whether: (1) the administrator acted within the scope of his/her authority; (2) the decision was within the range of options allowed by the applicable statutes; (3) the relevant factors were considered; (4) the administrator made "a clear error of judgment"; and (5) the necessary procedures were followed. None of this was particularly new, but more followed.

Overton Park dealt with federal highway statutes instructing the secretary of the Department of Transportation to withhold approval of highway projects using land in public parks, recreation areas, wildlife and waterfowl refuges, or historic sites unless there was "no feasible and prudent alternative." The statutory provisions also required minimizing the harm to such areas when roads were built through them. Transportation Secretary John Volpe approved a six-lane interstate highway project that would have severed Overton Park, a 342-acre city park in Memphis, Tennessee.

Volpe provided no formal statement of factual findings indicating why there was no feasible and prudent alternative or why the design could not be changed to reduce harm to the park. Instead, he offered "'post hoc' rationalizations." These did not constitute a whole record—or even an adequate record—for review. The Supreme Court remanded the case to the district court for full review of the administrative record on which Volpe made his decision. It noted that the lower court might require Volpe and other officials who participated in the decision to explain their action (*Citizens to Preserve Overton Park, Inc. v. Volpe* 1970:411, 415–416, 419).

The district court eventually held that Volpe either never made an analysis of alternative routes or made it incorrectly. The case was then remanded back to Volpe for a new decision based on the statutory criteria. In the end, Volpe found that Interstate 40 could not legally be built through Overton Park. The effect of *Overton Park* is to prompt agencies to keep formal records explaining their discretionary actions, especially if they are likely to provoke significant litigation. The case also encouraged agencies to keep more copious records when engaging in informal rule-making.

Adjudication. Formal adjudication is subject to substantial evidence review and can also be challenged for procedural irregularity. The APA specifically provides that an agency's adjudicatory decision may be reversed if it is unwarranted by the facts "to the extent that the facts are subject to trial de novo [anew] by the reviewing court" (section 706[2][F]). These provisions encourage a hard look. The reviewing court will consider the whole record to determine whether the facts, in the context of the governing statutes or rules, reasonably support the agency's decision. This approach has been a staple of federal administrative law at least since 1951, when the Supreme Court outlined it in *Universal Camera Corp. v. National Labor Relations Board.*

Legislative Review of Administration

Judicial review of public administration in the United States is episodic. It takes place in distinct cases. Individual judicial decisions eventually aggregate into the legal and constitutional doctrines that govern administrative practice. Legislative review is more continuous and diffuse. It takes place whenever a legislature is in session and deals with the entire range of administrative concerns—budgets, personnel, implementation, organizational design, use of technology, strategic planning, policy choices, reporting, and even the architecture and location of agency buildings, offices, and other facilities.

At the federal level, the constitutional basis for congressional review of administrative activity is crystal-clear. The agencies implement legislative mandates with congressionally appropriated funds, often exercising delegated legislative authority. Therefore, Congress has a legitimate role in ensuring that agency actions are in keeping with legislative intent. It is well established that "keeping a watchful eye on the administration of the laws it has enacted is [an] important function of our National Legislature" (La Follette 1946:45). The more difficult issue is how Congress can exercise oversight of the agencies without undue micromanagement, causing needless inefficiency, or interfering with principled administrative decisionmaking. The following are the main mechanisms for congressional review of federal administration.

Oversight by Committees and Subcommittees

The Legislative Reorganization Act of 1946 charged the standing committees in the House of Representatives and Senate with exercising "continuous watchfulness" of the administrative execution of the laws under
their jurisdictions (section 136). In 1970, this language was strengthened
to require the committees to "review and study" agency implementation
"on a continuing basis" (Legislative Reorganization Act of 1970: section
118). This language is broad enough to support informal contacts between committee members or their staffs and agency personnel as well as
formal legislative hearings on administrative performance.

The most comprehensive empirical study of committee review of
agency activity yielded the following conclusions: (1) Communication
levels between congressional staff and administrators is "very extensive";
(2) slightly over half the committees engage in active or intermediate
monitoring of the agencies, the remainder being reactive; (3) "the nature
of congressional oversight is rather impressive"; and (4) "congressional
oversight probably improves policy at the margins" (Aberbach 1990:85,
95, 198). Additionally, the study found that almost all the committees had
intermediately or well-developed networks for obtaining information
from and about the agencies (Aberbach 1990:88).

Reporting Requirements

Congressional review of administration relies on agency reports, often
heavily, as Vice President Al Gore's National Performance Review made
clear in 1993:

> Today the annual calendar is jammed with report deadlines. On August 31
> of each year, the Chief Financial Officers (CFO) Act requires that agencies
> file a 5-year financial plan and a CFO annual report. On September 1, bud-
> get exhibits for financial management activities and high risk areas are due.
> November 30, IG [Inspector General] reports are expected, along with re-
> ports required by the Prompt Payment Act. On January 31, reports under
> the Federal Civil Penalties Inflation Report Adjustment Act of 1990 come
> due. On March 31, financial statements are due and on May 1 annual single-
> audit reports must be filed. On May 31 another round of IG reports are due.
> At the end of July and December, "high risk" reports are filed. On August
> 31, it all begins again. And these are just major reports!

In fiscal year 1993, Congress required executive branch agencies to prepare 5,348 reports. (Gore 1993:34)

One wonders how much of this material receives a careful congressional
read, but chances are that it is given a good agency write. Just knowing
that such reports must be filed probably influences agency behavior.

Research, Evaluation, Audit, and Investigation

Congressional review is assisted by a number of legislative agencies and
functionaries. The General Accounting Office, Congressional Research
Service, and Congressional Budget Office all play a role in assessing
agency performance. In particular, the GAO engages in investigations,
broad program reviews, and evaluations of administrative activity. The
CRS supplies Congress with policy and legal analyses, which often bear
upon federal administration. The CBO is mainly concerned with federal
budget matters, but it also undertakes program analyses of federal
spending at the request of congressional committees.

In addition to these agencies, Congress learns about administration
from the inspectors general and chief financial officers (CFOs) within the
agencies. The inspectors general are sometimes considered the eyes and
ears of Congress within the agencies (Moore and Gates 1986). They are
employed by the agencies to audit, investigate, and report maladministration both to Congress and the agency heads. The CFOs oversee the financial management of administrative operations. Their annual reports
are an invaluable source of financial information.

Sunset Legislation

Congressional and state legislation is sometimes subject to sunset provisions. These specify that whatever programs or administrative operations a law authorizes will terminate after a number of years—often
five—unless reauthorized by statute. Such provisions are intended to
force legislatures periodically to engage in probing evaluations of the
administrative implementation and efficacy of the laws they enact. Sun-
setting by Congress guards against the continuation of programs and
agencies that have outlived their usefulness. It seeks to reverse the effect
of legislative inertia by attaching specific consequences to inaction. The
threat of sunset also places agencies on notice that inadequate perfor-

mance may lead to the demise of the agency itself or some of its programs.

Although once viewed as a promising approach to legislative review
of public administrative operations, in practice sunset legislation has had
mixed results. In a sense, sunset laws are redundant. Congress and the
state legislatures evaluate agencies and programs in conjunction with
passing budgets, which is generally done on an annual or biennial basis.
Budget hearings ought to reveal what is not working as intended. Consequently, requiring the reauthorization of agencies and their programs at
fixed times, even when there is no sign of trouble, may involve an unnecessary investment of legislative effort and expense. Even when sunset
provisions prompt legislative review of administrative operations that
are somehow operating below the radar screen, they may not be cost-effective. In any case, most programs under sunset legislation are apparently reauthorized, and several states have lost interest in this form of
legislative review (Warren 1996:195–196).

Casework

Casework, or constituency service, is another means of congressional review, though a haphazard one. It runs the gamut from helping constituents arrange visits to Washington, D.C., to intervening in administrative processes to resolve their problems with federal agencies. Senators
and Representatives routinely write letters to the agencies on behalf of
constituents. The agencies generally refer to these as "congressionals"
and expedite attention to the matters involved. Casework is taxing on the
congressional offices, but the public expects it, and it helps members get
reelected. The volume is huge. In 1984, it exceeded 5,000–10,000 requests
per year in many congressional offices—a number that has no doubt
grown exponentially with the growing popularity of e-mail (Vogler
1988:219).

Much casework has no significant impact on federal administration, but
sometimes it prompts agencies to recognize "problems occurring at the
middle and lower levels of the bureaucracy ... and even search for patterns behind the complaints" (Dodd and Schott 1979:269). It may also reveal such ineptitude, abuse, or other ills that Congress will revamp an
agency's authority, organization, processes, or leadership. Casework
helped alert Congress to the abuses and poor administration addressed by
the Taxpayers' Bill of Rights legislation in 1986 and the Internal Service

Restructuring and Reform Act of 1998 (Burnham 1989:305; Roth and Nixon 1999).

Strategic Planning and Annual Performance Reports

The Government Performance and Results Act of 1993 was a congressional initiative aimed at substantially upgrading legislative review. It was premised partly on the finding that "congressional policymaking, spending decisions and program oversight are seriously handicapped by insufficient attention to [administrative] program performance and results" (section 2[a][3]). It requires the agencies to write five-year strategic plans in consultation with Congress (i.e., committees, subcommittees, or work teams). These are updated at least every three years and include a statement of goals and objectives. Additionally, the agencies must file two annual documents: (1) performance plans, which prospectively identify performance goals and indicators; and (2) performance reports, retrospectively assessing the past year's performance. The act emphasizes the need for quantifiable objectives and quantitative measurement. The overall intent is eventually to link congressional budget decisions to agency performance.

To date, the Government Performance and Results Act has not produced consistent legislative review of agency performance. The agencies have had trouble writing meaningful plans, and congressional attention to them has been uneven and somewhat marked by political grandstanding (Harris 1997; Barr 1998). The act's future effectiveness is uncertain, though potentially it remains a powerful tool for congressional review and direction of the agencies. Most notably, Congress's participation in the development of agency strategic plans can strengthen administrative understanding of legislative intent and improve implementation.

Congressional Review Act

Title II of the Small Business Regulatory Enforcement Fairness Act of 1996 includes a subtitle known as the Congressional Review Act. It requires the agencies to submit all covered final or interim rules to Congress and the GAO before they can take effect. Coverage extends to interpretive and procedural rules but excludes rules on a variety of subjects and those exempted from notice and comment for good cause under APA provisions.

The act provides for two levels of review, depending on whether a rule is *major* or *ordinary*. Major rules are those expected to have an annual economic impact of at least $100 million or have a substantial effect on key economic concerns such as costs, prices, employment, and productivity. With some exceptions, major rules are subject to a sixty-day review period in Congress during which it can pass a joint resolution of disapproval. The resolution is subject to presidential veto and legislative override. Rules that are not disapproved are published in the *Federal Register* and take effect as indicated therein.

Ordinary rules are also subject to congressional disapproval, but not the sixty-day review period. They can be published as final after being submitted to Congress and the GAO. No rule that is disapproved can be reissued in identical or similar form unless the agency receives specific statutory authorization to do so. The act specifically provides that congressional failure to disapprove a rule should not be taken by the courts or agencies as tacitly inferring any legislative intent.

Legislative review of agency rules is not a new idea. It was discussed in the 1940s in connection with drafting the APA. Michigan adopted it in 1944, and by 1970 Kansas, Nebraska, Virginia, and Wisconsin had followed suit (U.S. Senate 1970:1293). At least twenty-two states currently provide for review of rules by legislative committees of one kind or another. Joint committees are frequently used, as in Alabama, Illinois, Kansas, Maryland, Michigan, Ohio, Vermont, Washington, and Wisconsin (Bonfield 1986:482–483; Bonfield 1993:184–185). The first legislative disapproval of a federal rule occurred in 2001, when Congress voted down OSHA's ergonomics rule (Dewar 2001). The fact that OSHA had taken about a decade or so to write the rule suggests that agencies can be blindsided by political change unless they remain responsive to key committee members in Congress. Past legislative intent will not bind current congressional review.

Conclusion: Checks, Balances, and Federal Administration

During debate on an administrative law bill in 1940, a senator rose to contend that "the bureaucrats are drunk with power" and "believe that their ipse dixit [say-so] should settle all questions" (U.S. Congress 1940:7176; Senator Henry Ashurst [D–AZ]). Times have changed! Today's administrators are more apt to be frustrated by a lack of power and multiplicity of challenges to their expertise. Judicial review and legislative review have brought a substantial measure of checks and balances to bear on federal administrative processes. Although this encumbers administration, the expansion of both judicial and legislative review was fully predictable. U.S. constitutional government has been likened to "a machine that would go of itself," and as early as 1939, when the full-fledged administrative state was new, it was clear that "under our system of divided powers, the executive branch of the national government is not exclusively controlled by the President, by the Congress, or by the courts. All three have a hand in controlling it, each from a different angle and each in a different way" (Kamen 1987; Meriam 1939:131). It just took the judicial and legislative branches time to catch up with the strong "imperial presidency" that developed out of the New Deal, World War II, and the Cold War (Schlesinger 1973). Some criticize judicial and congressional review for gridlocking administration. Others see it as part of the normal messiness of the constitutional separation of powers. Almost everybody agrees that when the constitutional machine moves significantly in one direction or another, administrative law is sure to follow.

7

Staying Current

This book has described and analyzed the core premises, processes, and principles of administrative law in the United States, mostly with respect to the federal level. It should have a long shelf-life. The Administrative Procedure Act of 1946 still provides the federal government's basic administrative law framework. It has been able to accommodate substantial amendment because its fundamental principles have endured. Congress's key point in enacting it was that public administration should incorporate the democratic-constitutional values of representation, participation, transparency, fairness, and limited government intrusion on private activity. Major subsequent administrative law initiatives—including negotiated rulemaking, freedom of information, alternative dispute resolution, and paperwork reduction—have been intended to advance the achievement of these values. If folding them into administrative law and practice is sometimes bumpy, it is not because they run counter to the APA's initial purposes—in fact, national security policy aside, it is difficult to think of a single post-1946 administrative law statute that does undercut the APA's intent. Similarly, cases like *Nova Scotia* and *Cinderella*, decided decades ago, remain good law because they are firmly rooted in principles on which the APA is based (*United States v. Nova Scotia Food Products Corp.* 1977; *Cinderella Career and Finishing Schools, Inc. v. Federal Trade Commission* 1970).

Public managers can reasonably expect stability in the larger purposes of administrative law. However, they can also expect change in the particulars. Today, rulemaking, adjudication, transparency, and judicial review are not the same as in 1946. The constitutional law affecting public administration is radically different. How can public managers stay current? There are at least three relatively easy steps and one harder one.

The easy ones are: (1) Always keep the primary function of American administrative law in mind; (2) frequently consult administrative law publications and websites; and (3) talk to agency colleagues and attorneys about new administrative law developments. More difficult and expensive: Have experts conduct periodic administrative law audits to ensure compliance with newer requirements.

The Primary Function of U.S. Administrative Law

In many fields of study a couple of underlying principles go a long way in organizing thinking, research, and application. In economics, these are supply and demand; in sociology, stratification and mobility. In administrative law, the tension between constitutional contractarianism and administrative instrumentalism is the defining element. The primary function of administrative law is to funnel constitutional contractarian values into administrative practice in order to harmonize public administration with constitutional democracy. The simple secret of the APA's remarkable durability is that by focusing on procedure rather than substantive policy criteria (e.g., cost-benefit, environmental justice) it acts as such a funnel.

Constitutional Contractarianism

Constitutional contractarianism is based on natural rights theory. Its basic assumptions are that individuals are born with fundamental rights and they form governments to protect those rights. Rights are not created by governments; they preexist it. Government is a mechanism for preventing others from encroaching on our rights and for achieving common purposes. Perhaps nowhere are these principles more succinctly stated than in the Declaration of Independence and the Preamble of the U.S. Constitution.

In the Declaration's famous words, "We hold these Truths to be self-evident, that all Men are created equal, that they are endowed by their Creator with certain unalienable Rights, that among these are Life, Liberty, and the Pursuit of Happiness—That to secure these Rights, Governments are instituted among Men, deriving their just Powers from the Consent of the Governed." The Preamble is a compact between "We the People" that has as one of its prime objectives to "secure the Blessings of Liberty to ourselves and our Posterity."

Contractarianism pervades the Constitution's Bill of Rights. It identifies spheres of personal freedom, such as religion and speech, on which the government may tread only under extraordinary circumstances. It affords a wide variety of protections for persons accused of crimes. The Eighth Amendment's ban on cruel and unusual punishments protects those convicted as well. Here is one court's contractarian interpretation: "Inadequate resources can *never* be an adequate justification for the state's depriving *any* person of his constitutional rights. If the state cannot obtain the resources to detain persons awaiting trial in accordance with minimum constitutional standards, then the state simply will not be permitted to detain such persons" (*Hamilton v. Love* 1971:1194; emphasis added). Sounds radical, but the identical premise is written into the Fifth Amendment's Takings Clause: Government can take private property only for "public use" and with "just compensation"; if the state is unable to pay for someone's land, then it cannot have it—no matter how important the public purpose. Contractarian premises are also reflected in the construction of strict scrutiny in constitutional law, which requires government to show a compelling interest for some abridgments of equal protection and substantive rights and to narrowly tailor the infringement or make it the means of achieving the governmental purpose that is least restrictive of those rights (see Chapter 2).

Contractarianism is incorporated into several aspects of contemporary administrative law. For instance, the absence of standing requirements allows anyone to comment on proposed rules in informal rulemaking or to file a freedom of information request. The procedural due process protections provided in adjudications is another example. Executive orders seeking to protect disadvantaged groups from environmental injustice and to guard state sovereignty in federal rulemaking also embody contractarianism.

Public Administrative Instrumentalism

Public administration in the United States is instrumental, rather than contractarian, in its outlook. It emphasizes cost-effectiveness in achieving results. From the field's founding in the days of Woodrow Wilson in the 1880s through former Vice President Al Gore's National Performance Review in the 1990s, the public administrative purpose has been to make government "work better and cost less" (Wilson 1887; Gore 1993). This basic posture is captured in a classic statement on public budgeting that contrasts sharply with the Eighth Amendment interpretation quoted above:

> Budget decisions must be made on the basis of relative values. There is no absolute standard of value. It is not enough to say that an expenditure for a particular purpose is desirable or worth while. The results must be more valuable than they would be if the money were used for any other purpose.
>
> . . .
>
> Costs must be judged in relation to the results and the results must be worth their cost in terms of alternative results that are foregone or displaced. (Lewis 1952:213–214, 215)

Is the best possible use of public money really to reduce jail crowding? To the contractarian judge the question is irrelevant; to administrative budgeters and much budget reform since the 1940s, it is central.

It is an uncomfortable reality that, however aberrant, public administration's instrumentalism has often led to a remarkably callous disregard for individual rights (Rosenbloom and O'Leary 1997). This is one reason why Congress considered the APA necessary in the 1940s and the federal courts began building constitutional rights into individuals' encounters with public administration in the 1950s. As late as 1993, a federal circuit court of appeals had the following to say in response to a prison warden's manual for search procedures, which literally compelled male guards to sexually abuse female prisoners:

> A bland American civil servant can be as much of a beast as a ferocious concentration camp guard if he does not think about what his actions are doing. . . . Half the cruelties of human history have been inflicted by conscientious servants of the state. The mildest of bureaucrats can be a brute if he does not raise his eyes from his task and consider the human beings on whom he is having an impact. . . .
>
> How did a civilized country and a civilized state like Washington get into this fix where it takes federal judges to tell a responsible state official to stop his approval of indecency because he is violating the Constitution? (*Jordan v. Gardner* 1993:1544)

The primary function of U.S. administrative law is to ensure that administrators do raise their eyes to the broad contractarian values that underlie constitutional democracy—at the very least when legally or constitutionally required to do so.

The tension between contractarianism and instrumentalism necessarily results in compromises. Instrumental public administration also has roots in the Preamble, which calls for promoting the common defense and general welfare. Cost-effectiveness is not irrelevant to public policy. The constitutional law regarding procedural due process in administrative contexts recognizes this. The cost of more elaborate procedural protections is balanced along with the individual's interest and the relative efficacy of the procedures in place. Consequently, in the metaphor of administrative law as a funnel, the funnel has a filter. Pure contractarianism is not feasible. A government cannot really release potentially dangerous persons indicted for predatory crimes because it cannot afford constitutional jails. Rulemaking by appointed administrators is far less democratic than legislation by elected representatives; administrative evidentiary adjudication affords individuals less protection than judicial trials in terms of procedure, quality of evidence, and availability of juries; transparency has exemptions and exceptions.

Administrative law's compromises between contractarianism and instrumentalism cannot satisfy everyone all the time. Some critics will want more contractarianism, others more instrumentalism. If the debate did not begin with the framing of the Constitution, it certainly goes back that far. In *The Federalist* (1787–1788), James Madison argued for checks and balances as "auxiliary precautions," necessary to ensure that the government would "control itself." Alexander Hamilton maintained that a strong, independent executive was required to prevent "bad execution," for "a government ill-executed, whatever it may be in theory, must be, in practice, a bad government" (Publius 1787–1788: No. 51, 322; No. 70, 423). In the 1990s, the Hamiltonians favored reinventing government to make it results-oriented rather than procedure-oriented. They condemned the one-size-fits-all approach that administrative law promotes (Gore 1993:1–9). Madisonians might have responded in the words of Senator Pat McCarran (D–NV), a leading sponsor of the APA in 1946: "It is sometimes said that . . . the substantive and procedural law applicable to an administrative agency should be prescribed piecemeal, for that agency alone. . . . Diversity merely feeds confusion, which is a great vice in any form of government and operates to defeat the very purposes of good government" (McCarran 1946:829). After the September 11, 2001, terrorist attacks on the United States, the debate over constitutional contractarianism and administrative instrumentalism focused more sharply on transparency versus national security (Nakashima 2002). Keeping the tension between the contractarian and instrumental outlooks in mind usually makes it easier to understand such controversies and to assimilate change in administrative law.

Periodicals and Websites

For the reader of this book, continuing self-education in administrative law should be straightforward. It ought to be relatively easy to follow and understand any general discussion or development. Technical changes may present more difficulty, but few should be impenetrable. There are a variety of sources worth consulting periodically.

1. The American Bar Association's Section of Administrative Law and Regulatory Practice publishes an invaluable quarterly newsletter, *Administrative and Regulatory Law News*. It contains reviews of major court cases and developments in state administrative law as well as discussions of leading law-review articles. Subscription is open to libraries and individuals (membership in the American Bar Association is not necessary). Contact the ABA Section of Administrative Law and Regulatory Practice, 740 15th Street, NW, Washington, DC 20005–1002 (Tel. 202-662-1529).

2. The *Administrative Law Review* contains highly readable articles on the entire range of administrative law topics, including frequent analyses on recent developments in specific areas, such as paperwork reduction and sunshine. Careful attention to its contents is an excellent way of staying current. It is published by American University's Washington College of Law and the Section of Administrative Law and Regulatory Practice of the American Bar Association. Individuals and libraries may subscribe. Contact the American Bar Association, 750 North Lake Shore Drive, Chicago, IL 60611–4497 (Tel. 312-988-5522).

3. The American Bar Association's Section of Administrative Law and Regulatory Practice also publishes books on specific areas of administrative law. Consult www.abanet.org/administrativelaw.

4. The Administrative Codes and Registers Section of the National Association of Secretaries of State is another organization interested in administrative law. Consult www.nass.org/acr/acr/html.

5. The Reporters Committee publishes *Tapping Officials' Secrets*, which is chock-full of information about every state's open meetings and open records laws. Consult www.reporters committee.org/tapping2001/index.cgi. Additional information

about transparency can be found in the U.S. Department of Justice's *FOIA Reference Guide*, www.usdoj.gov/04foia/index.html; the American Civil Liberty Union's website, www.aclu.org/library/foia.html; and the American Society of Access Professionals, www.accesspro.org/.

6. The *Federal Register* can be followed at www.access.gpo.gov/su_docs/aces/aces140.html.

7. Florida State University maintains an administrative procedure database, www.law.fsu.edu/library/admin/.

8. Supreme Court cases are easily accessed through "Find Law," www.findlaw.com. Materials on administrative law are at www.findlaw.com/01topics/00administrative/index.html.

9. Administrative law developments in federal agencies can be tracked through the "FirstGov" portal, www.firstgov.gov, and OMB Watch's site, www.ombwatch.org.

Talk Administrative Law Talk

A well-known article entitled "Stories Managers Tell: Why They Are as Valid as Science" noted that "managers first and foremost communicate through stories that constitute or construct their world" (Hummel 1991:39). Public managers talk about human resources management, budgeting, organizational design, program evaluation, and other administrative practices. They learn a great deal through such talk. Talking about administrative law will solidify and expand one's understanding and knowledge. Today administrative law is too central to administrative practice to be considered a technical specialty best left to the lawyers. Typically it is the public managers, not legal staff, who are called on to integrate administrative law into day-to-day administrative operations. As noted in Chapter 2, they are also the ones who may end up being sued personally for violating someone's clearly established constitutional or statutory rights.

Administrative Law Audits

The vast judicial intervention in prison administration during the last quarter of the twentieth century spawned "an emerging new specialty in the corrections field, which, according to some proponents of the idea, trains and designates officials to perform 'constitutional audits' of facilities and procedures in order to reduce legal liabilities" (though just to protect the prisoners' constitutional rights would be reason enough; Feeley and Hanson 1990:26). In 2000, the U.S. Department of Agriculture contracted out for civil rights audits. Administrative law audits can also be of great value. Many agencies lack systematic processes for learning of new court decisions on administrative law and integrating them into their operations. Over time, personnel and other procedural manuals can become dated and standard practices out of sync with the latest legal developments. Even where legal staffs copiously attempt to adjust agency operations to new administrative law requirements, there may be some gaps in what reaches frontline personnel. Periodic administrative law audits would systematically focus attention on practices that need updating. They could also serve as an educational tool for agency personnel. Financial audits (instrumental) are common; are administrative law audits (contractarian) less important?

The Next Level

The purpose of this book has been to equip public managers with the essentials to understand, follow, and integrate administrative law into their daily practice. It also provides a knowledge base for those who want to study administrative law further or dig more deeply into any of its major areas. There are several books that can take public administrators to the next level. The classic work emphasizing state-level administrative law is Michael Asimow, Arthur Bonfield, and Ronald Levin, *State and Federal Administrative Law* (2nd ed., 1998). A good next step for those primarily interested in federal-level law would be Kenneth Warren's encyclopedic *Administrative Law in the Political System* (3rd ed., 1996) or Kenneth Culp Davis's older but still thought-provoking *Administrative Law and Government* (1975). Following either of these, one cannot go wrong with Peter Strauss et al.'s 1,463-page *Gellhorn and Byse's Administrative Law: Cases and Comments* (9th ed., 1995). Administrative law is a key part of the hard work of modern democracy. One can never learn too much about it.

REFERENCES

Abbott Laboratories v. Gardner. 1967. 387 U.S. 136.

Aberbach, Joel. 1990. *Keeping a Watchful Eye.* Washington, DC: Brookings Institution.

Aberbach, Joel, and Bert Rockman. 2000. *The Web of Politics.* Washington, DC: Brookings Institution.

Adarand Constructors v. Pena. 1995. 515 U.S. 200.

Administrative Dispute Resolution Act. 1990. PL 101–552. 104 Stat. 2736. 5 U.S.C. 571.

Administrative Procedure Act of 1946. PL 79–404. 60 Stat. 237. 5 U.S.C. 551.

Allen, Mike, and George Lardner Jr. 2001. "Veto Over Presidential Papers." *Washington Post*, November 2, p. A1.

Allen v. Wright. 1984. 468 U.S. 737.

Allison, Graham. 1979. "Public and Private Management: Are They Fundamentally Alike in All Unimportant Respects?" In David Rosenbloom, Deborah Goldman, and Patricia Ingraham, eds., *Contemporary Public Administration.* New York: McGraw Hill, 1994, pp. 151–171.

American Bar Association. 1934. "Report of the Special Committee on Administrative Law." In U.S. Congress, Senate, Committee on the Judiciary, Subcommittee on Separation of Powers (1970). *Separation of Powers and the Independent Agencies: Cases and Readings.* 91st Cong., 1st sess. Document 91–49, pp. 214–239. Washington, DC: U.S. Government Printing Office.

American Federation of Government Employees, Local 32 v. Federal Labor Relations Authority. 1985. 774 F.2d. 498.

Asimow, Michael, Arthur Bonfield, and Ronald Levin. 1998. *State and Federal Administrative Law*, 2nd ed. St. Paul: West Group.

Assessment of Federal Regulations and Policies on Families Act. 1998. PL 105–277. 112 Stat. 2681. 5 U.S.C. 601.

Association of American Physicians and Surgeons, Inc. v. Hillary Rodham Clinton. 1993. 997 F.2d 898.

Atwater v. City of Lago Vista. 2001. U.S. Supreme Court, No. 99–1408.

Automotive Parts & Accessories Association v. Boyd. 1968. 407 F.2d 330.

Baker v. City of St. Petersburg. 1968. 400 F.2d 294.

Ball, Howard. 1986. "Downwind from the Bomb." *New York Times Magazine*, February 9, pp. 33 ff.

Bardach, Eugene, and Robert Kagan. 1982. *Going by the Book*. Philadelphia: Temple University Press.

Barger, Harold. 1984. *The Impossible Presidency*. Glenview, IL: Scott, Foresman.

Barr, Stephen. 1998. "GOP Sees No Results in Results Act." *Washington Post*, June 9, p. A4.

Barr, Stephen. 2000. "Some Pessimism on 'Reinvention.'" *Washington Post*, March 31, p. 427.

Barron, Jerome, and C. Thomas Dienes. 1999. *Constitutional Law in a Nutshell*. St. Paul: West Group.

Bazelon, David. 1976. "The Impact of the Courts on Public Administration." *Indiana Law Journal*, Vol. 52 (No. 1): 101–110.

Bernstein, Marver. 1955. *Regulating Business by Independent Commission*. Princeton, NJ: Princeton University Press.

Bi-Metallic Investment Co. v. State Board of Equalization of Colorado. 1915. 239 U.S. 441.

Board of County Commissioners, Wabaunsee County v. Umbehr. 1996. 518 U.S. 668.

Board of Curators of University of Missouri v. Horowitz. 1978. 435 U.S. 78.

Board of Education of Independent School District No. 92 of Pottawatomie County v. Earls. 2002. U.S. Supreme Court, No. 01–332.

Board of Trustees of the University of Alabama v. Garrett. 2001. 121 S.Ct. 955.

Bonfield, Arthur. 1986. *State Administrative Rule Making*. Boston: Little, Brown.

Bonfield, Arthur. 1993. *State Administrative Rule Making: Supplement*. Boston: Little, Brown.

Bonfield, Arthur, and Michael Asimow. 1989. *State and Federal Administrative Law*. St. Paul: West Publishing.

Brentwood Academy v. Tennessee Secondary School Athletic Association et al. 2001. 121 S.Ct. 924.

Bryan v. Moore. 2000. 528 U.S. 1133.

Buckley v. American Constitutional Law Foundation. 1999. 525 U.S. 182.

Bureau of National Affairs, Inc. v. U.S. Department of Justice. 1984. 742 F.2d 1484.

Burnham, David. 1989. *A Law Unto Itself*. New York: Random House.

C & A Carbone, Inc. v. Town of Clarkstown. 1994. 511 U.S. 383.

Carter v. Carter Coal Co. 1936. 298 U.S. 238.

Central Intelligence Act. 1949. PL 81–110. 63 Stat. 208.

Chamber of Commerce of the United States, et al. v. Reich. 1996. 74 F.3d 1322.

Chevron U.S.A., Inc. v. Natural Resources Defense Council. 1984. 467 U.S. 837.

Chicago Teachers Union v. Hudson. 1986. 475 U.S. 292.

Cinderella Career and Finishing Schools, Inc. v. Federal Trade Commission. 1970. 425 F.2d 583.

Citizens to Preserve Overton Park, Inc. v. Volpe. 1971. 401 U.S. 402.

City of Canton v. Harris. 1989. 489 U.S. 378.

City of Erie v. Pap's A.M. 2000. 529 U.S. 277.

Civil Service Reform Act. 1978. PL 95–454. 92 Stat. 111. 5 U.S.C. 1101.

Cleveland Board of Education v. La Fleur. 1974. 414 U.S. 632.

Cleveland Board of Education v. Loudermill. 1985. 470 U.S. 532.

Coglianese, Cary. 1997. "Assessing Consensus: The Promise and Performance of Negotiated Rulemaking." *Duke Law Journal*, Vol. 46 (No. 6): 1255–1349.

Coyle, Marcia. 1995. "Agencies Ask for Less Sunshine." *National Law Journal*, September 25, p. A12.

Craig v. Boren. 1976. 429 U.S. 190.

Davis, Kenneth Culp. 1975. *Administrative Law and Government*. St. Paul: West Publishing.

Delaware v. Prouse. 1979. 440 U.S. 648.

Department of the Air Force v. Rose. 1976. 425 U.S. 352.

Dewar, Helen. 2001. "Ergonomics Repeal Prompts Look Back." *Washington Post*, March 9, p. A16.

Dodd, Lawrence, and Richard Schott. 1979. *Congress and the Administrative State*. New York: Wiley.

Dolan v. City of Tigard. 1994. 512 U.S. 374.

Dworkin, Terry. 1992. "Legal Approaches to Whistleblowing." In Marcia Miceli and Janet Near, *Blowing the Whistle*. New York: Lexington Books, pp. 232–279.

Edwards, George III, and Stephen Wayne. 1985. *Presidential Leadership*. New York: St. Martin's Press.

Executive Order 8802. 1941. 6 *U.S. Federal Register* 3109.

Executive Order 12,044. 1978. 3 *Code of Federal Regulations* 152.

Executive Order 12,291. 1981. 3 *Code of Federal Regulations* 127.

Executive Order 12,498. 1985. 3 *Code of Federal Regulations* 323.

Executive Order 12,606. 1987. 3 *Code of Federal Regulations* 241.

Executive Order 12,612. 1987. 3 *Code of Federal Regulations* 252.

Executive Order 12,866. 1993. 3 *Code of Federal Regulations* 638.

Executive Order 12,898. 1994. 3 *Code of Federal Regulations* 859.

Executive Order 12,954. 1995. 3 *Code of Federal Regulations* 329.

Executive Order 13,233. 2001. 3 *Code of Federal Regulations* 815.

False Claims Act. 1863. 12 Stat. 696.

Federal Advisory Committee Act. 1972. PL 92–463. 86 Stat. 770. 5 U.S.C. Appendix 2.

Federal Trade Commission v. Cement Institute. 1948. 333 U.S. 683.

Federal Trade Commission v. Ruberoid. 1952. 343 U.S. 470.

Federal Trade Secrets Act. 1948. PL 80–772. 62 Stat. 791. 18 U.S.C. 1905.

Feeley, Malcolm, and Roger Hanson. 1990. "The Impact of Judicial Intervention on Prisons and Jails." In John DiIulio Jr., ed., *Courts, Corrections, and the Constitution*. New York: Oxford University Press, pp. 12–46.

Ferguson v. City of Charleston. 2001. 121 S.Ct. 1281.

Fiorina, Morris. 1977. *Congress: Keystone of the Washington Establishment*. New Haven: Yale University Press.

Flast v. Cohen. 1968. 392 U.S. 83.

Foerstel, Herbert N. *Freedom of Information and the Right to Know*. Westport, CT: Greenwood Press, 1999.

Ford Motor Company v. FTC. 1981. 673 F.2d 1008.

Fox, William Jr. 2000. *Understanding Administrative Law*. New York: Lexis Publishing.

Freedom of Information Act 1966. PL 89–487. 80 Stat. 250. 5 U.S.C. 552.

Frothingham v. Mellon. 1923. 262 U.S. 447.

Funk, William. 1987. "When Smoke Gets in Your Eyes: Regulatory Negotiation and the Public Interest—EPA's Woodstove Standards." *Environmental Law*, Vol. 18 (Fall): 55–98.

Funk, William, Jeffrey Lubbers, and Charles Pou, eds. 2000. *Federal Administrative Procedure Sourcebook*, 3rd ed. Chicago: American Bar Association.

Funk, William, Sidney Shapiro, and Russell Weaver. 1997. *Administrative Procedure and Practice*. St. Paul: West Group.

Garcia v. San Antonio Metropolitan Transit Authority. 1985. 469 U.S. 528.

Garvey, Jane. 1999. "FAA Is Doing the Right Thing." *USA Today*, December 20, p. 26A.

Gellhorn, Ernest, and Ronald Levin. 1997. *Administrative Law and Process in a Nutshell*. St. Paul: West Publishing.

Gilbert v. Homar. 1997. 520 U.S. 924.

Goldberg v. Kelly. 1970. 397 U.S. 254.

Golden, Marissa Martino. 1998. "Interest Groups in the Rulemaking Process: Who Participates?" *Journal of Public Administration Research and Theory*, Vol. 8 (April): 245–270 (proquestmail@bellhowell.infolearning.com version).

Goldman, Deborah, and David Rosenbloom. 1998. "Whistleblower." In Jay Shafritz, ed., *International Encyclopedia of Public Policy and Administration*. Boulder: Westview Press, pp. 2397–2400.

Goldstein, Amy. 2001. "'Last-Minute' Spin on Regulatory Rite." *Washington Post*, June 9, pp. A1 ff.

Gore, Al. 1993. *From Red Tape to Results: Creating a Government That Works Better & Costs Less*. Washington, DC: U.S. Government Printing Office.

Gore, Al. 1995. *Common Sense Government Works Better & Costs Less*. Washington, DC: U.S. Government Printing Office.

Goss v. Lopez. 1975. 419 U.S. 565.

Government in the Sunshine Act. 1976. PL 94–409. 90 Stat. 1241. 5 U.S.C. 552b.

Government Performance and Results Act. 1993. PL 103–62. 107 Stat. 285.

Graham, John. 2002. "Open Reviews, Better Data Improve Regulations." *Federal Times*, January 7, p. 15.

Griggs v. Duke Power Co. 1971. 401 U.S. 424.

Grunwald, Michael. 2001. "Business Lobbyists Asked to Discuss Onerous Rules." *Washington Post*, December 4, p. A3.

Hamilton, Alexander. 1788. "Federalist Paper No. 78." In *The Federalist Papers*, ed. Clinton Rossiter. New York: Mentor, 1961, pp. 464–472.

Harlow v. Fitzgerald. 1982. 457 U.S. 800.

Harris, Christy. 1997. "Agency Goals Score an F." *Federal Times*, September 8, p. 5.

Hawes, Leonard, and Richard Rieke. 1998. "Alternative Dispute Resolution." In Jay Shafritz, ed., *International Encyclopedia of Public Policy and Administration*. Boulder: Westview Press, pp. 104–107.

Heckler v. Campbell. 1983. 461 U.S. 458.

Heckler v. Chaney. 1985. 470 U.S. 821.

Heclo, Hugh. 1977. *A Government of Strangers*. Washington, DC: Brookings Institution.

Heclo, Hugh. 1978. "Issue Networks and the Executive Establishment." In Anthony King, ed., *The New American Political System*. Washington, DC: American Enterprise Institute, pp. 87–124.

Hope v. Pelzer. 2002. U.S. Supreme Court, No. 01–309.

Housing Study Group v. Kemp. 1990. 736 F.Supp. 321.

Hummel, Ralph. 1991. "Stories Managers Tell: Why They Are as Valid as Science." *Public Administration Review*, Vol. 51 (January/February): 31–41.

Humphrey's Executor v. United States. 1935. 295 U.S. 602.

Industrial Union Department, AFL-CIO v. American Petroleum Institute. 1980. 448 U.S. 607.

J. W. Hampton, Jr., & Co. v. United States. 1928. 276 U.S. 394.

Jordan v. Gardner. 1993. 986 F.2d 1521.

Kamen, Michael. 1987. *A Machine That Would Go of Itself*. New York: Knopf.

Kelley v. Johnson. 1976. 425 U.S. 238.

Kendall v. United States. 1838. 37 U.S. 524.

Kerwin, Cornelius. 1999. *Rulemaking*, 2nd ed. Washington, DC: CQ Press.

Kerwin, Cornelius, and Scott Furlong. 1992. "Time and Rulemaking: An Empirical Test of Theory." *Journal of Public Administration Research and Theory*, Vol. 2 (April): 113–138.

La Follette, Robert Jr. 1946. "Congress Wins a Victory Over Congress." *New York Times Magazine*, August 4, pp. 11ff.

Lardner, George Jr. 2001. "Bush Urged to Rescind Order on Presidential Materials." *Washington Post*, November 7, p. A27.

Larrabee, Jennifer. 1997. "'DWB (Driving While Black)' and Equal Protection: The Realities of an Unconstitutional Police Practice." *Journal of Law and Policy*, Vol. 6 (No. 1): 291–328.

Leahy, Patrick. 1976. *A Report on Advisory Committees in the Department of Agriculture and Department of Defense*. Washington, DC: Office of U.S. Senator Leahy.

Legislative Reorganization Act. 1946. PL 79–601. 60 Stat. 812.

Legislative Reorganization Act. 1970. PL 91–510. 84 Stat. 1140.

Lewis, Vern. 1952. "Toward a Theory of Budgeting." In Jay Shafritz and Albert Hyde, eds., *Classics of Public Administration*, 2d ed. Chicago: Dorsey Press, 1987, pp. 213–229.

Light, Paul. 1995. *Thickening Government*. Washington, DC: Brookings Institution.

Lipsky, Michael. 1980. *Street-Level Bureaucracy*. New York: Russell Sage Foundation.

Local 2677, American Federation of Government Employees v. Phillips. 1973. 358 F.Supp. 60.

Lowi, Theodore. 1969. *The End of Liberalism*. New York: Norton.

Lubbers, Jeffrey. 1994. "Management of Federal Agency Adjudication." In David Rosenbloom and Richard Schwartz, eds., *Handbook of Regulation and Administrative Law*. New York: Marcel Dekker, pp. 287–323.

Lubbers, Jeffrey, 1997. "Paperwork Redux: The (Stronger) Paperwork Reduction Act of 1995." *Administrative Law Review*, Vol. 49 (Winter): 111–121.

Lujan v. Defenders of Wildlife. 1992. 504 U.S. 555.

Madison, James. 1999. *James Madison: Writings*. Comp. and annot. Jack Rakove. New York: Library of America.

Marbury v. Madison. 1803. 5 U.S. 137.

Marshall v. Barlow's, Inc. 1978. 436 U.S. 307.

Mashaw, Jerry, Richard Merrill, and Peter Shane. 1992. *Administrative Law.* St. Paul: West Publishing.

Mathews v. Eldridge. 1976. 424 U.S. 319.

May, Randolph. 1997. "Reforming the Sunshine Act: Report and Recommendation by the Special Committee to Review the Government in the Sunshine Act." *Administrative Law Review,* Vol. 49 (Spring): 415–428.

McCarran, Pat. 1946. "Improving 'Administrative Justice.'" *American Bar Association Journal,* Vol. 32: 827ff.

McMillian v. Monroe Co. 1997. 520 U.S. 781.

Memphis Light, Gas & Water Division v. Craft. 1978. 436 U.S. 1.

Meriam, Lewis. 1939. *Reorganization of the National Government, Part I: An Analysis of the Problem.* Washington, DC: Brookings Institution.

Michigan v. Tyler. 1978. 436 U.S. 499.

Milbank, Dana. 2002. "GAO Sues Administration for Task Force Records." *Washington Post,* February 23, A7.

Miller, Bill. 2001. "Records Order Spurs Lawsuit." *Washington Post,* November 29, A31.

Miller, Bill. 2002a. "$37.7 Billion for Homeland Defense Is a Start, Bush Says." *Washington Post,* January 25, p. A15.

Miller, Bill. 2002b. "More Help Sought for Those Who Blow Whistle." *Washington Post,* February 28, p. A21.

Model State Administrative Procedure Act. 1981. *Selected Federal and State Administrative and Regulatory Laws.* In William Funk, Sidney Shapiro, and Russell Weaver, eds. St. Paul: West Group, pp. 299–353.

Moore, Mark, and Margaret Gates. 1986. *The Inspectors-General.* New York: Russell Sage.

Moreno, Angel. 1994. "Presidential Coordination of the Independent Regulatory Process." *Administrative Law Journal of the American University,* Vol. 8 (Fall): 461–516.

Morgan v. United States. 1936. 298 U.S. 468.

Morgan v. United States. 1938. 304 U.S. 1.

Morris, Kim. 1977. "Judicial Review of Non-reviewable Administrative Action." *Administrative Law Review,* Vol. 29 (Winter): 65–86.

Morrison v. Olson. 1988. 487 U.S. 654.

Motor Vehicles Manufacturers Association of the United States, Inc. v. State Farm Mutual Automobile Insurance Co. 1983. 463 U.S. 29.

Nader v. Allegheny Airlines, Inc. 1976. 426 U.S. 290.

Nakashima, Ellen. 2001a. "Rule-Making Process to Be Tightened." *Washington Post,* September 26, p. A23.

Nakashima, Ellen. 2001b. "Environmental Group Sues for Records of Energy Task Force." *Washington Post,* December 12, p. A33.

Nakashima, Ellen. 2002. "Bush View of Secrecy Is Stirring Frustration: Disclosure Battle Unites Right and Left." *Washington Post,* March 3, p. A4.

National Association of Government Employees v. Federal Labor Relations Authority. 1985. 770 F.2d 1223.

Negotiated Rulemaking Act. 1990. PL 101–648. 104 Stat. 4969. 5 U.S.C. 561.

New York v. Burger. 1987. 482 U.S. 691.

New York v. United States. 1992. 505 U.S. 144.

Nixon v. Administrator of General Services. 1977. 433 U.S. 425.

Nixon v. United States. 1993. 506 U.S. 224.

Office of the Federal Register. 1999. *The United States Government Manual, 1999/2000.* Washington, DC: U.S. Government Printing Office.

O'Hare Truck Service, Inc. v. City of Northlake. 1996. 518 U.S. 712.

O'Leary, Rosemary, and Susan Raines. 2001. "Lessons Learned from Two Decades of Alternative Dispute Resolution Programs and Processes at the U.S. Environmental Protection Agency." *Public Administration Review*, Vol. 61 (November/December): 682–692.

Olson, William, and Alan Woll. 1999. "Executive Orders and National Emergencies: How Presidents Have Come to 'Run the Country' by Usurping Legislative Power." *Policy Analysis*, No. 358 (October 28). Washington, DC: Cato Institute.

Ombwatch. 2001. www.ombwatch.org/info/2001/access.html.

Owen v. City of Independence. 1980. 445 U.S. 622.

Paperwork Reduction Act. 1980. PL 96–511. 94 Stat. 2812. 44 U.S.C. 3501.

Paperwork Reduction Act. 1995. PL 104–13. 109 Stat. 163. 44 U.S.C. 3501.

Pembaur v. City of Cincinnati. 1986. 475 U.S. 469.

Pike v. Bruce Church, Inc. 1970. 397 U.S. 137.

Piotrowski, Suzanne, and David Rosenbloom. 2002. "The Problem of Nonmission Based Values in Results Oriented Public Management: The Case of Freedom of Information." *Public Administration Review,* Vol. 62 (November/December): 643–657.

Presidential Records Act. 1978. PL 95–591. 92 Stat. 2523. 44 U.S.C. 2201.

Printz v. United States. 1997. 521 U.S. 898.

Pritchett, C. Herman. 1977. *The American Constitution.* New York: McGraw-Hill.

Privacy Act (1974). PL 93–579. 88 Stat. 1896. 5 U.S.C. 552a.

Professional Airways Systems Specialists, MEBA, AFL-CIO v. Federal Labor Relations Authority. 1987. 809 F.2d 855.

Publius. 1787–1788. *The Federalist Papers,* ed. Clinton Rossiter. New York: Mentor Books, 1961.

Quirk, Paul. 1980. "Food and Drug Administration." In James Q. Wilson, ed., *The Politics of Regulation.* New York: Basic Books, pp. 191–235.

Rankin v. McPherson. 1987. 483 U.S. 378.

Regulatory Flexibility Act. 1980. PL 96–354. 94 Stat. 1164. 5 U.S.C. 601.

Reich, Charles. 1964. "The New Property." *Yale Law Journal,* Vol. 73 (April): 733–787.

Richardson v. McKnight. 1997. 521 U.S. 399.

Richardson v. Perales. 1971. 402 U.S. 389.

Rivenbark, Leigh. 1998. "Cases Swamp EEOC." *Federal Times,* August 10, p. 3.

Roe v. Wade. 1973. 410 U.S. 113.

Rohr, John. 1989. *Ethics for Bureaucrats,* 2nd ed. New York: Marcel Dekker.

Rosenbloom, David. 1971. *Federal Service and the Constitution*. Ithaca: Cornell University Press.

Rosenbloom, David. 1992. "The Federal Labor Relations Authority." In Patricia Ingraham and David Rosenbloom, eds., *The Promise and Paradox of Civil Service Reform*. Pittsburgh: University of Pittsburgh Press, pp. 141–156.

Rosenbloom, David. 2000. *Building a Legislative-Centered Public Administration: Congress and the Administrative State, 1946–1999*. Tuscaloosa: University of Alabama Press.

Rosenbloom, David H., James Carroll, and Jonathan Carroll. *Constitutional Competence for Public Managers: Cases and Commentary*. F. E. Peacock: Itasca, IL, 2000.

Rosenbloom, David, and Robert Kravchuk. 2002. *Public Administration: Understanding Management, Politics, and Law in the Public Sector*, 5th ed. New York: McGraw-Hill.

Rosenbloom, David, and Rosemary O'Leary. 1997. *Public Administration and Law*, 2nd ed. New York: Marcel Dekker.

Roth, William Jr., and William Nixon. 1999. *The Power to Destroy*. New York: Atlantic Monthly Press.

Rourke, Francis. 1993. "Whose Bureaucracy Is This, Anyway? Congress, the President, and Public Administration." *PS: Political Science and Politics*, Vol. 26 (December): 687–692.

Rutan v. Republican Party of Illinois. 1990. 497 U.S. 62.

Sargentich, Thomas. 1997. "The Small Business Regulatory Enforcement Fairness Act." *Administrative Law Review*, Vol. 49 (Winter): 123–137.

Schechter Poultry Corp. v. United States. 1935. 295 U.S. 495.

Schlesinger, Arthur Jr. 1973. *The Imperial Presidency*. Boston: Houghton Mifflin.

Scholz, John. 1994. "Managing Regulatory Enforcement in the United States." In David Rosenbloom and Richard Schwartz, eds., *Handbook of Regulation and Administrative Law*. New York: Marcel Dekker, pp. 423–462.

Schwartz, Bernard. 1994. "Some Crucial Issues in Administrative Law." In David Rosenbloom and Richard Schwartz, eds., *Handbook of Regulation and Administrative Law*. New York: Marcel Dekker, pp. 207–222.

Schweiker v. Hansen. 1981. 450 U.S. 785.

Shafritz, Jay, David Rosenbloom, Norma Riccucci, Katherine Naff, and Albert Hyde. 2001. *Personnel Management in Government, 5th ed.* New York: Marcel Dekker.

Simon v. Eastern Kentucky Welfare Rights Organization. 1976. 426 U.S. 26.

Skidmore v. Swift & Co. 1944. 323 U.S. 134.

Skrzycki, Cindy. 1998. "Congress: Fewer Forms or Budgets Will Suffer." *Washington Post*, August 14, pp. G1ff.

Skrzycki, Cindy. 2001a. "OMB to Revisit Costs, Benefits of Rules." *Washington Post*, May 29, p. E1.

Skrzycki, Cindy. 2001b. "Critics Assail Review of 'Final' Rules." *Washington Post*, April 3, p. E1.

Small Business Regulatory Enforcement Fairness Act. 1996. PL 104–121. 110 Stat. 857. 5 U.S.C. 601.

Soeken, Donald. 2002. "Whistleblower Act Falls Short of Protection." *Federal Times*, January 7, p.15.

South Dakota v. Dole. 1987. 483 U.S. 203.

Spady v. Mount Vernon. 1974. 419 U.S. 983.

Sparrow, Malcolm. 1994. *Imposing Duties*. Westport, CT: Praeger.

Stanley v. Illinois. 1972. 405 U.S. 645.

Steadman v. Securities and Exchange Commission. 1981. 450 U.S. 91.

Steck, Henry. 1984. "Politics and Administration: Private Advice for Public Purpose in a Corporatist Setting." In Jack Rabin and James Bowman, eds., *Politics and Administration: Woodrow Wilson and American Public Administration*. New York: Marcel Dekker, pp. 147–174.

Steel Co. v. Citizens for a Better Environment. 1998. 523 U.S. 83.

Stewart, Richard. 1975. "The Reformation of American Administrative Law." *Harvard Law Review*, Vol. 88 (June): 1669–1813.

Strauss, Peter, Todd Rakoff, Roy Schotland, and Cynthia Farina. 1995. *Gellhorn and Byse's Administrative Law: Cases and Comments*, 9th ed. Westbury, NY: Foundation Press.

Taylor, Gary. 1993. "The State of Whistleblower Statutes." *National Law Journal*. September 20, p. 37.

Toilet Goods Association, Inc. v. Gardner. 1967. 387 U.S. 158.

United States v. Florida East Coast Railway Co. 1973. 410 U.S. 224.

United States v. International Boxing Club of New York, Inc. 1955. 348 U.S. 236.

United States v. Lopez. 1995. 514 U.S. 549.

United States v. Mead Corp. 2001. 121 S.Ct. 2164.

United States v. Morrison. 2000. 529 U.S. 598.

United States v. National Treasury Employees Union. 1995. 513 U.S. 454.

United States v. Nixon. 1974. 418 U.S. 683.

United States v. Nova Scotia Food Products Corp. 1977. 568 F.2d 240.

United States v. Richardson. 1974. 418 U.S. 166.

Universal Camera Corp. v. National Labor Relations Board. 1951. 340 U.S. 474.

USA Today. 1999. "Requiring Child Safety Seats on Planes Masks Deeper Dangers." *USA Today*, December 20, p. 26A.

U.S. Congress. 1939. *Congressional Record*. Vol. 84, 76th Cong., 1st sess. Washington, DC: U.S. Government Printing Office.

U.S. Congress. 1940. *Congressional Record*. Vol. 86, 76th Cong., 3rd sess. Washington, DC: U.S. Government Printing Office.

U.S. Congress. 1946. *Congressional Record*. Vol. 92, 79th Cong., 2nd sess. Washington, DC: U.S. Government Printing Office.

U.S. Congress. 1966. *Special Inquiry on Invasion of Privacy*. House Committee on Government Operations, 89th Cong., 1st. sess. Washington, DC: U.S. Government Printing Office.

U.S. Department of Defense v. Federal Labor Relations Authority. 1994. 510 U.S. 487.

U.S. Department of Health and Human Services. 1978. "Residual Functional Capacity: Maximum Sustained Work Capability Limited to Light and Medium Work as a Result of Severe Medically Determinable Impairment(s)." *Federal Register*, Vol. 43 (November 28): 55369–55370.

U.S. Department of Justice. 2000. *FOIA Reference Guide.* www.usdoj.gov/04foia/index.html.

U.S. Department of Justice. 2001. "FOIA Post." Office of Information and Privacy. www.usdoj.gov/oip/foiapost/2001/foiapost19.html.

U.S. General Accounting Office. 1998. *Federal Rulemaking: Agencies Often Published Final Actions Without Proposed Rules.* Washington, DC: U.S. General Accounting Office.

U.S. General Services Administration. 1999. *Twenty-seventh Annual Report of the President on Federal Advisory Committees, Fiscal Year 1998.* Washington, DC: U.S. General Services Administration, March.

U.S. House of Representatives. 2001. *Oversight Hearing on Presidential Records Act.* Subcommittee on Government Efficiency, Financial Management and Intergovernmental Relations. November 6. www.house.gov/reform/gefmir/hearings/1106_presidential_records/1106.

U.S. Merit Systems Protection Board. 1995. *Sexual Harassment in the Federal Workplace.* Washington, DC: U.S. Merit Systems Protection Board.

U.S. Merit Systems Protection Board. 1997. *Adherence to Merit Principles in the Workplace: Federal Employees' Views.* Washington, DC: U.S. Merit Systems Protection Board.

U.S. Merit Systems Protection Board. 1998. *Issues of Merit.* Washington, DC: U.S. Merit Systems Protection Board, February.

U.S. Merit Systems Protection Board. 2002a. *Issues of Merit.* Washington, DC: U.S. Merit Systems Protection Board, January.

U.S. Merit Systems Protection Board. 2002b. *Issues of Merit.* Washington, DC: U.S. Merit Systems Protection Board, April.

U.S. Senate. 1970. *Separation of Powers and the Independent Agencies: Cases and Selected Readings.* Committee on the Judiciary, Subcommittee on Administrative Practice and Procedures. 93rd Cong., 2nd sess. Washington, DC: U.S. Government Printing Office.

U.S. Senate. 1974. *Freedom of Information Act Source Book.* Committee on the Judiciary, Subcommittee on Administrative Practice and Procedure, 93rd Cong., 2nd sess. Washington, DC: U.S. Government Printing Office.

U.S. Senate. 1978. *Federal Advisory Committee Act (Public Law 92–463): Source Book: Legislative History, Texts, and Other Documents.* Committee on Governmental Affairs, Subcommittee on Energy, Nuclear Proliferation, and Federal Services. 95th Cong., 2nd sess. Washington, DC: U.S. Government Printing Office.

U.S. Senate. 1989. *Negotiated Rulemaking Act of 1989: Report.* Committee on Governmental Affairs, 101st Cong., 1st sess. Report 101–97 (August 1). Washington, DC: U.S. Government Printing Office.

Vaughn, Robert. 1992. "The U.S. Merit Systems Protection Board and the Office of Special Counsel." In Patricia Ingraham and David Rosenbloom, eds., *The Promise and Paradox of Civil Service Reform.* Pittsburgh: University of Pittsburgh Press, pp. 121–140.

Vermont Yankee Nuclear Power Corporation v. Natural Resources Defense Council, Inc. 1978. 435 U.S. 519.

Vernonia School District 47J v. Acton. 1995. 515 U.S. 646.

Village of Willowbrook v. Olechon. 2000. 528 U.S. 562.

Vogler, David. 1988. *The Politics of Congress*, 5th ed. Boston, MA: Allyn and Bacon.

Wald, Patricia. 1994. "Regulation at Risk: Are the Courts Part of the Solution or Most of the Problem?" *Southern California Law Review*, Vol. 67 (March): 621–657.

Warren, Kenneth. 1996. *Administrative Law in the Political System*, 3rd ed. Upper Saddle River, NJ: Prentice-Hall.

Weinberg, Steven. 2000. "Author's Research on John Lennon Is a Textbook on How to Use the Freedom of Information Act." *St. Louis Post-Dispatch*, February 13, p. F11.

West v. Atkins. 1988. 487 U.S. 42.

Westin, Alan. 1967. *Privacy and Freedom.* New York: Antheneum.

Wharton, Dale. 1995. "Blank Check." www.eco.utexas.edu/~archive/chiapas95/1995.05/msg00201.html.

Whistleblower Protection Act. 1989. PL 101–12. 103 Stat. 16. 5 U.S.C. 1201.

White, Leonard. 1926. "Preface" *(Introduction to the Study of Public Administration),* in Jay Shafritz and Albert Hyde, eds., *Classics of Public Administration*, 2nd ed. Chicago: Dorsey Press, 1987, pp. 55–64.

Whren v. United States. 1996. 517 U.S. 806.

Wickard v. Filburn. 1942. 317 U.S. 111.

Willoughby, W. F. 1927. *Principles of Public Administration.* Washington, DC: Brookings Institution.

Willoughby, W. F. 1934. *Principles of Legislative Organization and Administration.* Washington, DC: Brookings Institution.

Wilson, Woodrow. 1887. "The Study of Administration." In Jay Shafritz and Albert Hyde, eds., *Classics of Public Administration*, 2d ed. Chicago: Dorsey Press, 1987, pp. 1–25.

Woll, Peter. 1977. *American Bureaucracy*, 2nd ed. New York: W.W. Norton.

Wood, B. Dan, and Richard Waterman. 1994. *Bureaucratic Dynamics.* Boulder: Westview Press.

Wyatt v. Stickney. 1971. 325 F.Supp. 781; 334 F.Supp. 1341.

Wyman v. James. 1971. 400 U.S. 309.

Youngstown Sheet and Tube v. Sawyer. 1952. 343 U.S. 579.

Zifcak, Spencer. 1998. "Freedom of Information." In Jay Shafritz, ed., *International Encyclopedia of Public Policy and Administration.* Boulder: Westview Press, pp. 941–944.

INDEX